The Valley Of Zermatt And The Matterhorn: A Guide

Edward Whymper

THE VALLEY OF ZERMATT AND THE MATTERHORN

A GUIDE

BY

EDWARD WHYMPER

AUTHOR OF "A GUIDE TO CHAMONIX AND THE RANGE OF MONT BLANC," "SCRAMBLES AMONGST THE ALPS," ETC. ETC.; HONORARY MEMBER OF THE SWISS AND ITALIAN ALPINE CLUBS, ETC. ETC.

WITH ILLUSTRATIONS & MAPS

LONDON
JOHN MURRAY, ALBEMARLE STREET
GENEVA: GEORG & CO., 10 RUE CORRATERIE
1897

Printed by R. & R. CLARK, LIMITED, *Edinburgh*

INTRODUCTION.

THIS little Guide to Zermatt is written upon the same lines as the Guide to Chamonix which was published by Mr. Murray last year. It treats more or less of what may be called the Zermatt *district*, embracing the Cream of the Alps; but it is not easy to define the limits of the district, which includes the Saas Thal as well as the Nicolai Thal, and extends right and left into Switzerland, and southwards into Italy. The prevailing idea has been to give greater prominence to the excursions which can be made in the basin of the Zermatt Valley (that is, the Nicolai Thal) than to those which may be made outside it. It is assumed that a visitor will desire to know something about the history of the place, and concerning people who have been associated with it, and so the topographical matter is preceded by a slight historical sketch.

About fifty of the Illustrations have been engraved expressly for the work, and the remainder are chiefly drawn from my *Scrambles amongst the Alps.* I am indebted to the Italian Alpine Club for permission to reproduce the portrait of my old guide and comrade Jean-Antoine Carrel which is given on p. 88; to the Zermatt Railway Company for the basis of the Plan of Zermatt; and for assistance of various kinds to the Rev. L. S. Calvert, Mr. W. E. Davidson, Rev. J. Llewelyn Davies, Sir John Evans, Mr. H. A. Grueber, Mons. X. Imfeld, MM. Alexandre and Joseph Seiler, Rev. Christopher Smyth, Canon J. G. Smyth, Rev. J. Sowerby, Rev. E. W. Stevenson, and Mr. H. Schütz-Wilson, to all of whom I tender my sincere thanks.

The following remarks may be of some service to those who visit the Zermatt district for the first time.

Expenses.—More will be got for money by settling down at a few places than by constantly moving from one place to another. *Pensionnaires* are taken at nearly all the hotels mentioned in this volume. Low rates are quoted at the beginning and at the end of the season.

Money.—Take some Napoleons (20-franc pieces), a small quantity of French silver for wayside expenses, and the rest in sovereigns and £5 Bank of England notes. The notes can be changed at Geneva, Lausanne, or Zermatt. Sovereigns go everywhere, except at the very smallest places. English silver is not understood, and will not pass. Beware of small Italian silver coins, which are supposed to be withdrawn from circulation.

Clothing.—Woollen goods and flannels are most suitable. It answers better to have several changes of thin garments than to be provided with a few thick ones. **Mountain-boots** should be taken out, and got into use before starting. The *nailing* is best done on the spot. **Knickerbockers.**—The musquitoes of the Rhone Valley display partiality for the calves of those who adopt this form of attire.

Rope.—If excursions are contemplated on which it will be desirable to use rope, it will be best to take rope out. There is none in the market equal to the Manilla rope which is specially manufactured by Mr. John Buckingham, 194, 196 Shaftesbury Avenue, London, W.C., which *ought* to be identified (amongst other ways) by a red thread woven among the strands. It is to be regretted that there are several spurious imitations abroad, in which this red thread is fraudulently copied. Beware of them.

Ice-axes can be obtained at Zermatt at the establishment of Melchior Anderegg, or at Châtillon of Carrel (the maker).

Soap.—There is a great opening for soap in Alpine regions, and at the present time it pays to carry a cake.

Baggage.—The minimum of baggage sometimes means the maximum of comfort. Anyone who has no more than he himself can transport conveniently, can travel more quickly, pleasantly, and economically than those who exceed that limit. On the other hand, innkeepers look with suspicion upon travellers with little or no baggage, and are apt to thrust them into the very worst rooms.

The most convenient method of sending luggage to Switzerland is per Messrs. Stockwell and Co., 15 King Street, Cheapside, London, E.C., *who are sole English Agents for the Swiss Postal Service viâ Calais and Bale.* For Rates see Advertisement.

The Swiss Post.—Travellers to Zermatt (or anywhere in Switzerland) will do well to procure the little book entitled *Tarif Postal de poche pour la Suisse et l'Étranger*, publié par la Direction Générale des Postes Suisses. Price 40 centimes. This gives much information as to Postal Rates for Letters, Parcels, etc. Luggage is forwarded by the Swiss Post at low rates. A package, for example, weighing not more than 44 lbs. (20 kilos.) and not exceeding £40 (1000 francs) in value, can be sent for 1 fr. 80 cts. between any two Post Offices in Switzerland.

Time.—In Switzerland, 'Central Europe' time is kept, which is 55 min. in advance of Paris time, and Paris time is 8 min. in advance of Greenwich time. When crossing and re-crossing the frontier it is well to keep these facts in mind. At Geneva (Cornavin Station), trains leaving for France start at Paris time, and those for Switzerland depart at Central Europe time.

Custom-houses.—In going to Zermatt *viâ* Paris—Dijon—Pontarlier—Lausanne, baggage is examined at Vallorbes. Travellers from Zermatt into Italy (or from Italy to Zermatt) by the high snow passes are not usually troubled by douaniers.

In by-gone years the baggage of tourists was seldom taxed upon entry into Switzerland. Of late years duties have been levied upon little coils of Alpine rope and other trifles. Although such inflictions are annoying, my recommendation is *to pay* without murmuring; and 1. to take (and to preserve) a receipt for the amount paid; 2. to obtain the name of the douanier; 3. to have the transaction witnessed, if possible; 4. to make exact notes of the occurrence.

Passports should be carried. Though a prolonged tour may be made in France, Switzerland, and Italy without finding any use for them, occasions sometimes arise when they are desirable or necessary, and it is best to be on the safe side.

Maps.—The Maps and Plans given in this volume will be found sufficient for most purposes. Those who desire greater detail can turn to the Government Maps of Switzerland and Italy.

1. The Swiss portions of the Zermatt district are included in Sheets xxii, xxiii of the *Carte topographique de la Suisse* (commonly called the Carte Dufour), scale $\frac{1}{100000}$, engraved on copper. Price 2 francs each.

2. They are also contained in the following sheets of the *Atlas topographique de la Suisse* (commonly called the Siegfried Map), scale $\frac{1}{50000}$. Sheet 482, Sierre; 487, Vissoye; 528, Evolena; 531, Matterhorn; 496, Visp; 500, St. Niklaus; 533, Mischabel; 535, Zermatt; 497, Brig; 501, Simplon; 534, Saas; 536, Monte Moro. Price 1 franc each.

3. Nos. 528, 531, 533 and 535 are put together, and sold as one sheet, entitled EVOLÈNE—ZERMATT—MONT-ROSE. Price 2 francs.

4. A very useful Map will be found in Sheet iii of the *Carte Générale de la Suisse*, scale $\frac{1}{250000}$. This embraces all between Geneva and the Simplon Pass, and from Thun to the Italian frontier. Price 2 francs.

5. Those who cross from Zermatt or Saas into Italy may find it useful to have the following sheets of the *Carta d'Italia*, scale $\frac{1}{50000}$. No. 29 (iv), Valtournanche; 29 (i), Monte Rosa; 30 (iv), Bannio (this includes Macugnaga and the Val Anzasca). Price 50 centimes each.

The above-mentioned Maps can be obtained of Messrs. Georg and Co., 10 Rue Corraterie, Geneva.

Language.—German is the language for the Zermatt district. French is useful, although it is not understood by the majority of the peasants in the Nicolai Thal and in the Saas Thal. In most of the hotels at Zermatt English is spoken. In the Val Tournanche and Valpelline French is sufficient. Some of the younger guides in the Zermatt district speak English.

Religion.—The Canton Valais is the most Catholic Canton in the Swiss Confederation. At the Census of 1888, 100,925 persons were returned as Catholic, and only 865 as Protestant. Protestantism is tolerated. English-speaking people, when in the Zermatt district, do not always recognise the fact that they are in a Catholic country, and sometimes do things which may excite differences of opinion.

Upon engaging Guides.—The recommendations that I should make in regard to the choice of guides at Zermatt are just those which I should make in regard to guides at any other place. 1. Before engaging a guide, make enquiry as to his antecedents from those who know. 2. Avoid men notorious for accidents, and those who are addicted to drink. 3. For difficult or long excursions give preference to men of middle age rather than to the youngest or oldest.

There is no *Bureau des Guides* at Zermatt, and enquiries have to be made to learn what men are available. During "the season," besides the Valaisan Guides whose names are given in the List in the Appendix, one often finds Oberlanders at Zermatt, or men from Macugnaga (Val Anzasca), from the Val Tournanche and other parts.

Some guides carry on the reprehensible practice of soliciting employment in the trains from Visp to Zermatt. *Those who introduce and recommend themselves are generally of an inferior class.*

I do not attempt to decide whether a traveller should employ guides. Some persons are competent to carry out by themselves all the excursions that are mentioned. A large number, however, are not equal to this. Inasmuch as I am unacquainted with the various capacities of my readers, I am unable to say whether they need not, or should employ guides. Everyone must decide that for himself.[1]

Mendicity.—Before the Zermatt Railway was constructed, mendicity had become a nuisance between Visp—Zermatt. Since the opening of the Railway, the *road* has been clear of beggars, *because it no longer pays to beg.* Cripples of sorts, however, have in the last few years broken out at Zermatt, and even at the Riffelalp. I am told that they do not belong to the Village or even to the Valley. If they are not patronized, they will no doubt disappear. If they are encouraged, they will multiply.

The **Société Suisse des Hôteliers** published in 1896 a small book containing the following remarks, which shew the views of Swiss Hotelkeepers upon several matters of general interest.[2]

Ordering Rooms in advance.—It is said that "A rather remarkable confusion of ideas prevails among the travelling public as to this frequently occurring question, which, in the height of the season especially, causes numerous unpleasant discussions."

"In a great measure this is owing to the advice contained in travellers' guide-books, advice, which, we are willing to admit, is given in good faith, and with the intention of guarding the interest both of traveller and of landlord. This advice is to the effect, 'that rooms should be ordered in advance especially when one is due to arrive at a late hour.' But owing to the fact that in the respective notices in guide-books, neither the question of *right* nor the *commercial* aspect of such ordering of apartments has been in the least discussed, there has arisen among a great many travellers the one-sided opinion, that ordering beforehand will, to a certain extent, ensure to the guest a claim, a power of disposal, without binding him to any reciprocal obligation."

[1] It is presupposed that my readers are acquainted with the various technical terms which are employed. If they should not be, I refer them to *Scrambles amongst the Alps.*

[2] The book is published in English, French and German editions, and is entitled *The Hotels of Switzerland*, Basle, 1896. Price 50 centimes. It gives a considerable amount of information,—and discusses a variety of topics,—from the reasonableness of wanting hot dishes at night to bringing Monkeys into Hotels. It is said that "Rooms are often considerably soiled and damaged by such uncouth inhabitants."

Let us now examine the following considerations:

1. Which traveller has the greater claim to accommodation,
   (a) the one who arrives early at the hotel, or (b) the one who by letter, by telegram, or only by telephone makes known his intention to put up there, and either arrives late at night or does not even arrive at all; whereas the former by his timely presence appears to be the better customer.

2. An agreement, a contract in which claims and counter-claims are stipulated, must be concluded by at least *two* parties.
   A *one-sided* order from the traveller does not give him the slightest *legal claim* to consideration, for in such a case there is lacking:
   (a) a declaration on the part of the second party (the landlord) that he *can* and *will* accept the order; (b) *the traveller's guarantee* that he will fulfil the obligation *entered into* by giving the order.

With the increase in the number of travellers there is also an increase in the number of those *who believe they may bind the hotel-keeper by ordering apartments in advance, without being themselves in any way bound by such an order.*

Hence the efficiency of such orders is diminishing daily, and the landlord is all the less to be blamed if he first attends to the guests that have actually arrived, and refuses to comply with any orders from persons unknown to him, unless recommended by trustworthy parties.

A prepaid reply seems, in a certain measure, to increase the probability of having an order for rooms attended to; it may, according to the more or less definite answer of the landlord, bring about, if not a legal, yet a moral obligation on his part. Still even then it cannot be said to be binding, as an *effectual guarantee is wanting on the part of the traveller* for the fulfilment of the obligation entered into, which alone can give the order the character of an agreement."[1]

Ordering rooms for arrivals early in the Morning.

"If the room has been reserved for a guest overnight in consequence of his order, he should only be charged for it *once; provided* he occupies it only during the day, and places it, by early notice, at the disposal of the landlord for the same evening.

"Should the latter be prevented from disposing of it for the ensuing night, the traveller must, especially during the season or when there is a great rush of visitors, be willing to pay for the room for *two* nights, even though he may not have occupied the room for fully 24 hours."

Landlord's responsibility. Depositing Objects of Value.

"The traveller will do well, in order to avoid losses and disagreeable law-suits, to follow the advice of guide-books and the request of landlords, *to hand over all valuables to the landlord personally.*"

Payment by Coupons, and preparation of Hotel-bills.

"If payment is to be by coupons, notice to this effect *must* be given *on arrival.* The guest should not be surprised if such payments, especially at the last minute, and in the bustle of leaving, are rejected as insufficient. In this case also the traveller should mind the advice to ask for, and examine, his bill in proper time, and to provide the means for paying it in time also.

[1] To this may be added that in the height of the season, *in Switzerland*, the telegraph is much used, and one not unfrequently arrives *before the telegram.*

"Landlords, on the other hand, should always make out their accounts in good time, and not, as unfortunately happens too often, allow travellers to ask for them repeatedly and in vain. This makes them ill-tempered and distrustful."

Some hotels at Zermatt are open throughout the year, and attempts are being made to establish 'a winter season.' Casual tourists arrive in every month of the year, and occasional ascents of a few of the great peaks have been made even in December and January. But the **Season** may be said to begin in June and to end in September, though the weather is *sometimes* fit for the majority of the excursions that can be made as early as the middle of May and for a little while into October. Usually, tourists thin off at the beginning of October, and by the middle of the month only *habitués* and stragglers are left. It is 'the end of the Season.'

EDWARD WHYMPER.

June, 1897.

ERRATUM (IN SOME COPIES)

Page 120, sixth and seventh lines from top, "Sir W. M. Conway" should read "Mr. Mich. Carteighe."

CONTENTS.

CHAPTER I.

ON THE EARLY HISTORY AND RISE OF ZERMATT.

CHAPTER II.

UPON SOME ATTEMPTS TO ASCEND THE MATTERHORN.

CHAPTER III.

THE FIRST ASCENT OF THE MATTERHORN.

CHAPTER IV.

DESCENT OF THE MATTERHORN.

CHAPTER V.

SUBSEQUENT HISTORY OF THE MATTERHORN.

CHAPTER VI.

HOW TO GET TO ZERMATT.

CHAPTER VII.

UPON THE VALLEY OF ZERMATT (NICOLAI THAL).

CHAPTER VIII.

UPON THE VILLAGE OF ZERMATT.

CHAPTER IX.

EXCURSIONS FROM ZERMATT.

CHAPTER X.

EXCURSIONS FROM THE RIFFELALP AND RIFFELBERG HOTELS.

CHAPTER XI.

EXCURSIONS FROM THE LAC NOIR HOTEL.

CHAPTER XII.

ON THE VALLEY OF SAAS (SAAS THAL).

APPENDIX.

LIST OF ILLUSTRATIONS.

VISP (VIÈGE).

CHAPTER I.

ON THE EARLY HISTORY AND RISE OF ZERMATT.

A LEGEND—THE BISHOP OUTWITS SATAN—DISCOVERY OF ROMAN COINS UPON THE THEODUL PASS—EARLIEST MENTION OF VISP AND ST. NICHOLAS—THE LORDS OF THE VALLEY OF VIÈGE—EARLIEST MENTION OF ZERMATT—TREATY BETWEEN THE MEN OF ZERMATT AND THOSE OF VAL ANZASCA—ZERMATT A CAUSE OF DISSENSION—THE DE LA TOUR FAMILY—MURDER OF THE COMPTESSE DE VIÈGE AND HER SON—WAR IN THE VALAIS—THE END OF BISHOP TAVELLI—NEW MASTERS AT ZERMATT—THE ZERMATTERS BECOME FREEHOLDERS, AND RÉPUBLICANS SOON AFTERWARDS—DESCRIPTION BY BOURRIT—ZERMATT ANNEXED TO THE FRENCH EMPIRE—THE VALAIS JOINS THE SWISS CONFEDERATION—DE SAUSSURE—VISIT OF THE FIRST ENGLISHMAN TO ZERMATT—GROWTH IN POPULARITY—THE FIRST ASCENT OF MONTE ROSA—ALEXANDRE SEILER I.

THE Village of Zermatt (formerly called Prato Borno or Pratoborno, Pra Borno, Pratoburnoz, Praborgne or Praborny) lies at the southern end of a valley which is one of the lateral branches of the great Valley of the Rhone. It is an older place than one would suspect from its appearance. From documentary evidence which will be referred to presently, it is apparent that the valley in which it is situated was *peopled* six to seven centuries ago. It was *known* in much earlier times. There is a tradition current in the Valais to the effect that the pass called the Col Theodul (Théodule) is named after the first Bishop of Sion,[1] and that he crossed it under remarkable circumstances.

"The Pope of this time—it was in the fourth century—had

[1] St. Théodule is said to have been Bishop of Sion from 381-391 A.D.

presented a very fine bell to the saintly prelate of the Valley of the Rhone, recently converted to Christianity. But what a task, at the beginning of the *moyen âge*, to transport such a mass of brass from the banks of the Tiber to the bosom of the Alps! Grateful as the holy Bishop was to the sovereign Pontiff for this act of generosity, he scarcely dared cherish the hope of seeing the faithful drawn to church by the sonorous tones of the papal bell, for the expense of transport was out of all proportion to the value of the gift.

What could be done?

The Bishop might have reflected a long time without finding a solution of the problem, if Satan, ever on the watch to pick up a soul, hadn't offered to transport the bell on his back, from Rome to Sion, in a single night;—on one condition, namely, that if he arrived within the walls of the Valaisan capital before cock-crow, the soul of St. Théodule should be his for ever.

The Bishop closed with the offer, and, the same evening, Satan set out with the heavy bell and the Bishop clinging to it. The only *souvenir* of this wonderful journey is that the Col du Théodule, by which the Valais was entered, took the name of the holy man from this period.

The Devil reached the Valley of the Rhone and the city" [Sion] "long before dawn, and, joyous at having bagged the soul of a bishop, had already taken a bound to clear the walls, when the Saint cried out from the bell—

> Coq, chante!
> Que tu chantes!
> Ou que jamais plus tu ne chantes!

and immediately a piercing concert rent the air—all the cocks of Sion awoke at the voice of the worthy prelate, and it is from this moment that they began to crow so early in the morning.

At this noise, the demon let fall the bell (which buried itself several feet in the ground), and vanished without a word to express his disgust." [1]

M. Alfred Cérésole, *pasteur à Vevey*, gives another version of the same legend.

"It is known," he says, "that Théodule, the first bishop of Sion and patron of the Valais, was a saint to whom popular tradition attributed remarkable influence, even over demons. One day at Sion, he learnt suddenly that the Pope, at Rome, was in great danger, and that it was his duty to warn him, to save his life. Troubled in spirit, and not knowing how to send a speedy message to the Holy Father, he opened his window and saw three devils dancing merrily on a roof. The saintly bishop beckoned to them to come near, and asked which was the liveliest. 'I,' answered one, 'I am as swift as the wind.' 'I,' said another, 'I fly like a bullet' [*comme une balle de fusil*].[2] 'This couple,' said the third, 'are idle talkers, I am as quick as the thought of a woman.' 'Well,' said Théodule, 'I treat with *you;* and I declare that I am yours, if, before the sound of cock-crow, you take me to Rome and back again.' The bargain was concluded. Satan

[1] Quoted from *Les Veillées des Mayens* by L. Courthion, Geneva (no date).

[2] Whence it appears that fire-arms were known in the fourth century!

selected a fine black cock, and set it as a sentinel, against his return, on the wall around the town. The bishop put a white cock on the roof of his château, and told it not to go to sleep until he came back. The journey to Rome was as quick as lightning. The Holy Father expressed his gratitude to Théodule by presenting him with a bell for his church, and the Devil undertook to carry the gift to the Cathedral of Sion. Before two o'clock in the morning, the bishop with his bell and its porter were back again. Satan took a short cut, and scaled the Alps at a bound by the pass between the Cervin[1] and Breithorn. The episcopal cock, wide awake on the roof, heard a great row, and crowed lustily as he saw his master flying through the air, and the black cock did the same. The Devil, on arriving at Sion, furious at finding he had lost his bet, hurled the bell with such force to the ground that it was buried nine arms-lengths in the soil."

From these accounts it seems that St. Théodule was acquainted with the Devil, and to have been even more astute than the Prince of Darkness. The Diabolical One appears to have been badly treated upon this occasion; for, according to both the relations, he carried out a difficult undertaking very successfully, and got nothing for his trouble,—which must have added to the many 'sorrows of Satan.'

There is a strong presumption, approaching certainty, that the Theodul Pass was traversed long before the fourth century.[2] At different times, many Roman coins have been discovered upon it, even upon its summit (10,890 feet). In the collection which has been formed by Mons. Joseph Seiler[3] of Brieg, the dates of the Roman coins which have been found upon the Theodul Pass range from about B.C. 200 to 400 A.D. Amongst others, the collection embraces examples of

NERVA.	VICTORINUS.
FAUSTINA I.	CLAUDIUS II.
MARCUS AURELIUS.	DIOCLETIANUS.
FAUSTINA II.	CONSTANTINUS I.
SEPT. SEVERUS.	VALENS.
MAXIMINUS I.	VALENTINIAN II.
GALLIENUS.	THEODOSIUS.

In some instances these coins may have been simply lost *en route*. In others, it is very likely that they were deposited intentionally; but, whichever supposition is adopted, one is led to conclude that the pass was traversed at a very early date.

One of the most curious 'finds' of Roman coins that has occurred

1 Sometimes called Col du Mont Cervin, or Matterjoch. Upon the current Government Maps of Switzerland it is termed Matterjoch or Theodulpass.

2 The neighbouring pass of the Simplon was in regular use in the third century, if not earlier. "Une colonne milliare érigée (au III siècle) sous les césars Volusianus et Gallus découverte à Sion porte le Leuga XVII, distance exacte de cette ville au point culminant du Simplon." "Les gazettes piémontaises ont parlé de la découverte récente d'une autre colonne milliare dans la vallée d'Ossola dont l'inscription indiquerait que la route du Simplon fut ouverte dans les dernières années du *deuxième siècle.*" —*Developpement de l'indépendance du Haut-Vallais et conquête du Bas-Vallais*, par M. Fréd. de Gingins-la-Sarraz, 8vo, Lausanne, 1844, p. 72.

3 Mons. Joseph Seiler very kindly favoured me by transmitting his collection to London for examination. I am much indebted to Sir John Evans for the determinations. There were *two* coins of Gallienus and *two* of Diocletian, but only single examples of all the others.

upon the Theodul Pass happened in 1895, close to the summit. On August 24 of that year, a girl employed in the kitchen of the inn went out to fetch some water; and, about fifty mètres down, upon the Italian side, spied two coins sticking out from underneath a thin, flat stone, which had a large, square stone on the top of it. She lifted off the two stones and found fifty-four coins underneath the lower one, all together in a clump, and they had apparently been enveloped in a bag, which had rotted. The flat stone had been used to conceal them, and the square, heavy one to keep the other in its place, and they had possibly remained in this position for centuries. Sir John Evans has identified in this collection three coins of AURELIANUS, A.D. 270-275, eight of PROBUS, A.D. 276-282, nineteen of CONSTANTIUS II, A.D. 335-361, nine of CONSTANTIUS GALLUS, A.D. 351-354, one of MAGNENTIUS, A.D. 350-353, and two of DECENTIUS, A.D. 351-353. One of these latter is given below.[1]

COIN OF DECENTIUS (A.D. 351-353), WITH CHRISTIAN SYMBOL.

Nothing is known about the Valley of Zermatt during these remote times, and one has to come down to the beginning of the 13th century for the first documentary references to it. The earliest is given in the great work by the Abbé Gremaud.[2] It is a declaration, dated 1218, that Guillaume, *chevalier*, of Viège (Vespia) *gave* to the *Curé* of that place his rights over tithes at Lalden (Laudona), a small village in the Valley of the Rhone, a little higher up than Viège. This is followed in Gremaud's work by a deed [No. 274], dated 1218, which states that one Conradus *sold* tithes to the same *Curé;* and that document is witnessed, amongst others, by Henselmus, *major* of

[1] The place where this 'find' was made is 160 to 170 feet from the inn at the summit, and 50 to 60 feet below it, and is away from the track usually followed when crossing the pass. The girl's duties led her in that direction. She went to fetch water, which is collected there from the dribbles of snow-water running off the rocks; and she made her discovery through the rocks (in August, 1895) being unusually free from snow. Eleven of the coins were sold to passers-by and others, at fifty francs apiece and downwards, before I had an opportunity to examine the collection.

[2] *Documents relatifs à L'Histoire du Vallais*, recueillis et publiés par l'Abbé J. Gremaud, 7 vols., 8vo, Lausanne, 1875-94. The first five volumes of this work were brought out at the expense of the Société d'histoire de la Suisse romande. The publication was then suspended for nine years from want of funds, and it has been continued by means of subsidies from the Confederation and the Valaisan Government. The seven volumes extend to more than 4300 pages, and include 2817 documents (from the earliest times down to A.D. 1431), which embrace Wills, Treaties and Deeds, largely intermingled with records of disputes, threats, and other unpleasant matters.

Chouson (St. Nicholas).[1] The *majors* of these times were hereditary officials, who exercised jurisdiction in their districts; received complaints, imposed fines, and enjoyed various privileges; and, as *majories* were confined to the larger places, this shews that, even at the beginning of the 13th century, the Village of St. Nicholas was accounted of some importance.

In the *middle* of the 13th century the property in the Valley of St. Nicholas, or a large part of it, belonged to the Comtes de Biandrate. According to the Baron Frédéric de Gingins-la-Sarraz, who wrote a Memoir[2] upon the family, the Biandrates[3] were, from the 11th century, amongst the most powerful barons in Piedmont. He says that they took their name from a small but very old town in the Province of Novara, and mentions three different branches of the family, one of them being the Comtes de Biandrate of the Valais. It is with this branch we are alone concerned.

Godefroi III, Count of Biandrate, *seigneur* of the Val Sesia, married Aldise daughter of Pierre de Castello, who was *seigneur* of neighbouring valleys. This latter bestowed upon his son-in-law his possessions in the Val Anzasca, by a deed dated June 8, 1250; and by his marriage the Count also acquired property in the Valais, which had come to his wife by the maternal side. Her mother is said to have belonged to the house of the *seigneurs* de Viège, which was rich and powerful in the 13th century. "The domains of these lords extended over the Valley of Viège" (Nicolai Thal or Valley of St. Nicholas), "which ends at Monte Rosa"; and, in the Valley of the Rhone, up to the sources of that river.[4] The property gained by marriage appears to have been acquired before 1250, for in the deed of that date the Comte de Biandrate reserves to himself right to transfer a portion of his Valaisan serfs to the Italian valleys; and, according to Gingins-la-Sarraz, this was actually done at a later date.[5] The same author says that upon the death of two uncles, in about 1258, the ancestral domains devolved upon the Countess Aldise.

The Count Godefroi III died in or about 1270, leaving three sons —Guillaume, Jocelin, and Pierre, the latter of whom died about two years after his father. Guillaume had the property in Piedmont as his share of the family possessions; and Jocelin took that in the Valais, with the exception of the Château of Viège and its *dépendances*, which were reserved to the mother for life. The domains of the two brothers were subsequently augmented by a gift from their grandfather, Pierre de Castello, who made over to them all that belonged to him on the Simplon between Crevola (near Domo d'Ossola) and Brigue. Jocelin also appears to have come into

1 In the Gremaud documents, the following variations in spelling can be found. Chauson, Schosun, Schauson, Schouson, and Zauxon.

2 *Documents pour servir à l'histoire des Comtes de Biandrate recueillis dans les Archives du Vallais*, et précédés d'une notice par le Baron Frédéric de Gingins-la-Sarraz, 4to, Turin, 1847.

3 Blandratae or Blandrate, in Latin; Biandrate or Biandra, in Italian; and Blandrà in the dialect of the Upper Valais.

4 Gingins-la-Sarraz, p. 21.

5 The aim of this transplantation (which it is said was expressed in the deed) was to put an end to ceaseless quarrels between the Valaisans and Piedmontese about pasturages.

possession of some of the Novara property which had passed to his younger brother; to have added to his wealth by marriage; and ultimately, when he "inherited the estates of his mother, he found himself one of the richest *seigneurs* in the Upper Valais."

It does not seem, however, that the Biandrates had absolute dominion in the Nicolai Thal, for there is a document in existence [Gremaud, No. 737] dated Rarogne, May 12, 1268, in which Rudolph of Rarogne makes over his rights and possessions in the parish and valley of St. Nicholas to his wife, daughter of Girold de la Tour; and there is evidence which leads to the same conclusion in a deed printed by Ruden in his *Familien-Statistik*,[1] which runs thus:—

"All believers in Christ are hereby informed that I Walter de Ried with the pious consent of my son Peter, and of my daughters Salome and Hemma (my other children were under age), and of Johannes de Ried guardian of the said children, have sold and devised for twelve pounds, which he has paid, to Walter son of Emke and his heirs, my meadow in Finellen[2] and the house which is built upon it, with the cellarage, and my share in the ekkun,[3] with the water and with everything else that may pertain to the said property. I have caused a deed to be drawn and duly signed by witnesses, who are Matthä de Stadel, Jacobus in spisce, Thomas de Wiestin, and Walter priest of Pratoborno,[4] who completed this deed at the place of Normandus, precentor and chancellor sedunensis,[5] in which place I Peter sworn chaplain have written it. He who shall dare to oppose this deed let the curse of God be upon him and pay to the King sixty pounds and a gold obolus. Done at Pratoborno A.D. 1280, on the 27th of the wine-month.[6]

Ruden (who was Curé of Zermatt from 1845 to 1865) says that this deed is preserved in the parish archives. It shews that there was a priest at Zermatt in 1280, and doubtless there was a church there at that time, inasmuch as the Normandus (Precentor of Sion) who is mentioned in it left by his will, dated 1285, a legacy to the Church of Pra Borno [Gremaud, No. 1153]. The property sold by Walter of Ried was at Findelen, which is at the present time the most elevated and the most remote of the hamlets round about the main village of Zermatt. The more distant hamlets would naturally be the last to be peopled; and, as Findelen clearly was in existence in 1280, it may fairly be presumed that Zermatt itself was an established place at some much earlier date.

In 1291, Jocelin, compte de Biandrate, and his nephew Jean (son of his brother William), with the men of Saas, St. Nicholas, and Zermatt on the one part, made a treaty of peace with the men of the Val Anzasca on the other part [Gremaud, No. 1021], and this is evidence that the Biandrates were lords in those districts, and that there were communications between the Valaisan and the Italian valleys in those remote times. But this family would seem

1 *Familien-Statistik der löblichen Pfarrei von Zermatt, mit beilagen.* Gesammelt und geordnet von Joseph Ruden, 8vo, Ingenbohl, 1869. The original deed is in Latin. A German translation is appended.

2 Findelen.

3 There is an 'alp' called Eggen close to the village of Findelen.

4 The old name of Zermatt.

5 Of the cathedral of Sion.

6 The original reads "Actum apud Pratobornum anno Domini M.CC.LXXX.V. Kal. Octob. Rudolpho regnante, Petro episcopante." The former was Rudolph of Habsburg, and the latter was Pierre d'Oron, Bishop of Sion from 1274 to 1287.

to have parted with some of its possessions not long afterwards, for in the Will of Pierre de la Tour, *seigneur* of Châtillon, which was made in 1350, the valleys of St. Nicholas and Zermatt were bequeathed to his three sons.[1]

About this time, the Valley of Zermatt became a cause of dissension. In the 12-14th centuries the greatest family in the Valais was that of De la Tour de Châtillon. The origin of this family is lost in the mist of ages. Dr. Schiner stated[2] that *he* possessed a manuscript which shewed that it was in existence before A.D. 1000. The De la Tours were strong enough to defy and to fight the Bishops of Sion, and they were frequently in hot water.[3] They were vassals both of the Bishop of Sion and of the Count of Savoy, and in the event of war between the Valais and Savoy were bound to supply soldiers to the former, and personal aid to the latter—a dual responsibility which from a business point of view was not likely to work well.

Pierre de la Tour, whose will has been quoted, "quarrelled with the Bishop about his *fiefs* at St. Nicholas and Zermatt, which the prelate claimed in default of *hommage;* and in 1351, along with some confederates, he took up arms against his spiritual superior. 'In the month of August, these Sons of Belial threw themselves upon the Bishop and his people, wounded them, killed a clerk and other persons, and pillaged upon several occasions the episcopal castles and lands.'" So said the sentence of excommunication which was pronounced against the *Seigneur* de la Tour and his accomplices. Pierre died a few years afterwards, and transmitted the quarrel as well as the property. Antoine de la Tour, who succeeded his father, also 'refused to pay homage for his *fiefs* in the Valley of St. Nicholas,'[4] and this led to war between the *Seigneur* and the Bishop,[5] which was carried on more or less continuously from 1362 to 1375.

During this strife an incident occurred which had particular interest for the inhabitants of the Valley of Zermatt. At that time, their former lords the Biandrates were represented by Isabelle, comptesse de Viège, and her son Antoine, compte de Biandrate. In 1365, while the quarrel between Antoine de la Tour and Bishop Tavelli was proceeding, Count Antoine and his mother let their castle at Viège to Pierre de Platea, and on November 3, to avoid

1 "In primis animam meam Altissimo meo Creatori recommendo, etc. Et quia heredis institutio fundamentum et caput est totius testamenti, idcirco heredes mihi instituo Antonium, Johannem et Petrum, filios meos, pro equalibus portionibus, eo salvo quod dono et concedo dicto Antonio in avantagium, ultra portionem sibi competentem in bonis meis cum fratribus suis, castrum meum de Castellione una cum vallibus de Liech, de Schauson et de Praborny, cum pertinentiis et appendentiis omnibus dictorum locorum" [Gremaud, No. 1971].

There is another document in Gremaud [No. 2040] from which it appears that a certain John de Mont had rights or property in Zermatt in 1357.

2 *Description du Département du Simplon, ou de la ci-devant République du Valais.* Par Mr. Schiner, Docteur en Médicine de la Faculté de Montpellier, 8vo, Sion, 1812, p. 278.

3 The very first reference to them in Gremaud is in connection with some differences they had with the Abbey of St. Maurice, in 1158.

4 *Le Vallais historique*, par l'Abbé B. Rameau, 4to, Sion, 1886, pp. 88-9.

5 This bishop was Guichard Tavelli, who held the see from 1342 to 1375.

the dangers of war, went towards Brigue, intending to take refuge in their tower at Naters, close by; but at night-time, when near the bridge over the Rhone, they encountered some of the episcopal troops, who murdered both and flung them into the river.

This crime was so much talked about that the Pope sent his Legate to the Valais to open an enquiry and to punish the guilty; and a decree [Gremaud, No. 2107] was issued by him, ordering the Bishop to bring the murderers to justice, to recover the bodies of the victims and to inter them in the cathedral church in a manner befitting their rank; to found two chapels with two chaplains apiece for perpetual mass for the repose of their souls; and, further, that all their property which had been seized by the partizans of the Bishop was to be restored to the family. Some of it, it is said, went to a half-brother of Count Antoine, but the *fiefs* which were held from the Chapter of Sion were absorbed in the bishopric, and in course of time the Plateas of Viège (formerly vassals of the Biandrates) came into possession of part of them.[1]

The war still went on. The Bishop besieged Antoine de la Tour in his castle of Bas-Châtillon (or Niedergestelen) near Raron, and burned his villages. The Count of Savoy then intervened, and ordered the *Seigneur* to give the required homage, and condemned the Bishop to pay 16,000 francs for the damage he had done. Finally, five years later (Aug. 8, 1375), Antoine de la Tour put an end to his rival by hiring assassins; who, assisted by some of his own men, broke into the Bishop's castle of la Soie (near Sion) in the early morning, seized him and his Chaplain whilst they were walking in a garden which extended to the battlements of the ramparts, and hurled both over, on the side where the rocks beneath were perpendicular [Gremaud, No. 2165]. This, even in the fourteenth century, was a rough way of handling a bishop, and it was not approved by the people. The Valaisans rose against De la Tour, burned his castles and "rid the country for ever from this ambitious family."

The brothers Antoine and Jean de la Tour sold the castle of Châtillon and all their possessions in the Valais to the Count of Savoy. The deed recording this transaction is dated St. Maurice, August 8, 1376 [Gremaud, No. 2214].[2] The Count of Savoy, like a keen man of business, made sure of a *sale* before he effected the *purchase*. There is another deed in existence [Gremaud, No. 2212], dated at Turin, from which it appears that he sold the Castle and the Lötschen Thal to the new Bishop of Sion on *July* 9, 1376, for 40,000 golden florins; which, although a good round sum, was, as auctioneers would say, a ridicuously small and inadequate price for a domain of such extent.

But, although the Bishop made the purchase, it appears that he had still to get into possession, for there is a document dated Aug. 14, 1376, which sets forth that, having bought the Château of Châtillon, he promised full pardon *to those who still defended it* [Gremaud, No. 2215]. Wrangles went on between the Bishops of

[1] Quoted from Baron Gingins-la-Sarraz.

[2] This important document occupies twenty-two pages of print.

Sion and the Valaisans about the property of the De la Tours for more than fifty years. A good deal of it, including the district with which we are concerned, got in course of time into the hands of the Esperlinis (Asperlini), the De Plateas, and the De Werras. These families were important ones in the Upper Valais even when the De la Tours were at their greatest, and it was only in the natural order of things that some of the possessions of the *Seigneur* of Châtillon drifted into their nets. They all belonged to the neighbourhood of Visp (Viège)—a district which, according to Chanoine de Rivaz, 'historians agree is the cradle of the chief *noblesse* of the country.' Regarding these noble families Dr. Schiner says "their number was large, and their pride extreme; so much so that they built a church" [at Visp] "for their own especial use, namely that down below, in order that they should not mix with the populace, as they considered it too low a thing to assemble together in the house of God."

Ruden tells us (pp. 114, etc.) that several De Werras[1] are mentioned in a deed of 1435 as part lords of the vale of Zermatt. He says, also, it appears from a long roll of parchment, that three Esperlinis were lords of *half* the vale of Zermatt in 1448. In 1515, Johann Werra, of Leuk, bought the property of the Esperlinis, and then, in all, he had dominion over 115 families. These families, by a charter dated 1538, bought their freedom for the sum of 700 'Mörserpfund' from the heirs of the said Werra; and on Jan. 25, 1540, the seniors assembled together in Zermatt Church to devise statutes for the future government of their community.

At the same period 'the noble Philip Perrini of Leuk' was lord of 35 families, and the De Plateas had 39 more. The Perrini men secured their freedom in 1562 by payment of 655 'Mörserpfund,' but their friends and relatives under the Plateas remained serfs until 1618, when they delivered themselves from bondage for the sum of 450 'Mörserpfund' and *four fat sheep!*[2] "With what burning desire," says Ruden, "must they have longed for the freedom which their brothers had so long enjoyed." Three years later, "still intoxicated with joy," the heads of these families met to arrange their affairs upon the same footing as the others; but it would seem, from subsequent passages in Ruden, that the whole were not fused into a single commune until the year 1791.

It may be inferred, from the considerable number of persons who were living at Zermatt during the periods referred to by Ruden, that the conditions of life there were not much harder in those early times than they are now, and this although the people of the Valais

1 The name of Willermus Werra appears in the Gremaud documents as early as the year 1247 [No. 507]. Petrus de Platea de Uesbia is in one of 1255 [No. 625].

2 Ruden gives the names and abodes of those who were freed upon these three occasions, and from his lists it appears that those who were enfranchised belonged strictly to Zermatt and its surroundings, and not to places lower down the valley. The total number of families (or households) amounts to 189. If there were no more than four persons to a household, the population of Zermatt three centuries ago must have been considerably larger than it is now. The list of those who were freed in 1538 contains names which will be familiar to visitors to Zermatt,—such as Perren, Ruden, and Weltschen.

were more or less in a state of bondage.[1] Yet, even when in bondage, they had rights of some sort,[2] though no political influence. All power then was in the hands of the Bishops of Sion and the *Seigneurs*, whose relations to each other were somewhat complex. A student of the early history of the Valais may be excused if he does not comprehend the precise relations which existed between the Bishops and the *Seigneurs*, and their serfs or vassals, as it is abundantly clear that the Valaisans did not understand them themselves. The history of their country in medieval times is principally composed of records of interminable disputes and petty warfare, arising from differences about rights which were or were not possessed. The Abbé Gremaud, in speaking of these contests, divides them into three groups. There were 1. The wars between the lord paramount and his vassals. 2. Little private wars between individual lords, and 3. others between the lords and the communes.

One can hardly tell what the Valais should be called during these times. It was neither Kingdom nor County, Empire or Republic. Gingins-la-Sarraz terms it a principality, and says—

> "La principauté temporelle des évêques de Sion se composa dans l'origine d'un assemblage de diverses possessions féodales éparses tant dans le Haut-Vallais que dans le Bas; mais, loin de former entr'elles un territoire arrondi et compacte, ces propriétés seigneuriales se trouvaient, au contraire, séparées les unes des autres et entrecoupées par les fiefs dépendants médiatement ou immédiatement de la maison de Savoie, qui possédait des seigneuries importantes non-seulement dans les quartiers inférieurs, mais aussi dans les régions supérieures de la longue vallée du Rhône."

How the Counts of Savoy became masters of this part of the Valais, says the Abbé Gremaud, is unknown; and he makes the same confession in respect to the origin of the Bishopric. From the 12th to the 15th centuries, the Bishops of Sion were very important personages, who declared war on their own account, and exercised sovereign powers, with little to check their authority and pretensions. Down to the end of the 14th century they were not drawn exclusively from the Valais. Several were Vaudois, and others were Genevese or French, or came from the Valley of Aosta; but for the last 500 years nearly all have been people of the country, and some have sprung from a very low origin.[3] The right of the Chapter to

[1] In feudal times they were bought and sold, and transferred with the land. Thus, in 1257 Guillaume de Mœrell sold his men in the valley of the Simplon to Jocelin, vidomne of Sion [Gremaud, No. 638]. In 1279, Guillaume de Scala of Brigue sold three men to Pierre de Louèche, Canon of Sion [Gremaud, No. 880]. In 1280, Jean de Miège sold a man to Jacques, Canon of Sion [Gremaud, No. 886]. In 1292, Nantelme d'Ayent sold to the Chapter of Sion some men and his rights in the Val d'Hérens [Gremaud, No. 1110]. In 1358, Jean, *seigneur* of Anniviers, sold some '*taillable*' men to Tavelli, Bishop of Sion [Gremaud, No. 2046]; and, in 1408, Antoine de la Rochiz sold men to Perret de la Chapelle [Gremaud, No. 2587].

[2] Ruden says [p. 122] that Jodok Kalbermatter of Visp bought a portion of the Platea property at Zermatt in 1528, and upon May 10 met his purchased vassals in the Church, to receive their submission and oath of fidelity, and in return promised not to curtail their *rights and privileges*.

[3] England has been visited by two Bishops of Sion. Ermanfroid, who held the see from 1055 to 1082, came as Pope's Legate in 1070, and presided at the Council at Windsor when Stigand, Archbishop of Canterbury, was deposed; and Cardinal Schiner (nominal bishop from 1499 to 1522) came to London in the reign of Henry VIII.

elect the Bishop was sometimes upset by the Pope, and the people had no voice in the matter until recent times. The disputes which recurred upon this subject were only terminated in 1807; and now, when a vacancy occurs, the Chapter selects four Canons, from whom the Bishop is chosen by the *Grand Conseil* of the Canton. The election is confirmed by the Pope.

After the end of the fourteenth century, the power of the great lords was gradually shorn and shattered, the privileges of the Bishop were curtailed, and in course of time the people acquired the management of their own affairs and a voice in the election of their rulers. It took much to rouse them to action against their spiritual chiefs. Valaisans have always been good Catholics. "How blessed it is," said the mother of Thomas Platter, "to be the mother of a priest"; and this feeling, to which she gave expression four centuries ago, exists amongst the people of the Valais at the present time. But there are some things which flesh and blood cannot endure. While it is annoying to be frequently menaced with eternal damnation, it is more than aggravating, when you bring a basket of trout to market, to have the biggest picked out by your Bishop, the next best by his Vice-lord (*vidomne*), and to have only the refuse left for sale; and, it may be, the revolt of the Valaisans against the authority of their Bishops, and against the *Seigneurs*, was more stimulated by a desire to rid themselves from such petty oppressions than by a wish to found a model Republic, or from a profound belief that all men are born free and equal. Sometimes they chased their Bishops from the diocese. They shut one up, and kept him a prisoner, refusing to release him until he had assented to their demands; and another (who is said to have been remarkable for his learning and eloquence) was told to his face "We are a free people. Understand that if the Bishops of Sion have exercised sovereign powers they have done it simply through our good-nature. . . As you will not sign, we are off at once; and we will go from *dizain* to *dizain*, to tell the people. . . Don't mistake, they will rise in fury, and will destroy your *châteaux*, and you will learn from experience that you would have done better to have paid attention to our wishes."

In 1628 (ten years after the Zermatters had freed themselves from their lords) the Valais was first termed a Republic, and for some length of time afterwards the country enjoyed comparative repose. The condition of affairs towards the end of the 18th century was thus described by Marc Bourrit.[1]

"The confederation is made up of seven little republics, called *Dixains*,[2] and at different times each one of them has contracted its own particular alliances; but they felt that unity was strength, and could only bring about

[1] *Description des Alpes Pennines et Rhetiennes*, par M. T. Bourrit, 8vo, Geneva, 1781; vol. i, pp. 105-6.

[2] Schiner (*Description du Département*, p. 9) says, the Upper Valais was divided into seven districts "which the Valaisans called *Disains* or *Dixains*, in Latin *Deseni*, and in German *Zenden*. One does not know the origin of this term. However, it cannot be derived from the word *ten*, as there are only seven and not ten." The Abbé Gremaud (vol. v, pp. lxxxi-ii) adopts a different view. This author says that the term *dixain* was first employed in 1417.

unity by a well-considered confederation. The *Dixains* appoint the Bishop to preside over their assemblies. This is not altogether a voluntary choice; but exhausted by long troubles they could only terminate them by associating the Bishop with the Government. . . To-day he is called Prince. He has the right to strike money in certain cases, and to pardon. . . The election of a Bishop is a matter of importance,"

and he then went on to shew how it was managed at that time.

Bourrit (writing in 1781) spoke favourably of the Valaisans, particularly of those in the neighbourhood of Visp. "One finds there," he said, "an enchanting openness and sweetness of character. . . The children seemed to us to be the most beautiful in the Valais; they followed us in troops, from house to house, with a familiarity to which we were not quite accustomed. . . We were very much surprised that they refused some money which we offered to them. . . This corner of the world seemed to possess all that could contribute to render life happy." But it would appear that this pastoral simplicity and almost angelic condition did not prevail universally, and he rather spoiled his picture by mentioning upon an earlier page that he found himself "by the side of a gibbet, having bits of corpses fastened to it,—heads and limbs being nailed up. This horrible sight, which we came upon unexpectedly, *is very common throughout the Valais*, where justice is severe—where they hang a man for robberies which elsewhere are punished at the most with a whipping."

'This corner of the world,' a few years later, was again the theatre of sanguinary and barbarous scenes. The Republicans of the Upper Valais did not regard favourably the advances which were made upon them by the French Republic in 1799; and, when fortune temporarily favoured their arms, took the opportunity to bury a French officer to the waist, and to stone him to death. "Quelques jours auparavant, trois Vaudois surpris pillant l'église de ce premier village" [Varone] "avaient eu le crâne fracassé sur l'enclume d'une forge."[1] These barbarities appear to have caused the reprisals which a few months later were made in the Valley of Zermatt and elsewhere.

From 1802 to 1810 the Valais formed an independent Republic; and after that, for a short time, Zermatt became part of the French Empire. The *Moniteur*, one morning in 1810, contained the following decree.

"Napoleon, etc., considering that the route over the Simplon, which unites the empire with our kingdom of Italy, is useful to more than sixty millions of persons, that it has cost France and Italy more than eighteen millions, an expenditure which would become useless unless commerce could be carried on conveniently and in perfect safety; that the Vallais has not kept any of the engagements which it entered into when we commenced the works of this great line of communication, wishing also to put an end to the anarchy which afflicts the country, and to cut short the pretensions of one part of the population to sovereignty over the other, let it be decreed as follows. Art. I. The Vallais is united to the Empire. Art. II. The territory shall form a department under the title the *Département du Simplon.*"

The Valais was incorporated forthwith, and remained a Department

[1] Both these statements are taken from Hilaire Gay's *Histoire du Vallais*, vol. ii, p. 110.

of the French Empire for about three years. After the battle of Leipzig the allies speedily penetrated into Switzerland; and, on Dec. 24, 1813, the Préfet of the Département du Simplon, learning of their approach, made himself scarce, and went off in hot haste to Chambery with all the cash, leaving his guns behind him. A provisional Government for the Valais was established shortly afterwards, and on Sept. 12, 1814, "it was received, as the twentieth Canton, into the bosom of the Swiss Confederation."[1]

Down to the end of the 18th century Zermatt was not much visited by strangers. To *gens du pays*, however, it must have been a well-known place. So long back as 1414, Guichard de Rarogne dated a proclamation from Zermatt (Pratoborno),[2] which he would not have done if the name had been unfamiliar to those he addressed; and in 1364 and 1428 Zermatt paid Peter's Pence [Gremaud, Nos. 2090 and 2784], and may therefore have been heard of at Rome. To some extent, at least, it was known to the outer world. When De Saussure went there in 1789 he clearly had obtained some previous knowledge of the place. He was led to believe in the Val d'Ayas that he would be able to get from St. Jacques to Zermatt in a day —a fair day's work at the present time; and, although he did not accomplish this (being compelled by bad weather to make for Breuil), he actually took mules across from Breuil to Zermatt, and this seems to have been an ordinary proceeding at that time, although it is not now. His reception at Zermatt was somewhat frigid. There was no inn, and he says that the *cabaretiers* were either away or refused to take him in, and that the *Curé* declined to sell him anything. The first Englishman who is known to have visited Zermatt fared better.

Mr. George Cade, a native of York, passed that way in 1800.[3] The people flocked together in the Val Tournanche to regard the novel spectacle, and when he crossed into Switzerland the *Curé* of St. Nicholas told him that he had *never before seen an Englishman.* Mr. Cade left Chamonix at the beginning of Sept. 1800, accompanied by the Marie Coutet (Couttet) who had been guide to De Saussure in 1789, and in earlier years. They crossed the Great St. Bernard together, went up the Val Tournanche, and over the Theodul Pass to Zermatt, and thence to Visp and down the Rhone Valley. In connection with the Val Tournanche, Mr. Cade refers to a man named Erin, who was said to be 'the best guide in the country.' He accompanied them to the top of the Theodul, whence he was sent back. 'He went whistling away . . . without pikes or precaution.' This would appear to be the same Jean-Baptiste Erin who had conducted De Saussure, and, as it is stated that he was a *guide*, one may presume that travellers or tourists were not altogether unknown. But

1 *Histoire du Vallais depuis les temps les plus anciens jusqu'à nos jours*, par Hilaire Gay, 8vo, Geneva and Paris, 1889, vol. ii, pp. 124-6, 129.

2 Ordering the men of Louèche and elsewhere to guard the passes against the Bernese [Gremaud, No. 2623].

3 In the *Alpine Journal*, vol. vii, pp. 431-436, the Rev. J. Sowerby drew attention to a manuscript account of Mr. Cade's journey, and printed a portion of it. By the favour of its present owner, I have been permitted to examine this manuscript, and to make the extracts which are given.

Mr. Cade says that since the journey of De Saussure 'no attempts have been made to cross this famous passage' (the Theodul Pass), though he observes shortly afterwards

"that there is still some commerce carried on through this pass . . . which is probably the highest in the world for any man or animal. . . Nine mules had made the ascent this year. . . It is not uncommon for the passage to be shut up the whole year. Indeed the mules never cross from one side to the other if they sink much in the snow, or suffer from the rarefaction of the air. They are immediately unloaded, and the muleteers make shift themselves to transport their merchandize; otherwise, they proceed slowly to the Col, deposit their goods there and retire, either unloaded or in charge of articles left there perhaps several weeks before, purposely for them. Thus the Vallaisans send iron into Piedmont, and receive in exchange different wines."

His experience at Zermatt is thus described. "They addressed us in High Dutch, too high indeed for our weak understandings," but the *Curé* behaved well, and sent a message that he "wished for nothing so much as to be of service," and in the evening they had a chat.

"The conversation grew spirited. Politics were soon introduced by a detail of the entry of the French in the Valley of St. Nicholas: but why retrace the crimes with which it was accompanied, the violation of Wives and Virgins? Children, like the old, were murdered without mercy. . . When the enemy reached Zermatt the same cruelties were repeated, with an extortion of 500,000 livres. Meanwhile our host, this excellent old man, was bound, and a poignard was held at his breast till the demand was exacted.[1] The brave and generous villagers sacrificed everything for their Priest."

During the first half of the nineteenth century Zermatt was not unfrequently visited both by Swiss and strangers,[2] but the total number per annum was inconsiderable. This may be inferred from the slight notice bestowed upon it in "*The Traveller's Guide through Switzerland*, by Mr. J. G. Ebel, a new edition, arranged and improved by Daniel Wall," London, 1818, which was one of the earliest guide-books to Switzerland published in English.[3] The first edition of Murray's *Handbook for Travellers in Switzerland and the Alps of Savoy and Piedmont*, published in 1838, devotes, however, several pages to the Valleys of Saas and Zermatt; and from the details which are given, it is obvious that the district was becoming somewhat more visited, though, at that time, there was still no inn at Zermatt.

"The house of the curé offers its hospitalities, and a worthier host than Jean François de la Costa cannot be found. In the little plain of Zermatt, situated amidst the grandest scenery of nature, surrounded by forests of pines

[1] These appear to have been reprisals for the barbarities mentioned on p. 12.

[2] Amongst the better-known persons who went there may be mentioned W. Brockedon, the Artist (1825); Elie de Beaumont (1834); Engelhardt (1835); Desor and Studer (1839); Agassiz, Charpentier and Topffer (1840); J. D. Forbes (1841); John Ball (1845); and John Ruskin (1849).

[3] It said, "A place which may perhaps interest the tourist is the VALLEY OF PRABORGNE, which communicates with that of St. Nicholas. It is bounded by enormous glaciers, which descend to the bottom of the valley. The village of Praborgne is very lofty: it overlooks these glaciers from an immense height." It seems that the writer of this paragraph had not been on the spot, and he appears to be doubtful whether the tourist *would* be interested.

and vast glaciers, is placed, with its neat church, this elevated and retired village, with more cleanness and comfort among its inhabitants than is to be found in many places of greater pretensions: this has perhaps been effected by the influx of strangers, for many mineralogists, botanists, and entomologists, come here to collect rich harvests in the neighbourhood."

Until 1852, the only hotel at Zermatt was a little inn kept by the village doctor (Lauber), which was started in 1839. Though small and humble, it was sufficient for the wants of the place.[1] In 1852, the Hotel du Mont Cervin was opened, at what was then the northern end of the village.[2] In 1854, the Laubor inn was acquired by Mons. Alexandre Seiler, who christened it Hotel du Mont Rose. M. Seiler understood the art of inn-keeping. He knew how to welcome the coming and to speed the parting guest; and admirably seconded by his estimable wife, he soon made a name for the Mont Rose. There was no need to advertise the house by the ordinary methods, for it was advertised sufficiently by its *clientèle.* If any-one enquired What is the best hotel in Zermatt? or Where shall we go? the answer was 'Go to the Monte Rosa,' or 'Go to Seiler's.' Success, however, was not immediate. In the first years that he kept the house, the total number of visitors amounted to about eighty per annum. Perhaps as many more, or a slightly larger number, patronised the Hotel du Mont Cervin, but this hotel was not popular and was never full, and people used to leave it to come to the Mont Rose.

ALEXANDRE SEILER I.

Nearly simultaneously with the foundation of the latter hotel, the outburst of British energy occurred which led to the subjugation of all the High Alps around Zermatt. Down to 1853, the Breithorn was the only one of the great peaks in this district which had been ascended. Between 1854 and 1865 all of the rest were conquered. The ball, so to speak, was opened by the three brothers Smyth, —gentlemen who, happily, are all still alive. In 1854, Captain (now Colonel) Edmund Smyth, the Rev. Christopher Smyth, and the Rev. (now Canon) J. G. Smyth,[3] made the first ascent of the Strahlhorn

[1] The Lauber inn is incorporated in the present Monte Rosa Hotel, and forms part of its southern end. It had apparently, only one story, and a very narrow frontage to 'the street.' The bureau of the present hotel, the smoking-room, and the rooms above, belonged to the original building.

[2] The original Mont Cervin Hotel was scarcely a quarter of the size of the present hotel of that name, in which it is now incorporated.

[3] All three of the Smyths were climbers in the days of their youth. Canon Smyth when at Westminster is said to have clambered up by the School to the top of the Chapter House, where, finding a ladder, he was enabled to continue his explorations as far as the clock in the West Tower! Col. Smyth is 'Crab Jones.' Don't you know Crab Jones? "Here he comes, sauntering along with a straw in his mouth, the queerest, coolest fish in Rugby. If he were tumbled into the moon this minute, he would just pick himself up without taking his hands out of his pockets or turning a hair."—*Tom Brown's School-Days.* When Capt. Smyth went to the Himalayas, the natives used to

HOTEL DU MONT ROSE, ZERMATT.

from the Adler Pass, and they then turned their attention to Monte Rosa. The first ascent of the highest mountain in Switzerland (the second in elevation in the Alps) might have been expected to have received a good deal of attention. The comparatively small notice that has been given to it has been due, I think, to the fact that no adequate account of the expedition has been published.[1]

These two ascents were quickly followed by those of the other mountains which are enumerated in the accompanying Table. The number of visitors to Zermatt increased rapidly during this period, though all who came could still be accommodated in the two hotels. After 1865, there was a notable augmentation in numbers, which was due to the publicity given by the *Times* newspaper to an account of the first ascent of the Matterhorn. From this relation, which was reprinted throughout the world, millions of people heard the names of Zermatt and the Matterhorn for the first time. The Monte Rosa Hotel benefited most from this, and in 1867 Mons. Seiler was able to make himself master of *both* hotels, and under his able management the Mont Cervin lost its old reputation. The large building called the Hotel Zermatt was erected by the Commune, but it now forms part of the Seiler Hotels; and in 1884 the great establishment at the Riffelalp was opened by the enterprise of Alexandre Seiler I. No one who knows the facts will dispute that the capacity and tact with which he directed his affairs, the geniality with which he received his patrons, and the kindliness which he and his esteemed wife extended to all who were in difficulty, had much to do with the development of the place, and that they occupy a very prominent position amongst the makers of Zermatt.

say 'he could climb where birds could not fly,'—which is an Oriental equivalent for 'Monsieur has the agility of a chamois!'

1 A reference to, rather than an account of it was published in the 2nd ed. of the book entitled *Where there's a Will there's a Way*, 8vo, London, 1856, and some notice of it was taken in the *Illustrated London News*, and in a Norfolk newspaper; but with these exceptions nothing of the nature of an account has, I believe, been published of the first ascent of Monte Rosa.

First Ascents of the principal Peaks in the Zermatt District, arranged in Chronological Order.

Year.	Name of Peak.	Height in Feet.	First Ascent made by
1854	Stralhhorn .	13,750	Rev. Christopher Smyth, Capt. Edmund Smyth, and Rev. J. Grenville Smyth, with — Andermatten of Saas.
1855	Monte Rosa, highest point	15,217	Mr. J. Birkbeck, Rev. Charles Hudson, Rev. Christopher Smyth, Rev. J. Grenville Smyth, and Rev. E. Stevenson, with Ulrich Lauener and other guides.
1856	Allalinhorn .	13,235	Mr. E. L. Ames, with Franz Andermatten and — Imseng of Saas.
1858	Dom . . .	14,941	Rev. J. Llewelyn Davies, with Johann zum Taugwald, — Kronig of Zermatt, and a man from Randa.
1859	Rimpfischhorn .	13,790	Rev. Leslie Stephen and Dr. R. Liveing, with Melchior Anderegg and Johann zum Taugwald.
1860	Alphubel . .	13,803	Rev. Leslie Stephen, with Melchior Anderegg.
1861	Lyskamm . .	14,889	Mr. W. E. Hall, Rev. J. F. Hardy, Mr. J. A. Hudson, Mr. C. H. Pilkington, Prof. Ramsay, Mr. T. Rennison, Dr. Sibson, Mr. R. Stephenson, with J. P. Cachat, Franz Lochmatter, Peter Perrn, J. M. Perrn, and Stephan zum Taugwald.
,,	Weisshorn . .	14,803	Dr. John Tyndall, with J. J. Bennen and — Wenger.
,,	Castor . .	13,878	Mr. William Mathews and Mr. F. W. Jacomb, with Michel Croz and Jean-Baptiste Croz.
,,	Nord End, Monte Rosa	15,132	Mr. E. N. Buxton, Sir T. Fowell Buxton, and Mr. J. J. Cowell, with Michel Payot and other guides.
1862	Dent Blanche .	14,318	Mr. T. S. Kennedy and Mr. Wigram, with Jean-Baptiste Croz and — Kronig.
,,	Täschhorn . .	14,757	Rev. J. Llewelyn Davies and Rev. J. Hayward, with Johann and Stephan zum Taugwald.
1864	Pollux . .	13,432	Mons. Jacot, with ?
,,	Rothhorn (Moming)	13,855	Mr. F. Craufurd Grove and Rev. Leslie Stephen, with Melchior Anderegg and Jakob Anderegg.
1865	Ober Gabelhorn	13,363	Mr. A. W. Moore and Mr. Horace Walker, with Jakob Anderegg.
,,	Matterhorn .	14,705	Lord Francis Douglas, Mr. Hadow, Rev. Charles Hudson, and Mr. Edward Whymper, with Michel Croz, Peter Taugwalder *père*, and Peter Taugwalder *fils*.

CHAPTER II.

UPON SOME ATTEMPTS TO ASCEND THE MATTERHORN.

ATTEMPTS BY THE CHASSEURS OF VAL TOURNANCHE (1858-9)—MESSRS. PARKER IN 1860—MR. VAUGHAN HAWKINS IN 1860—SECOND ATTEMPT BY MESSRS. PARKER IN 1861—MY FIRST NIGHT ON THE MATTERHORN (1861)—CAMP ON THE COL DU LION—WINTER ATTEMPT BY MR. T. S. KENNEDY IN 1862—RENEWED ATTACKS WITH MR. R. J. S. MACDONALD—A SOLITARY SCRAMBLE ON THE MATTERHORN—A NIGHT ALONE—A TUMBLE—MY FIFTH AND SIXTH ATTEMPTS IN 1862—PROFESSOR TYNDALL REACHES 'THE SHOULDER'—MY SEVENTH ATTEMPT (1863)—ABANDONMENT OF THE SOUTH-WEST RIDGE—MY EIGHTH ATTEMPT (1865)—BAMBOOZLED AND HUMBUGGED—A FLANK MARCH.

THE name of Zermatt is inseparably connected with that of the Matterhorn. This grand mountain, though not the loftiest of its district,[1] is *the* peak above all others that people wish to see. Trainloads of tourists pass the Weisshorn daily without emotion, but they raise a cheer when Mont Cervin comes in sight.

Most tourists obtain their first view of the mountain either from the valley of Zermatt or from that of Tournanche. From the former direction the base of the mountain is seen at its narrowest, and its ridges and faces seem to be prodigiously steep. The view of the mountain from Breuil, in the Val Tournanche, is scarcely less striking than that on the other side; but it perhaps makes less impression, because the spectator grows accustomed to the sight while coming up the valley. From this direction the mountain is seen to be broken up into a series of pyramidal wedge-shaped masses. It was natural to suppose that a way would more readily be found to the summit on a side thus broken up than in any other direction. The eastern face, fronting the Riffel, seemed one smooth, inaccessible cliff, from summit to base. The ghastly precipices which face the Z'Mutt Glacier forbade any attempt in *that* direction. There remained only the side of Val Tournanche; and it will be found that nearly all the earliest attempts to ascend the mountain were made upon that side.

The first efforts to ascend the Matterhorn of which I have heard were made in the years 1858-9, from the direction of Breuil, by some chasseurs of the Val Tournanche. The highest point that was attained was about as far as the place which is now called the 'Chimney'

[1] It is exceeded in elevation by Monte Rosa, the two highest points of the Mischabelhörner, the Lyskamm, and the Weisshorn.

CAMP

THE MATTERHORN, FROM THE RIFFELBERG.

(cheminée), a height of about 12,650 feet. Those who were concerned in these expeditions were Jean-Antoine Carrel, Jean-Jacques Carrel, Victor Carrel, the Abbé Gorret, and Gabrielle Maquignaz.[1]

Attempt by Messrs. Parker (1860).—The next attempt was made by the Messrs. Alfred, Charles, and Sandbach Parker, of Liverpool, in July 1860. These gentlemen, without guides, endeavoured to storm the peak by attacking its eastern face. The brothers went along the ridge between the Hörnli and the peak until they came to the point where the ascending angle is considerably increased. This place is marked on Dufour's map of Switzerland 3298 mètres (10,820 feet). They were then obliged to bear a little to the left to get on to the face of the mountain; and, afterwards, they turned to the right, and ascended about 700 feet higher, keeping as nearly as was practicable to the crest of the ridge, but, occasionally, bearing a little to the left—that is, more on to the face of the mountain. Clouds, a high wind, and want of time, were the causes which prevented them from going farther. Their highest point was under 12,000 feet.

Attempt by Mr. Vaughan Hawkins (1860).—Another attempt to ascend the mountain was made towards the end of August 1860, by Mr. Vaughan Hawkins, from the side of the Val Tournanche. Mr. Hawkins inspected the Matterhorn in 1859, with the guide J. J. Bennen, and formed the opinion that the south-west ridge[2] would lead to the summit. He engaged J.-Jacques Carrel, who was concerned in the first attempts, and, accompanied by Bennen (and by Professor Tyndall, whom he had invited to take part in the expedition), he started for the gap between the little and the great peak.[3]

Mr. Hawkins' party, led by Bennen, climbed the rocks abutting against the Couloir du Lion, on its south side, and attained the Col du Lion, although not without difficulty. They then followed the south-west ridge, passed the place at which the earliest explorers had turned back (the Chimney), and ascended about 300 feet more. Mr. Hawkins and J.-J. Carrel then stopped, but Bennen and Professor Tyndall mounted a few feet higher. They retreated, however, in less than half-an-hour, finding that time ran short; and, descending to the Col by the same route as they had followed on the ascent, proceeded thence to Breuil, down the Couloir instead of by the rocks. The point at which Mr. Hawkins stopped is easily identified from his description. Its height is about 12,990 feet above the sea. Bennen and Tyndall could not have ascended more than 50 or 60 feet beyond this in the few minutes they were absent from the others, as they were upon one of the most difficult parts of the mountain. This party therefore accomplished an advance of about 350 or 400 feet.

[1] Gabrielle Maquignaz is still alive, and is proprietor of the Hotel des Jumeaux at Breuil.

[2] This ridge is seen on the left of the engraving upon page 29; and if the reader consults this view, the explanatory outlines, and the maps, he will be able to form a fair idea of the points which were attained on this and upon the subsequent attempts.

[3] Since this time the small peak has received the name Tête du Lion. The gap is now called the Col du Lion; the glacier at its base, the Glacier du Lion; and the gully which connects the Col with the glacier, the Couloir du Lion.

Second Attempt by Messrs. Parker (1861).—Mr. Hawkins did not try again, and the next attempt was made by the Messrs. Parker, in July 1861. They again started from Zermatt; followed the route they had struck out on the previous year, and got a little higher than before; but they were defeated by want of time, shortly afterwards left Zermatt on account of bad weather, and did not again renew their efforts. Mr. Parker said—"In neither case did we go as high as we could. At the point where we turned we saw our way for a few hundred feet farther; but, beyond that, the difficulties seemed to increase." I am informed that both attempts should be considered as excursions undertaken with the view of ascertaining whether there was any encouragement to make a more deliberate attack on the north-east side.

My first night on the Matterhorn (1861).—I arrived at Breuil on the 28th of August 1861, with an Oberland guide, and found that Professor Tyndall had been there a day or two before, but had done nothing. On the way up we enquired for another man of all the knowing ones, and they, with one voice, proclaimed that Jean-Antoine Carrel, of the village of Val Tournanche, was the cock of the valley. We sought, of course, for Carrel; and found him a well-made, resolute-looking fellow, with a certain defiant air which was rather taking. Yes, he would go. Twenty francs a-day, whatever was the result, was his price. I assented. But I must take his comrade. "Why so?" Oh, it was impossible to get along without another man. As he said this an evil countenance came forth out of the darkness and proclaimed itself the comrade. I demurred, and the negotiations broke off.

I had seen the mountain from nearly every direction, and an ascent of it seemed much more than was likely to be accomplished in twenty-four hours. I intended to sleep out upon it, as high as possible, and to attempt to reach the summit on the following day. At Breuil, we endeavoured to induce another man to accompany us, but without success. Matthias zum Taugwald and other well-known guides were there at the time, but they declined to go on any account. A sturdy old fellow—Peter Taugwalder by name—said he would go! His price? "Two hundred francs." "What, whether we ascend or not?" "Yes—nothing less." The end of the matter was, that all the men who were more or less capable shewed a strong disinclination, or positively refused to go (their disinclination being very much in proportion to their capacity), or else asked a prohibitive price. This, it may be said once for all, was the reason why so many futile attempts were made upon the Matterhorn. One guide after another was brought up to the mountain, and patted on the back, but all declined the business. The men who went had no heart in the matter, and took the first opportunity to turn back.[1] For they were, with the exception of the man to whom reference will be made presently, universally impressed with the belief that the summit was entirely inaccessible.

[1] The guide Bennen must be excepted.

We resolved to go alone, and anticipating a cold bivouac, begged the loan of a couple of blankets from the innkeeper. He refused them; giving the curious reason, that we had bought a bottle of brandy at Val Tournanche, and had not bought any from him! No brandy, no blankets, appeared to be his rule. We did not require them that night, as it was passed in the highest cow-shed in the valley, which is about an hour nearer to the mountain than the hotel. The cowherds, good fellows, seldom troubled by tourists, hailed our company with delight, and did their best to make us comfortable; brought out their little stores of simple food, and, as we sat with them round the great copper pot which hung over the fire, bade us in husky voice, though with honest intent, to beware of the perils of the haunted cliffs. When night was coming on, we saw, stealing up the hill-side, the forms of Jean-Antoine Carrel and the comrade. "Oh ho!" I said, "you have repented?" "Not at all; you deceive yourself." "Why then have you come here?" "Because we ourselves are going on the mountain to-morrow." "Oh, then it is *not* necessary to have more than three." "Not for *us*." I admired their pluck, and had a strong inclination to engage the pair; but, finally, decided against it. The *comrade* turned out to be the J.-J. Carrel who had been with Mr. Hawkins, and was nearly related to the other man. Both were bold mountaineers; but Jean-Antoine was incomparably the better man of the two, and was the finest rock-climber I have ever seen. He was the only man who persistently refused to accept defeat, and who continued to believe, in spite of all discouragements, that the great mountain was not inaccessible, and that it could be ascended from the side of his native valley.

The night wore away without any excitement. The two Carrels crept noiselessly out before daybreak, and went off. We did not leave until nearly seven o'clock, and followed them leisurely, leaving all our properties in the cow-shed; sauntered over the gentian-studded slopes which intervene between the shed and the Glacier du Lion, left cows and their pastures behind, traversed the stony wastes, and arrived at the ice. Old beds of hard snow lay on its right bank (our left hand), and we mounted over them on to the lower portion of the glacier with ease. But, as we ascended, crevasses became numerous, and we were at last brought to a halt by some which were of very large dimensions; and, as our cutting powers were limited, we sought an easier route, and turned, naturally, to the lower rocks of the Tête du Lion, which overlook the glacier on its west. Some good scrambling took us in a short time on to the crest of the ridge which descends towards the south; and thence, up to the level of the Col du Lion, there was a long natural staircase, on which it was seldom necessary to use the hands. I dubbed the place 'The Great Staircase.' Then the cliffs of the Tête du Lion, which rise above the Couloir, had to be skirted. This part varies considerably in different seasons, and in 1861 we found it difficult; for the fine weather of that year had reduced the snow-beds abutting against it to a lower level than usual, and the rocks which were left exposed at the junction of the snow with the cliffs had few ledges or cracks to which we could hold. But by half-past

THE COL DU LION; LOOKING TOWARDS THE TÊTE DU LION.

ten o'clock we stood on the Col, and looked down upon the magnificent basin out of which the Z'Mutt Glacier flows. We decided to pass the night upon the Col, for we were charmed with the capabilities of the place, although it was one where liberties could not be taken. On one side a sheer wall overhung the Tiefenmatten

Glacier. On the other, steep, glassy slopes of hard snow descended to the Glacier du Lion, furrowed by water and by falling stones. On the north there was the great peak of the Matterhorn,[1] and on the south the cliffs of the Tête du Lion. Throw a bottle down to the Tiefenmatten—no sound returns for more than a dozen seconds.

> * * * 'how fearful
> And dizzy 'tis, to cast one's eyes so low!"

But no harm could come from that side. Neither could it from the other. Nor was it likely that it would from the Tête du Lion, for some jutting ledges conveniently overhung our proposed resting-place. We waited for a while, basked in the sunshine, and watched or listened to the Carrels, who were sometimes seen or heard, high above us, upon the ridge leading towards the summit; and, leaving at midday, we descended to the cow-shed, packed up the tent and other properties, and returned to the Col, although heavily laden, before six o'clock. This tent was not a success. It looked very pretty when set up in London, but it proved thoroughly useless in the Alps. It was made of light canvas, and opened like a book; had one end closed permanently and the other with flaps; it was supported by two alpenstocks, and had the canvas sides prolonged so as to turn in underneath. Numerous cords were sewn to the lower edges, to which stones were to be attached; but the main fastenings were by a cord which passed underneath the ridge and through iron rings screwed into the tops of the alpenstocks, and were secured by pegs. The wind, which playfully careered about the surrounding cliffs, was driven through our gap as through a blow-pipe; the flaps of the tent would not keep down, the pegs would not stay in, and it exhibited so marked a desire to go to the top of the Dent Blanche, that we thought it prudent to take it down and sit upon it. When night came on we wrapped ourselves in it, and made our camp as comfortable as the circumstances would allow. The silence was impressive. No living thing was near our solitary bivouac; the Carrels had turned back and were out of hearing; the stones had ceased to fall, and the trickling water to murmur.

It was bitterly cold. Water froze hard in a bottle under my head. Not surprising, as we were actually on snow, and in a position where the slightest wind was at once felt. For a time we dozed, but about midnight there came from high aloft a tremendous explosion, followed by a second of dead quiet. A great mass of rock had split off, and was descending towards us. My guide started up, wrung his hands, and exclaimed, "O my God, we are lost!" We heard it coming, mass after mass pouring over the precipices, bounding and rebounding from cliff to cliff, and the great rocks in advance smiting one another. They seemed to be close, although they were probably distant, but some small fragments, which dropped upon us at the same time from the ledges just above, added to the alarm.

We put ourselves in motion at daybreak, and commenced the

[1] The engraving is made after a sketch taken from the rocks of the Matterhorn, just above the Col.

ascent of the south-west ridge. There was no more sauntering with hands in the pockets,—each step had to be earned by downright climbing. But it was the most pleasant kind of climbing. The rocks were fast and unencumbered with débris; the cracks were good, although not numerous; and there was nothing to fear except from one's-self.

Hardly an hour passed before we arrived at the 'Chimney.' A smooth, straight slab of rock was fixed, at a considerable angle, between two others equally smooth. My companion essayed to go up, and, after crumpling his long body into many ridiculous positions, he said that he would not, for he could not, manage it. With some little trouble I got up unassisted, and then my guide tied himself on to the end of our rope, and I endeavoured to pull him up. But he was so awkward that he did little for himself, and so heavy that he proved too much for *me*, and after several attempts he untied himself, and quietly observed that he should go down. I told him he was a coward, and *he* mentioned his opinion of *me*. I requested him to go to Breuil, and to say that he had left his 'monsieur' on the mountain, and he turned to go; whereupon I had to eat humble pie and ask him to come back; for, although it was not very difficult to go up, and not at all dangerous with a man standing below, it was quite another thing to come down, as the lower edge overhung in a provoking manner.

The day was perfect; the sun was pouring down grateful warmth; the wind had fallen; the way seemed clear, no insuperable obstacle was in sight; but what could one do alone? I stood on the top, chafing under this unexpected contretemps, and remained for some time irresolute; but as it became apparent that the Chimney was swept more frequently than was necessary (it was a natural channel for falling stones), I turned at last, descended with the assistance of my companion, and returned with him to Breuil, where we arrived about mid-day.

The Carrels did not shew themselves. We were told that they had not got to any great height,[1] and that the 'comrade,' who for convenience had taken off his shoes and tied them round his waist, had managed to let one of them slip, and had come down with a piece of cord fastened round his naked foot. Notwithstanding this, they had boldly glissaded down the Couloir du Lion, J.-J. Carrel having his shoeless foot tied up in a pocket handkerchief.

The Matterhorn was not assailed again in 1861. I left Breuil with the conviction that it was little use for a single person to organise an attack upon it, so great was its influence on the morals of the guides; and persuaded that it was desirable at least two should go, to back each other when required: and departed with my guide over the Col Théodule, longing, more than before, to make the ascent, and determined to return, if possible, with a companion, to lay siege to the mountain until one or the other was vanquished.

[1] I learned afterwards from Jean-Antoine Carrel that they got considerably higher than upon their previous attempts, and about 250 or 300 feet higher than Professor Tyndall in 1860. In 1862, I saw the initials of J.-A. Carrel cut on the rocks at the place where he and his comrade had turned back.

A winter attempt by Mr. T. S. Kennedy (1862).—The year 1862 was still young, and the Matterhorn, clad in its wintry garb, bore but little resemblance to the Matterhorn of the summer, when a new force came to do battle with the mountain, from another direction. Mr. T. S. Kennedy of Leeds conceived the extraordinary idea that the peak might prove less impracticable in January than in June, and arrived at Zermatt in the former month to put his conception to the test. With stout Peter Perrn and sturdy Peter Taugwalder he slept in the little chapel at the Schwarzsee, and on the next morning, like the Messrs. Parker, followed the ridge between the peak called Hörnli and the great mountain. But they found that snow in winter obeyed the ordinary laws, and that wind and frost were not less unkind than in summer.

THOMAS S. KENNEDY.

"The wind whirled up the snow and spiculæ of ice into our faces like needles, and flat pieces of ice a foot in diameter, carried up from the glacier below, went flying past. Still no one seemed to like to be the first to give in, till a gust fiercer than usual forced us to shelter for a time behind a rock. Immediately it was tacitly understood that our expedition must now end; but we determined to leave some memento of our visit, and, after descending a considerable distance, we found a suitable place with loose stones of which to build a cairn. A tower six feet high was erected; a bottle, with the date, was placed inside, and we retreated as rapidly as possible."

This cairn was placed at the spot marked upon Dufour's Map of Switzerland 10,820 feet (3298 mètres), and the highest point attained by Mr. Kennedy was not, I imagine, more than two or three hundred feet above it. The cairn disappeared long ago.

Shortly after this Professor Tyndall gave an account of the reason why he had left Breuil, in August 1861, without doing anything.[1] It seems that he sent his guide Bennen to reconnoitre, and that the latter made the following report to his employer:—

"Herr, I have examined the mountain carefully, and find it more difficult and dangerous than I had imagined. There is no place upon it where we could well pass the night. We might do so on yonder Col upon the snow, but there we should be almost frozen to death, and totally unfit for the work of the next day. On the rocks there is no ledge or cranny which could give us proper harbourage; and starting from Breuil it is certainly impossible to reach the summit in a single day." "I was entirely taken aback," says Tyndall, "by this report. I felt like a man whose grip had given way, and who was dropping through the air. . . Bennen was evidently dead against any attempt upon the mountain. 'We can, at all events, reach the lower of

[1] See page 22.

the two summits,' I remarked. 'Even that is difficult,' he replied; 'but when you have reached it, what then? The peak has neither name nor fame.'"[1]

I was more surprised than discouraged by this report by Bennen. One half of his assertions I knew to be wrong. The Col to which he referred was the Col du Lion, upon which we had passed a night, less than a week after he had spoken so authoritatively; and I had seen a place not far below the 'Chimney'—a place about 500 feet above the Col—where it seemed possible to construct a sleeping-place. Bennen's opinions seem to have undergone a complete change. In 1860 he is described as having been enthusiastic to make an attempt; in 1861 he was dead against one.

The first attempt in 1862.—Undismayed by this, my friend Mr. Reginald Macdonald agreed to join me in a renewed assault from the south; and, although we failed to secure Melchior Anderegg and some other notable guides, we obtained two men of repute, namely, Johann zum Taugwald and Johann Kronig, of Zermatt. We met there early in July, but stormy weather prevented us for some days even from passing to the other side of the chain; and when we crossed the Col Théodule on the 5th the weather was thoroughly unsettled —it was raining in the valleys, and snowing upon the mountains.

We had need of a porter, and, by the advice of our landlord, descended to the châlets of Breuil in search of one Luc Meynet. We found his house a mean abode, encumbered with cheese-making apparatus, and tenanted only by some bright-eyed children; but as they said that uncle Luc would soon be home, we waited at the door of the little châlet and watched for him. At last a speck was seen coming round the corner of the patch of pines below Breuil, and then the children clapped their hands, dropped their toys, and ran eagerly forward to meet him. We saw an ungainly, wobbling figure stoop down and catch up the little ones, kiss them on each cheek, and put them into the empty panniers on each side of the mule, and then heard it come on carolling, as if this was not a world of woe: and yet the face of little Luc Meynet, the hunchback of Breuil, bore traces of trouble and sorrow, and there was more than a touch of sadness in his voice when he said that he must look after his brother's children. All his difficulties were, however, at length overcome, and he agreed to join us to carry the tent.

In the past winter I had turned my attention to tents, and that which we had brought with us was the result of experiments to devise one which should be sufficiently portable to be taken over the most difficult ground, whilst combining lightness with stability. Its base was just under six feet square, and a cross-section perpendicular to its length was an equilateral triangle, the sides of which were six feet long. It was intended to accommodate four persons. It was

[1] *Mountaineering in* 1861, *a Vacation Tour*, by John Tyndall; 8vo, London, 1862; pp. 86-7. Tyndall and Bennen were mistaken in supposing that the mountain has two summits; it has only one. They seem to have been deceived by the appearance of that part of the south-west ridge which is called 'the shoulder' (l'épaule), as seen from Breuil. Viewed from that place, its southern end has certainly, through foreshortening, the semblance of a peak; but when one regards it from the Col Théodule, or from any place in the same direction, the delusion is at once apparent.

THE MATTERHORN, FROM THE SUMMIT OF THE THÉODULE PASS.

supported by four ash-poles, six feet and a half long, and one inch and a quarter thick, tapering to the top to an inch and an eighth, which were shod with iron points.

Sunday, the 6th of July, was showery, and snow fell on the Matterhorn, but we started on the following morning with our three men, and pursued my route of the previous year. I was requested to direct the way, as none save myself had been on the mountain before. I did not distinguish myself on this occasion, and led my companions nearly to the top of the Tête du Lion before the mistake was discovered. The party becoming rebellious, a little exploration was made towards our right, and we found that we were upon the top of the cliff overlooking the Col du Lion. The day was far advanced before we arrived at our camping-place on the Col. Profiting by the experience of last year, we did not pitch the tent actually on the snow, but collected a quantity of débris from the neighbouring ledges, and after constructing a rough platform of the larger pieces, levelled the whole with the dirt and mud. Meynet had proved invaluable as a tent-bearer; for—although his legs were more picturesque than symmetrical, and although he seemed to be built on principle with no two parts alike—his very deformities proved of service; and we quickly found he had spirit of no common order, and that few peasants are more agreeable companions, or better climbers, than little Luc Meynet, the hunchback of Breuil.

A strong wind sprang up from the east during the night, and in the morning it was blowing almost a hurricane. The tent behaved nobly, and we remained under its shelter for several hours after the sun had risen, uncertain what it was best to do. A lull tempted us to move, but we had scarcely ascended a hundred feet before the storm burst upon us with increased fury. Advance or return was alike impossible; the ridge was denuded of its débris; and we clutched our hardest when we saw stones as big as a man's fist blown away horizontally into space. We dared not attempt to stand upright, and remained stationary, on all fours, glued, as it were, to the rocks. It was intensely cold, for the blast had swept along the main chain of the Pennine Alps, and across the great snow-fields around Monte Rosa. Our warmth and courage rapidly evaporated, and at the next lull we retreated to the tent; having to halt several times even in that short distance. Taugwald and Kronig then declared that they had had enough, and refused to have anything more to do with the mountain. Meynet also informed us that he would be required down below for important cheese-making operations on the following day. It was therefore needful to return to Breuil, and we arrived there at 2.30 P.M., extremely chagrined at our complete defeat.

Second attempt in 1862.—Jean-Antoine Carrel, attracted by rumours, had come up to the inn during our absence, and after some negotiations agreed to accompany us, with one of his friends named Pession, on the first fine day. We thought ourselves fortunate; for Carrel clearly considered the mountain a kind of *preserve*, and regarded our late attempt as an act of *poaching*. The wind blew itself out during the night, and we started again, with these two men and a porter, at

8 A.M. on the 9th, with unexceptionable weather. Carrel pleased us by suggesting that we should camp even higher than before; and we accordingly proceeded, without resting at the Col, until we overtopped the Tête du Lion. Near the foot of the 'Chimney,' a little below the crest of the ridge, and on its eastern side, we found a protected place; and by building up from ledge to ledge (under the direction of our leader, who at that time was a working mason), we at length constructed a platform of sufficient size and of considerable solidity. Its height was about 12,550 feet above the sea. We then pushed on, as the day was very fine, and, after a short hour's scramble, got to the foot of the Great Tower upon the ridge (that is to say, to Mr. Hawkins' farthest point), and afterwards returned to our bivouac. We turned out again at 4 A.M., and at 5.15 started upwards once more, with fine weather and the thermometer at 28°. Carrel scrambled up the Chimney, and Macdonald and I after him. Pession's turn came, but when he arrived at the top he looked very ill, declared himself to be thoroughly incapable, and said that he must go back. We waited some time, but he did not get better, neither could we learn the nature of his illness. Carrel flatly refused to go on with us alone. We were helpless. Macdonald, ever the coolest of the cool, suggested that we should try what we could do without them; but our better judgment prevailed, and, finally, we returned together to Breuil. On the next day my friend started for London.

Three times I had essayed the ascent of this mountain, and on each occasion had failed ignominiously. I had not advanced a yard beyond my predecessors. Up to the height of nearly 13,000 feet there were no extraordinary difficulties; the way so far might even become 'a matter of amusement.' Only 1800 feet remained; but they were as yet untrodden, and might present the most formidable obstacles. No man could expect to climb them by himself. A morsel of rock only seven feet high might at any time defeat him, if it were perpendicular. Such a place might be possible to two, or a bagatelle to three men. It was evident that a party should consist of three men at least. But where could the other two men be obtained. Carrel was the only man who exhibited any enthusiasm in the matter; and he, in 1861, had absolutely refused to go unless the party consisted of at least *four* persons. Want of men made the difficulty, not the mountain.

The weather became bad again, so I went to Zermatt on the chance of picking up a man, and remained there during a week of storms. Not one of the better men, however, could be induced to come, and I returned to Breuil on the 17th, hoping to combine the skill of Carrel with the willingness of Meynet on a new attempt, by the same route as before; for the upper part of the north-eastern ridge, which I had inspected in the meantime, seemed to be entirely impracticable. Both men were inclined to go, but their ordinary occupations prevented them from starting at once.

A solitary scramble on the Matterhorn (1862).—My tent had been left rolled up at the second platform, and whilst waiting for the men it occurred to me that it might have been blown away during the late stormy weather; so I started off on the 18th to see if this were so or not. The way was by this time familiar, and I mounted rapidly, astonishing the friendly herdsmen—who nodded recognition as I flitted past them and the cows—for I was alone, because no man was available. But more deliberation was necessary when the pastures were passed, and climbing began, as it was needful to mark each step, in case of mist, or surprise by night. It is one of the few things which can be said in favour of mountaineering alone (a practice which has little besides to commend it), that it awakens a man's faculties, and makes him observe. When one has no arms to help, and no head to guide him except his own, he must needs take note even of small things, for he cannot afford to throw away a chance; and so it came to pass, upon my solitary scramble, when above the snow-line, and beyond the ordinary limits of flowering plants, when peering about, noting angles and landmarks, that my eyes fell upon the tiny straggling plants—oftentimes a single flower on a single stalk—pioneers of vegetation, atoms of life in a world of desolation, which had found their way up—who can tell how?—from far below, and were obtaining bare sustenance from the scanty soil in protected nooks; and it gave a new interest to the well-known rocks to see what a gallant fight the survivors made (for many must have perished in the attempt) to ascend the great mountain. The Gentian, as one might have expected, was there, but it was run close by Saxifrages, and by *Linaria alpina*, and was beaten by *Thlaspi rotundifolium*, which latter plant was the highest I was able to secure, although it too was overtopped by a little white flower that I knew not, and was unable to reach.

The tent was safe, although snowed up; and I turned to contemplate the view, which, when seen alone and undisturbed, had all the strength and charm of complete novelty. The highest peaks of the Pennine chain were in front—the Breithorn (13,685 feet), the Lyskamm (14,889), and Monte Rosa (15,217); then, turning to the right, the entire block of mountains which separated the Val Tournanche from the Val d'Ayas was seen at a glance, with its culminating point the Grand Tournalin (11,086). Behind were the ranges dividing the Val d'Ayas from the Valley of Gressoney, backed by higher summits. More still to the right, the eye wandered down the entire length of the Val Tournanche, and then rested upon the Graian Alps with their innumerable peaks, and upon the isolated Pyramid of Monte Viso (12,643) in the extreme distance. Next, still turning to the right, came the mountains intervening between the Val Tournanche and the Val Barthélemy. Mont Rouss (a round-topped snowy summit, which seems so important from Breuil, but which is in reality only a buttress of the higher mountain, the Château des Dames) had long ago sunk, and the eye passed over it, scarcely heeding its existence, to the Becca Salle (or Bec de Sale),—a miniature Matterhorn—and to other, and more important heights. Then the grand mass of the Dent d'Hérens (13,714) stopped the way; a noble mountain, encrusted on its northern slopes with enormous hanging glaciers, which broke away at mid-day in immense slices, and thundered down on to the Tiefenmatten Glacier; and lastly, most splendid of all, came the Dent

Blanche (14,318), soaring above the basin of the great Z'Muttgletscher. Such a view is hardly to be matched in the Alps, and *this* view is very rarely seen, as I saw it, perfectly unclouded.

Time sped away unregarded, and the little birds which had built their nests on the neighbouring cliffs had begun to chirp their evening hymn before I thought of returning. Half mechanically I turned to the tent, unrolled it, and set it up. It contained food enough for several days, and I resolved to stay over the night. I had started from Breuil without provisions, or telling Favre—the innkeeper, who was accustomed to my erratic ways—where I was going. I returned to the view. The sun was setting, and its rosy rays, blending with the snowy blue, had thrown a pale, pure violet far as the eye could see; the valleys were drowned in purple gloom, whilst the summits shone with unnatural brightness: and as I sat in the door of the tent, and watched the twilight change to darkness, the earth seemed to become less earthy and almost sublime; the world seemed dead, and I, its sole inhabitant. By and by, the moon as it rose brought the hills again into sight, and by a judicious repression of detail rendered the view yet more magnificent. Something in the south hung like a great glow-worm in the air; it was too large for a star, and too steady for a meteor; and it was long before I could realise the scarcely credible fact that it was the moonlight glittering on the great snow-slope on the north side of Monte Viso, at a distance, as the crow flies, of 98 miles. Shivering, at last I entered the tent and made my coffee. The night was passed comfortably, and the next morning, tempted by the brilliancy of the weather, I proceeded yet higher in search of another place for a platform.

Solitary scrambling over a pretty wide area had shewn me that a single individual is subjected to many difficulties which do not trouble a party of two or three men, and that the disadvantages of being alone are more felt while descending than during the ascent. In order to neutralise these inconveniences, I devised two little appliances, which were now brought into use for the first time. One was a claw—a kind of grapnel—about five inches long, made of shear steel, one-fifth of an inch thick. This was of use in difficult places where there was no hold within arm's length, but where there were cracks or ledges some distance higher. The claw could be stuck on the end of the alpenstock and dropped into such places, or, on extreme occasions, flung up until it attached itself to something. The edges that laid hold of the rocks were serrated, which tended to make them catch more readily, and the other end had a ring to which a rope was fastened. It must not be understood that this was employed for hauling one's-self up for any great distance, but that it was used in ascending, at the most, for only a few yards at a time. In descending, however, it could be prudently used for a greater distance at a time, as the claws could be planted firmly; but it was necessary to keep the rope taut, and the pull constantly in the direction of the length of the implement, otherwise it had a tendency to slip away. The second device was merely a modification of a dodge practised by all climbers. It is often necessary for a solitary climber (or for the last man of a party during a descent) to make a loop in the end of his rope, to pass it over some rocks, and to come down holding the free end. The loop is then jerked off, and the process may be repeated. But as it sometimes happens that there are no rocks at hand which will allow a loose loop to be used, a slip-knot has to be resorted to, and the rope is drawn in tightly. Consequently, it will occur that it is not possible to jerk the loop off, and the rope has to be cut and left behind. To prevent this, I had a wrought-iron ring (two and a quarter inches in diameter and three eighths of an inch thick) attached to one end of my rope. A loop could be made in a moment by passing the other end of the rope through this ring, which of course slipped up and held tightly as I descended holding the free end. A strong piece of cord was also attached to the ring, and, on arriving at the bottom, this was pulled; the ring slid back again, and the loop was whipped off readily. By means of these two simple appliances I was able to ascend and descend rocks, which otherwise would have been completely impassable. The combined weight of these two things amounted to less than half-a-pound.[1]

It has been mentioned that the rocks of the south-west ridge are by no means difficult for some distance above the Col du Lion. This is true of them up to the level of the Chimney, but they steepen when that is passed, and remaining smooth and with but few fractures, and still continuing to dip outwards, present some steps of a very uncertain kind, particularly when they are glazed with ice. At this point (just above the Chimney) the climber is obliged to follow the southern (or Breuil) side of the ridge, but, in a few feet more, one must turn over to the northern (or Z'Mutt) side, where, in most years, nature kindly provides a snow-slope. When this is surmounted, one can again return to the crest of the ridge, and follow it, by easy rocks, to the foot of the Great Tower.[2] This was the highest point attained by Mr. Hawkins in 1860, and it was also our highest on the 9th of July.

This Great Tower is one of the most striking features of the ridge. It stands out like a turret at the angle of a castle. Behind it a battlemented wall leads upwards to the citadel. Seen from the Théodule pass it looks only an insignificant pinnacle, but as one approaches it (on the ridge) so it seems to rise, and, when one is at its base, it completely conceals the upper parts of the mountain. I found here a suitable place for the tent; which, although not so well protected as the second platform, possessed the advantage of being 300 feet higher up; and fascinated by the wildness of the cliffs, and enticed by the perfection of the weather, I went on to see what was behind.

The first step was a difficult one. The ridge became diminished to the least possible width—it was hard to keep one's balance—and just where it was narrowest, a more than perpendicular mass barred the way. Nothing fairly within arm's reach could be laid hold of;

[1] Illustrations of these appliances are given in *Scrambles amongst the Alps*.

[2] In consequence of rock-falls which have occurred, this description is no longer correct

it was necessary to spring up, and then to haul one's-self over the sharp edge by sheer strength. Progression directly upwards was then impossible. Enormous and appalling precipices plunged down to the Tiefenmatten Glacier on the left, but round the right-hand side it was just possible to go. One hindrance then succeeded another, and much time was consumed in seeking a way. I have a vivid recollection of a gully of more than usual perplexity at the side of the Great Tower, with minute ledges and steep walls; of the ledges dwindling away and at last ceasing; and of finding myself, with arms and legs divergent, fixed as if crucified, pressing against the rock, and feeling each rise and fall of my chest as I breathed; of screwing my head round to look for hold, and not seeing any, and of jumping sideways on to the other side. 'Tis vain to attempt to describe such places. Whether they are sketched with a light hand, or wrought out in laborious detail, one stands an equal chance of being misunderstood. Their enchantment to the climber arises from their calls on his faculties, in their demands on his strength, and on overcoming the impediments which they oppose to his skill. The non-mountaineering reader cannot feel this, and his interest in descriptions of such places is usually small, unless he supposes that the situations are perilous. They are not necessarily perilous, but I think it is impossible to avoid giving such an impression if the difficulties are particularly insisted upon.

There was a change in the quality of the rock, and there was a change in the appearance of the ridge. The rocks (talcose gneiss) below this spot were singularly firm; it was rarely necessary to test one's hold; the way led over the living rock, and not up rent-off fragments. But here, all was decay and ruin. The crest of the ridge was shattered and cleft, and the feet sank in the chips which had drifted down; while above, huge blocks, hacked and carved by the hand of time, nodded to the sky, looking like the grave-stones of giants. Out of curiosity I wandered to a notch in the ridge, between two tottering piles of immense masses, which seemed to need but a few pounds on one or the other side to make them fall; so nicely poised that they would literally have rocked in the wind, for they were put in motion by a touch; and based on support so frail that I wondered they did not collapse before my eyes. In the whole range of my Alpine experience I have seen nothing more striking than this desolate, ruined, and shattered ridge at the back of the Great Tower. It is needless to say that it is impossible to climb by the *crest* of the ridge at this part; still one is compelled to keep near to it, for there is no other way. Generally speaking, the angles on the Matterhorn are too steep to allow the formation of considerable beds of snow, but here there is a corner which permits it to accumulate, and it is turned to gratefully, for, by its assistance, one can ascend four times as rapidly as upon the rocks.

The Tower was now almost out of sight, and I looked over the central Pennine Alps to the Grand Combin, and to the chain of Mont Blanc. My neighbour, the Dent d'Hérens, still rose above me, although but slightly, and the height which had been attained could be measured by its help. So far, I had no doubts about my capacity to descend that which had been ascended; but, in a short time, on looking ahead, I saw that the cliffs steepened, and I turned back (without pushing on to them, and getting into inextricable difficulties), exulting in the thought that they would be passed when we returned together, and that I had, without assistance, got nearly to the height of the Dent d'Hérens, and considerably higher than any one had been before.[1] My exultation was a little premature.

About 5 P.M. I left the tent again, and thought myself as good as at Breuil. The friendly rope and claw had done good service, and had smoothened all the difficulties. I lowered myself through the Chimney, however, by making a fixture of the rope, which I then cut off, and left behind, as there was enough and to spare. My axe had proved a great nuisance in coming down, and I left it in the tent. It was not attached to the bâton, but was a separate affair, —an old navy boarding-axe. While cutting up the different snow-beds on the ascent, the bâton trailed behind fastened to the rope; and, when climbing, the axe was carried behind, run through the rope tied round my waist, and was sufficiently out of the way; but in descending, when coming down face outwards (as is always best where it is possible), the head or the handle of the weapon caught frequently against the rocks, and several times nearly upset me. So, out of laziness if you will, it was left in the tent. I paid dearly for the imprudence.

The Col du Lion was passed, and fifty yards more would have placed me on the 'Great Staircase,' down which one can run. But on arriving at an angle of the cliffs of the Tête du Lion, while skirting the upper edge of the snow which abuts against them, I found that the heat of the two past days had nearly obliterated the steps which had been cut when coming up. The rocks happened to be impracticable just at this corner, and it was necessary to make the steps afresh. The snow was too hard to beat or tread down, and at the angle it was all but ice; half-a-dozen steps only were required, and then the ledges could be followed again. So I held to the rock with my right hand, and prodded at the snow with the point of my stick until a good step was made, and then, leaning round the angle, did the same for the other side. So far well, but in attempting to pass the corner I slipped and fell.

The slope was steep on which this took place, and was at the top of a gully that led down through two subordinate buttresses towards the Glacier du Lion—which was just seen, a thousand feet below. The gully narrowed and narrowed, until there was a mere thread of snow lying between two walls of rock, which came to an abrupt termination at the top of a precipice that intervened between it and the glacier. Imagine a funnel cut in half through its length, placed at an angle of 45 degrees, with its point below and its concave side uppermost, and you will have a fair idea of the place.

[1] A remarkable streak of snow (marked 'cravate' in the outline of the Matterhorn, as seen from the Théodule) runs across the cliff at this part of the mountain. My highest point was somewhat higher than the lowest part of this snow, and was consequently nearly 13,500 feet above the sea.

The knapsack brought my head down first, and I pitched into some rocks about a dozen feet below; they caught something and tumbled me off the edge, head over heels, into the gully; the bâton was dashed from my hands, and I whirled downwards in a series of bounds, each longer than the last; now over ice, now into rocks; striking my head four or five times, each time with increased force. The last bound sent me spinning through the air, in a leap of fifty or sixty feet, from one side of the gully to the other, and I struck the rocks, luckily, with the whole of my left side. They caught my clothes for a moment, and I fell back on to the snow with motion arrested. My head fortunately came the right side up, and a few frantic catches brought me to a halt, in the neck of the gully, and on the verge of the precipice. Bâton, hat, and veil skimmed by and disappeared, and the crash of the rocks—which I had started—as they fell on to the glacier, told how narrow had been the escape from utter destruction. As it was, I fell nearly 200 feet in seven or eight bounds. Ten feet more would have taken me in one gigantic leap of 800 feet on to the glacier below.

The situation was sufficiently serious. The rocks could not be let go for a moment, and the blood was spirting out of more than twenty cuts. The most serious ones were in the head, and I vainly tried to close them with one hand, whilst holding on with the other. It was useless; the blood jerked out in blinding jets at each pulsation. At last, in a moment of inspiration, I kicked out a big lump of snow, and stuck it as a plaster on my head. The idea was a happy one, and the flow of blood diminished. Then, scrambling up, I got, not a moment too soon, to a place of safety, and fainted away. The sun was setting when consciousness returned, and it was pitch dark before the Great Staircase was descended; but, by a combination of luck and care, the whole 4900 feet of descent to Breuil was accomplished without a slip, or once missing the way. I entered the inn stealthily, wishing to escape to my room unnoticed. But Favre met me in the passage, demanded "Who is it?" screamed with fright when he got a light, and aroused the household. Two dozen heads then held solemn council over mine, with more talk than action. The natives were unanimous in recommending that hot wine mixed with salt should be rubbed into the cuts. I protested, but they insisted. It was all the doctoring they received. Whether their rapid healing was to be attributed to that simple remedy, or to a good state of health, is a question. They closed up remarkably quickly, and in a few days I was able to move again.[1]

Fourth attempt in 1862.—The news of this accident brought Jean-Antoine Carrel up to Breuil, and along with the haughty chasseur came one of his relatives, a strong and able young fellow named Cæsar. With these two men and Meynet I made another start on the 23rd of July. We got to the tent without any trouble, and on the following day had ascended beyond the Tower, and were picking our way cautiously over the loose rocks behind (where my traces

[1] I received much attention from a kind English lady (Mrs. J. H. Daniell) who was staying in the inn.

of the week before were well apparent) in lovely weather, when one of those abominable and almost instantaneous changes occurred, to which the Matterhorn is so liable on its southern side. Mists were created out of invisible vapours, and in a few minutes snow fell heavily. We stopped, as this part was exceedingly difficult, and, unwilling to retreat, remained on the spot several hours, in hopes that another change would occur; but, as it did not, we at length went down to the base of the Great Tower, and commenced to make a third platform,[1] at the height of 12,992 feet above the sea. It still continued to snow, and we took refuge in the tent. Carrel argued that the weather had broken up, and that the mountain would become so glazed with ice as to render any attempt futile; and I, that the change was only temporary, and that the rocks were too hot to allow ice to form upon them. I wished to stay until the weather improved, but my leader would not endure contradiction, grew more positive, and insisted that we must go down. We went down, and when we got below the Col his opinion was found to be wrong; the cloud was confined to the upper 3000 feet, and outside it there was brilliant weather.

Carrel was not an easy man to manage. He was perfectly aware that he was the cock of the Val Tournanche, and he commanded the other men as by right. He was equally conscious that he was indispensable to me, and took no pains to conceal his knowledge of the fact. If he had been commanded, or if he had been entreated to stop, it would have been all the same. But, let me repeat, he was the only first-rate climber I could find who believed that the mountain was not inaccessible. With him I had hopes, but without him none; so he was allowed to do as he would. His will on this occasion was almost incomprehensible. He certainly could not be charged with cowardice, for a bolder man could hardly be found; nor was he turning away on account of difficulty, for nothing to which we had yet come seemed to be difficult to *him;* and his strong personal desire to make the ascent was evident. There was no occasion to come down on account of food, for we had taken, to guard against this very casualty, enough to last for a week; and there was no danger, and little or no discomfort, in stopping in the tent. It seemed to me that he was spinning out the ascent for his own purposes, and that although he wished very much to be the first man on the top, and did not object to be accompanied by any one else who had the same wish, he had no intention of letting one succeed too soon,—perhaps to give a greater appearance of *éclat* when the thing was accomplished. As he feared no rival, he may have supposed that the more difficulties he made the more valuable he would be estimated; though, to do him justice, he never shewed any great hunger for money. His demands were fair, not excessive; but he always stipulated for so much per day, and so, under any circumstances, he did not do badly.

[1] This was at the position occupied by the higher of the two *cabanes* seen in the accompanying illustration, which is from a photograph taken by myself in 1895. The upper hut is now in a precarious condition. The lower one was put up in 1893.

THE GREAT TOWER, WITH THE OLD AND NEW CABANES.

Vexed at having my time thus frittered away, I was still well pleased when he volunteered to start again on the morrow, if it was fine. We were to advance the tent to the foot of the Tower, to fix ropes in the most difficult parts beyond, and to make a push for the summit on the following day.

Fifth attempt in 1862.—The next morning (Friday the 25th) when I arose, good little Meynet was ready and waiting, and he said that the two Carrels had gone off some time before, and had left word that they intended marmot-hunting, as the day was favourable for that sport. My holiday had nearly expired, and these men clearly could not be relied upon; so, as a last resort, I proposed to the hunchback to accompany me alone, to see if we could not get higher than before, though of reaching the summit there was little or no hope. He did not hesitate, and in a few hours we stood—for the third time together—upon the Col du Lion. It was the first time Meynet had seen the view unclouded. The poor little deformed peasant gazed upon it silently and reverently for a time, and then, unconsciously, fell on one knee in an attitude of adoration, and clasped his hands, exclaiming in ecstasy, "Oh, beautiful mountains!" His actions were as appropriate as his words were natural, and tears bore witness to the reality of his emotion.

Our power was too limited to advance the tent, so we slept at the old station, and starting very early the next morning, passed the place where we had turned back on the 24th, and, subsequently, my highest point on the 19th. We found the crest of the ridge so treacherous that we took to the cliffs on the right, although most unwillingly. Little by little we fought our way up, but at length we were both spread-eagled on the all but perpendicular face, unable to advance, and barely able to descend. We returned to the ridge. It was almost equally difficult, and infinitely more unstable; and at length, after having pushed our attempts as far as was prudent, I determined to return to Breuil, and to have a light ladder made to assist us to overcome some of the steepest parts.[1] I expected, too, that by this time Carrel would have had enough marmot-hunting, and would deign to accompany us again.

We came down at a great pace, for we were now so familiar with the mountain, and with each other's wants, that we knew immediately when to give a helping hand, and when to let alone. The rocks also were in a better state than I had ever seen them, being almost entirely free from glaze of ice. Meynet was always merriest on the difficult parts, and, upon the most difficult, kept on enunciating the sentiment, "We can only die once," a thought which seemed to afford him infinite satisfaction. We arrived at the inn early in the evening, and I found my projects summarily and unexpectedly knocked on the head.

[1] This appeared to be the most difficult part of the mountain. One was driven to keep to the edge of the ridge, or very near to it; and at the point where we turned back (which was almost as high as the *highest* part of the 'cravate,' and perhaps 100 feet higher than my scramble on the 19th) there were smooth walls seven or eight feet high in every direction, which were impassable to a single man, and which could only be surmounted by the assistance of ladders, or by using one's comrades as ladders.

Dr. Tyndall tries again (1862).—Professor Tyndall had arrived while we were absent, and had engaged both Cæsar and Jean-Antoine Carrel. Bennen was also with him, together with a powerful and active friend, a Valaisan guide, named Anton Walter. They had a ladder already prepared, provisions were being collected, and they intended to start on the following morning (Sunday). This new arrival took me by surprise. Bennen, it will be remembered, refused point-blank to take Professor Tyndall on the Matterhorn in 1861. "He was dead against any attempt on the mountain," says Tyndall. He was now eager to set out. Professor Tyndall has not explained in what way this revolution came about in his guide. I was equally astonished at the faithlessness of Carrel, and attributed it to pique at our having presumed to do without him. It was useless to compete with the Professor and his four men, who were ready to start in a few hours, so I waited to see what would come of their attempt.

Everything seemed to favour it, and they set out on a fine morning in high spirits, leaving me tormented with envy and all uncharitableness. If they succeeded, they carried off the prize for which I had been so long struggling; and if they failed, there was no time to make another attempt, for I was due in a few days more in London. When this came home clearly to me, I resolved to leave Breuil at once, but, when packing up, found that some necessaries had been left behind in the tent. So I went off about mid-day to recover them; caught the army of the Professor before it reached the Col, as they were going very slowly; left them there (stopping to take food), and went on to the tent. I was near to it when all at once I heard a noise aloft, and, on looking up, perceived a stone of at least a foot cube flying straight at my head. [See illustration on p. 42.] I ducked, and scrambled under the lee side of a friendly rock, while the missile went by with a loud buzz. It was the advanced guard of a perfect storm of stones, which descended with infernal clatter down the very edge of the ridge, leaving a trail of dust behind, with a strong smell of sulphur, that told who had sent them. The men below were on the look-out, but the stones did not come near them, and breaking away on one side descended to the glacier.

I waited at the tent to welcome the Professor, and when he arrived went down to Breuil. Early next morning some one ran to me saying that a flag was seen on the summit of the Matterhorn. It was not so, however, although I saw that they had passed the place where we had turned back on the 26th. I had now no doubt of their final success, for they had got beyond the point which Carrel, not less than myself, had always considered to be the most questionable place on the whole mountain. Up to it there was no choice of route. I suppose that at no one point between it and the Col was it possible to diverge a dozen paces to the right or left; but beyond it it was otherwise, and we had always agreed, in our debates, that if it could be passed success was certain. The accompanying outline from a sketch taken from the door of the inn at Breuil will help to explain. The letter B indicates the position of the Great Tower; C the 'cravate' (the strongly-marked streak of snow referred to on p. 40 which we just

A CANNONADE ON THE MATTERHORN.

failed to arrive at on the 26th); D the place where we now saw something that looked like a flag. Behind the point D a nearly level ridge leads up to the foot of the final peak. This will be understood by a reference to the outline upon p. 44, where the same letters indicate the same places. It was just now said, we considered that if the point C could be passed, success was certain. Tyndall was at D very early in the morning, and I did not doubt that he would reach the summit, although it yet remained problematical whether he would be able to stand on the very highest point. The summit was evidently

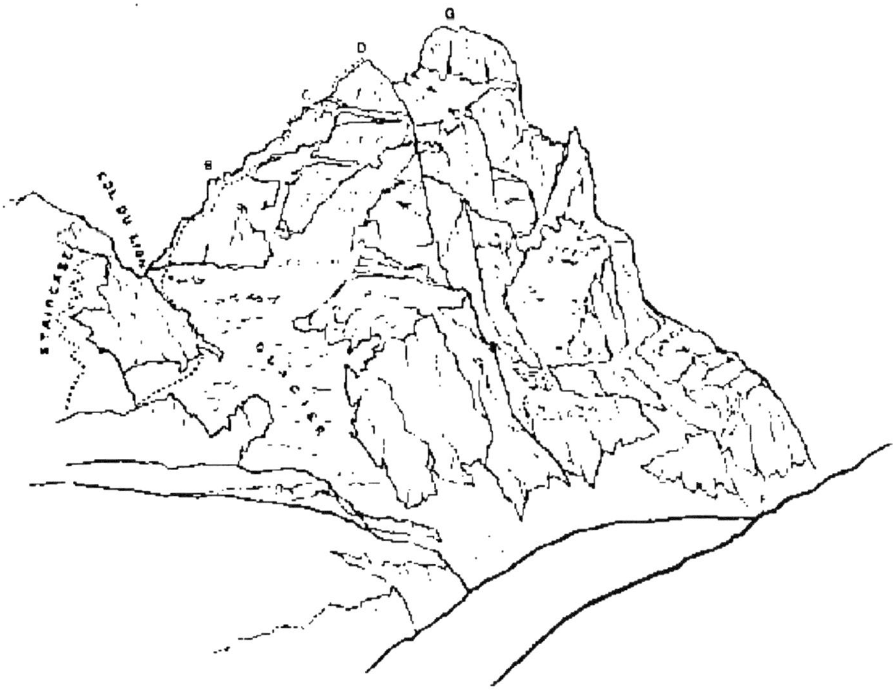

B. GREAT TOWER. C. CRAVATE.
D. END OF THE SHOULDER. F. GREAT COULOIR.

formed of a long ridge, on which there were two points nearly equally elevated—so equally that one could not say which was the highest—and between the two there seemed to be a deep notch marked G on the outline, which might defeat one at the very last moment.

My knapsack was packed, and I had drunk a parting glass of wine with Favre, who was jubilant at the success which was to make the fortune of his inn; but I could not bring myself to leave until the result was heard, and lingered about, as a foolish lover hovers round the object of his affections, even after he has been contemptuously rejected. The sun had set before the men were descried coming over the pastures. There was no spring in their steps—they, too, were defeated. The Carrels hid their heads, and the others said, as men will do when they have been beaten, that the mountain was horrible, impossible, and so forth. Professor Tyndall told me they had arrived *within a stone's-throw of the summit*, and admonished me to have nothing more to do with the mountain. I understood him to say that he should not try again, and ran down to the village of Val Tournanche, almost inclined to believe that the mountain was inaccessible; leaving the tent, ropes, and other matters in the hands of Favre, to be placed at the disposal of any person who wished to ascend it, more, I am afraid, out of irony than for generosity. There may have been those who believed that the Matterhorn could be ascended, but, anyhow, their faith did not bring forth works. No one tried again in 1862.

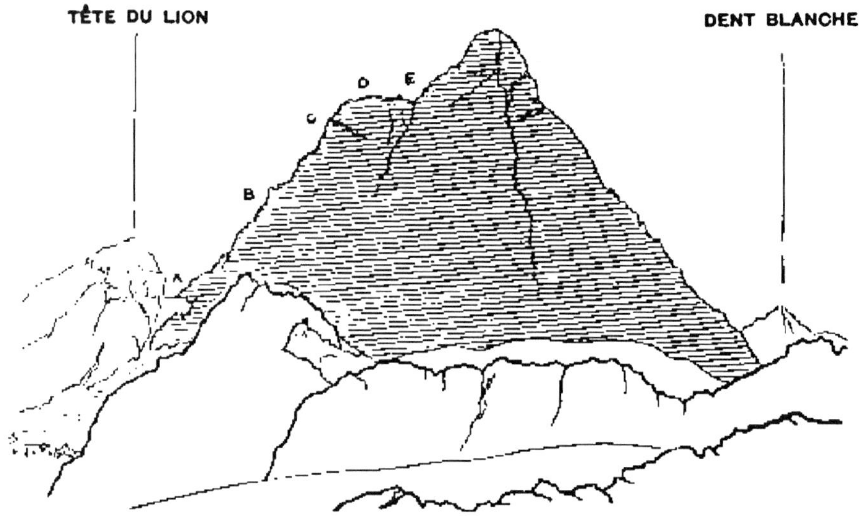

A. COL DU LION. B. GREAT TOWER. C. CRAVATE.
D. SHOULDER. E. TYNDALL'S FARTHEST.

My seventh attempt to ascend the Matterhorn (1863).—In the spring of 1863, I heard the cause of the failure of Professor Tyndall, and learnt that the case was not so hopeless as it appeared to be at one time. I found that he arrived as far only as the northern end of 'the shoulder.' The point at which, he says, they "sat down with broken hopes, the summit within a stone's-throw of us,[1] but still defying us," was not the notch or cleft at G (which is literally within a stone's-throw of the summit), but another and more formidable cleft that intervenes between the northern end of 'the shoulder' and the commencement of the final peak. It is marked E on the accompanying outline. Carrel and all the men who had been with me knew of the existence of this cleft, and of the pinnacle which rose between it and the final peak; and we had frequently talked about the best manner of passing the place. On this we disagreed, but we were both of

[1] It is not easy to understand how Dr. Tyndall and Bennen overlooked the existence of this cleft, for it is seen over several points of the compass, and particularly well from the southern side of the Théodule pass. Still more difficult is it to explain how the Professor came to consider that he was only 'a stone's-throw' from the summit; for, when he got to the end of 'the shoulder,' he must have been aware that the *whole height of the final peak was still above him.*

opinion that when we got to 'the shoulder,' it would be necessary to bear down gradually to the right or to the left, to avoid coming to the *top* of the notch. Tyndall's party, after arriving at 'the shoulder,' was led by his guides along the crest of the ridge, and, consequently, when they got to its northern end, they came to the top of the notch, instead of the bottom—to the dismay of all but the Carrels. Dr. Tyndall said "the mountain is 14,800 feet high, and 14,600 feet had been accomplished." He greatly deceived himself; by the barometric measurements of Signor Giordano the notch is no less than 800 feet below the summit.

I sauntered up the valley on July 31, and got to Breuil when all were asleep. A halo round the moon promised watery weather, and we were not disappointed, for, on the next day (August 1), rain fell heavily, and when the clouds lifted for a time, we saw that new snow lay thickly over everything higher than 9000 feet. J.-A. Carrel was ready and waiting (as I had determined to give the bold cragsman another chance); and he did not need to say that the Matterhorn would be impracticable for several days after all this new snow, even if the weather were to arrange itself at once. Whilst waiting, we made the tour of the mountain, and returned to Breuil after the absence of six days.

Carrel had *carte blanche* in the matter of guides, and his choice fell upon his relative Cæsar, Luc Meynet, and two others whose names I do not know. These men were now brought together, and our preparations were completed, as the weather was clearing up. We rested on Sunday, August 9, eagerly watching the lessening of the mists around the great peak, and started just before dawn upon the 10th, on a still and cloudless morning, which seemed to promise a happy termination to our enterprise.

By going always, though gently, we arrived upon the Col du Lion before nine o'clock. Changes were apparent. Familiar ledges had vanished; the platform, whereupon my tent had stood, looked very forlorn, its stones had been scattered by wind and frost, and had half disappeared; and the summit of the Col itself, which in 1862 had always been respectably broad, and covered by snow, was now sharper than the ridge of any church roof, and was hard ice. Already we had found that the bad weather of the past week had done its work. The rocks for several hundred feet below the Col were varnished with ice. Loose, incoherent snow covered the older and harder beds below, and we nearly lost our leader through its treacherousness. He stepped on some snow which seemed firm, and raised his axe to deliver a swinging blow, but, just as it was highest, the crust of the slope upon which he stood broke away, and poured down in serpentine streams, leaving long, bare strips, which glittered in the sun, for they were glassy ice. Carrel, with admirable readiness, flung himself back on to the rock off which he had stepped, and was at once secured. He simply remarked, "It is time we were tied up," and, after we had been tied up, he went to work again as if nothing had happened.

We had abundant illustrations during the next two hours of the value of a rope to climbers. We were tied up rather widely apart, and advanced, generally, in pairs. Carrel, who led, was followed closely by another man, who lent him a shoulder or placed an axe-head under his feet, when there was need; and when this couple were well placed the second pair advanced, in similar fashion,—the rope being drawn in by those above, and paid out gradually by those below. The leading men again advanced, or the third pair, and so on. This manner of progression was slow, but sure. One man only moved at a time, and if he slipped (and we frequently did slip) he could slide scarcely a foot without being checked by the others. The certainty and safety of the method gave confidence to the one who was moving, and not only nerved him to put out his powers to the utmost, but sustained nerve in really difficult situations. For these rocks (which, it has been already said, were easy enough under ordinary circumstances) were now difficult in a high degree. The snow-water which had trickled down for many days past in little streams, had taken, naturally, the very route by which we wished to ascend; and, refrozen in the night, had glazed the slabs over which we had to pass,—sometimes with a fine film of ice as thin as a sheet of paper, and sometimes so thickly that we could almost cut footsteps in it. The weather was superb, the men made light of the toil, and shouted to rouse the echoes from the Dent d'Hérens.

We went on gaily, passed the second tent platform, the Chimney, and the other well-remembered points, and reckoned, confidently, on sleeping that night upon the top of 'the shoulder'; but, before we had well arrived at the foot of the Great Tower, a sudden rush of cold air warned us to look out.

It was difficult to say where this air came from. It did not blow as a wind, but descended rather as the water in a shower-bath! All was tranquil again; the atmosphere *shewed* no signs of disturbance; there was a dead calm, and not a speck of cloud to be seen anywhere. But we did not remain very long in this state. The cold air came again, and this time it was difficult to say where it did *not* come from. We jammed down our hats as it beat against the ridge, and screamed amongst the crags. Before we had got to the foot of the Tower, mists had been formed above and below. They appeared at first in small, isolated patches (in several places at the same time), which danced and jerked and were torn into shreds by the wind, but grew larger under the process. They were united together, and rent again,—shewing us the blue sky for a moment, and blotting it out the next; and augmented incessantly, until the whole heavens were filled with whirling, boiling clouds. Before we could take off our packs, and get under any kind of shelter, a hurricane of snow burst upon us from the east. It fell very heavily, and in a few minutes the ridge was covered by it. "What shall we do?" I shouted to Carrel. "Monsieur," said he, "the wind is bad; the weather has changed; we are heavily laden. Here is a fine *gîte;* let us stop! If we go on we shall be half-frozen. That is *my* opinion." No one differed from him; so we fell to work to make a place for the tent, and in a couple of hours completed the platform which we had commenced in 1862. The clouds had blackened during that time, and we had hardly finished our task before a thunderstorm broke upon us with appalling fury. Forked lightning shot out at the turrets above, and at the crags below. It was so close that we quailed at its darts. It seemed to scorch us,—we were in the very focus of the storm. The thunder was simultaneous with the flashes; short and sharp, and more like the noise of a door that is violently slammed, multiplied a thousand-fold, than any noise to which I can compare it.

The wind during all this time seemed to blow tolerably consistently from the east. It smote the tent so vehemently (notwithstanding it was partly protected by rocks) that we had grave fears our refuge might be blown away bodily, with ourselves inside; so, during some of the lulls, we issued out and built a wall to windward. At half-past three the wind changed to the north-west, and the clouds vanished. We immediately took the opportunity to send down one of the porters (under protection of some of the others, a little beyond the Col du Lion), as the tent could not accommodate more than five persons. From this time to sunset the weather was variable. It was sometimes blowing and snowing hard, and sometimes a dead calm. The bad weather was evidently confined to the Mont Cervin, for when the clouds lifted we could see everything that could be seen from our gîte. Monte Viso, nearly a hundred miles off, was clear, and the sun set gorgeously behind the range of Mont Blanc. We passed the night comfortably—even luxuriously—in our blanket-bags, but there was little chance of sleeping, between the noise of the wind, of the thunder, and of the falling rocks. I forgave the thunder for the sake of the lightning. A more splendid spectacle than its illumination of the Matterhorn crags I do not expect to see.

We turned out at 3.30 A.M. on the 11th, and were dismayed to find that it still continued to snow. At 9 A.M. it ceased to fall, and the sun shewed itself feebly, so we packed up our baggage, and set out to try to get upon 'the shoulder.' We struggled upwards until eleven o'clock, and then it commenced to snow again. We held a council; the opinions expressed at it were unanimous against advancing, and I decided to retreat. For we had risen less than 300 feet in the past two hours, and had not even arrived at the rope which Tyndall's party left behind, attached to the rocks, in 1862. At the same rate of progression it would have taken us from four to five hours to get upon 'the shoulder.' Not one of us cared to attempt to do so under the existing circumstances; for besides having to move our own weight, which was sufficiently troublesome at this part of the ridge, we had to transport much heavy baggage, tent, blankets, and provisions, ladder, and 450 feet of rope, besides many other smaller matters. These, however, were not the most serious considerations. Supposing that we got upon 'the shoulder,' we might find ourselves detained there several days, unable either to go up or down.[1] I could not risk any such deten-

[1] Since then several persons have found themselves in this predicament for five or six consecutive days!

tion, being under obligations to appear in London at the end of the week.

We returned to Breuil in the course of the afternoon. It was quite fine there, and the tenants of the inn received our statements with evident scepticism. They were astonished to learn that we had been exposed to a snow-storm of twenty-six hours' duration. "Why," said Favre, the innkeeper, "*we* have had no snow; it has been fine all the time you have been absent, and there has been only that small cloud upon the mountain." Ah! that small cloud! None except those who have had experience of it can tell what a formidable obstacle it is.

I arrived at Châtillon at midnight on the 11th, defeated and disconsolate; but, like a gambler who loses each throw, only the more eager to have another try, to see if the luck would change; and returned to London ready to devise fresh combinations, and to form new plans.

Abandonment of the South-West Ridge.—All of my attempts up to this time, as well as those made by the chasseurs of Val Tournanche, Mr. Hawkins, and Prof. Tyndall, had been made by way of the south-west ridge. Why abandon a route which had been shewn to be feasible up to a certain point? I gave it up for four reasons. 1. On account of a growing disinclination for *arêtes*, and preference for snow, or rock-faces. 2. Because I was persuaded that meteorological disturbances were likely to baffle us again and again on the southern side of the mountain. 3. Because I found that the east face was a gross imposition—it looked not far from perpendicular, while its angle was, in fact, scarcely more than 40°. 4. Because I observed for myself that the strata of the mountain dipped to the west-south-west. Let us consider, first, why most persons receive such an exaggerated impression of the steepness of the eastern face.

When one looks at the Matterhorn from Zermatt, the mountain is regarded (nearly) from the north-east. The face that fronts the east is consequently neither seen in profile nor in full front, but almost half-way between the two; it looks, therefore, more steep than it really is. The majority of those who visit Zermatt go up to the Riffelberg, or to the Gornergrat, and from these places the mountain naturally looks still more precipitous, because its eastern face (which is almost all that is seen of it) is viewed more directly in front. From the Riffel hotel the slope seems to be set at an angle of 70°. If the tourist goes southwards, and crosses the Théodule pass, he gets, at one point, immediately in front of the eastern face, which then seems to be absolutely perpendicular. Comparatively few persons correct the erroneous impressions they receive in these quarters by studying the face in profile, and most go away with a very incorrect and exaggerated idea of the precipitousness of this side of the mountain, because they have considered the question from one point of view alone.

Several years passed away before I shook myself clear of my early and false impressions regarding the steepness of this side of the Matterhorn. First of all, I noticed that there were places on this eastern face where snow remained permanently all the year round. I do not speak of snow in gullies, but of considerable slopes which are about half-way up the face. Such beds as these could not continue to remain throughout the summer, unless the snow had been able to accumulate in the winter in large masses; and snow cannot accumulate and remain in large masses, in a situation such as this, at angles much exceeding 45°. Hence I was bound to conclude that the eastern face was many degrees removed from perpendicularity; and, to be sure on this point, I went to the slopes between the Z'Muttgletscher and the Matterhorngletscher, above the châlets of Staffel, whence the face could be seen in profile. Its appearance from this direction is amazing to those who have seen it only from the east. It looks so totally different from the apparently sheer and perfectly unclimbable cliff one sees from the Riffelberg, that it is hard to believe the two slopes are one and the same thing. Its angle scarcely exceeds 40°.

A step was made when this was learnt. This knowledge alone would not, however, have caused me to try an ascent by the eastern face instead of by the south-west ridge. Forty degrees may not seem a formidable inclination, nor is it for only a small cliff. But it is very unusual to find so steep a gradient maintained continuously as the general angle of a great mountain-slope, and very few instances can be quoted from the High Alps of such an angle being preserved over a rise of 3000 feet.

I do not think that the steepness or the height of this cliff would have deterred climbers from attempting to ascend it, if it had not, in addition, looked so repulsively smooth. Men despaired of finding anything to grasp. Now, some of the difficulties of the south-west ridge came from the smoothness of the rocks, although that ridge, even from a distance, seemed to be well broken up. How much greater, then, might not have been the difficulty of climbing a face which looked smooth and unbroken close at hand?

A

B

A more serious hindrance to mounting the south-west ridge is found in the dip of its rocks to the west-south-west. The great mass of the Matterhorn, it is now well ascertained, is composed of regularly stratified rocks,[1] which rise towards the east. It has been mentioned, more than once, that the rocks on some portions of the ridge leading from the Col du Lion towards the summit dip outwards, and that fractured edges overhang. This is shewn in the annexed diagram, Fig. A. It will be readily understood that such an arrangement is not favourable for climbers, and that the degree of facility with which rocks can be ascended

[1] Upon this subject see the note by Signor F. Giordano in the Appendix.

that are so disposed, must depend very much upon the frequency or paucity of fissures and joints. The rocks of the south-west ridge are sufficiently provided with cracks, but if it were otherwise, their texture and arrangement would render them unassailable.

It is not possible to go a single time upon the rocks of the south-west ridge, from the Col du Lion to the foot of the Great Tower, without observing the prevalence of their outward dip, and that their fractured edges have a tendency to overhang; nor can one fail to notice it is upon this account that most of the débris, which is rent off by frost, does not remain *in situ*, but pours down in showers over the surrounding cliffs.

The fact that the mountain is composed of a series of stratified beds was pointed out long ago. De Saussure remarked it, and recorded explicitly, in his *Travels* (§ 2243), that they "rose to the north-east at an angle of about 45°." Forbes noticed it also; and gave it as his opinion that the beds were "less inclined, or nearly horizontal." He added, "De Saussure is no doubt correct." The truth, I think, lies between the two.

I was acquainted with both of the above-quoted passages, but did not turn the knowledge to any practical account until I re-observed the same fact for myself. It was not until after my repulse in 1863, that I referred the peculiar difficulties of the south-west ridge to the dip of the strata; but when once persuaded that structure and not texture was the real impediment, it was reasonable to infer that the opposite side, that is to say the eastern face, might be comparatively easy. In brief, that an arrangement should be found like Fig. B, instead of like Fig. A. This trivial deduction was the key to the ascent of the Matterhorn.

The point was, Did the strata continue with a similar dip throughout the mountain? If they did, then the great eastern face, instead of being hopelessly impracticable, should be quite the reverse. In fact, it would be a great natural staircase, with steps inclining inwards; and, if it were so, its smooth aspect might be of no account, for the smallest steps, inclined in this fashion, afford good footing.

In June, 1865, when descending the Z'Muttgletscher, I brought these facts to the notice of my guides, Michel Croz, Christian Almer, and Franz Biener; but, although they readily admitted that they had been deceived as to the steepness of the eastern face, they were far from being satisfied that the slope would be easy to climb, and the two latter were averse to making an attempt upon it. I yielded to their reluctance, and went to examine an alternative route by a great gully[1] which leads from the Glacier du Mont Cervin to a point high up on the south-eastern ridge. We found that this gully was afflicted by falling rocks,[2] and unanimously agreed that it was not a suitable route. My renewed proposition to attack the eastern face did not find favour.

The men clustered together, and advocated leaving the mountain alone. Almer asked, with more point than politeness, "Why don't you try to go up a mountain which *can* be ascended?" "It is impossible," chimed in Biener.

[1] Marked F on the Map of the Matterhorn and its Glaciers, and on the outline upon p. 43.

[2] See *Scrambles amongst the Alps*, chap. XV.

"Sir," said Croz, "if we cross to the other side we shall lose three days, and very likely shall not succeed. You want to make ascents in the chain of Mont Blanc, and I believe they can be made. But I shall not be able to make them with you if I spend these days here, for I must be at Chamonix on the 27th." There was force in what he said, and his words made me hesitate. I relied upon his strong arms for some work which it was expected would be unusually difficult. Snow began to fall; that settled the matter, and I gave the word to retreat. We went back to Breuil, and on to the village of Val Tournanche, where we slept; and the next day proceeded to Châtillon, and thence up the Valley of Aosta to Courmayeur.

I cannot but regret that the counsels of the guides prevailed. If Croz had not uttered his well-intentioned words, he might still have been living. He parted from us at Chamonix at the appointed time, but by a strange chance we met again at Zermatt three weeks later, and two days afterwards he perished before my eyes on the very mountain from which we turned away, at his advice, on the 21st of June.

On the 7th of July, 1865,[1] I crossed the Va Cornère pass, in company with Christian Almer and Franz Biener, *en route* for Breuil. My thoughts were fixed on the Matterhorn, and my guides knew that I wished them to accompany me. They had an aversion to the mountain, and repeatedly expressed their belief that it was useless to try to ascend it. "*Anything* but Matterhorn, dear sir!" said Almer; "*anything* but Matterhorn." He did not speak of difficulty or of danger, nor was he shirking *work*. He offered to go *anywhere;* but he entreated that the Matterhorn should be abandoned. Both men spoke fairly enough. They did not think that an ascent could be made; and for their own credit, as well as for my sake, they did not wish to undertake a business which, in their opinion, would only lead to loss of time and money.

I sent them on to Breuil, and walked down to Val Tournanche to look for Jean-Antoine Carrel. He was not there. The villagers said that he, and three others, had started on the 6th to try the Matterhorn by the old way, on their own account. They will have no luck, I thought, for the clouds were low down on the mountains; and I walked up to Breuil, fully expecting to meet them. Nor was I disappointed. About half-way up I saw a group of men clustered around a châlet upon the other side of the torrent, and, crossing over, found that the party had returned. Jean-Antoine and Cæsar were there, C. E. Gorret, and J.-J. Maquignaz. They had had no success. The weather, they said, had been horrible, and they had scarcely reached the Glacier du Lion.

I explained the situation to Carrel, and proposed that we, with Cæsar and another man, should cross the Théodule by moonlight on the 9th, and that upon the 10th we should pitch the tent as high as possible upon the east face. He was unwilling to abandon the old route, and urged me to try it again. I promised to do so provided the new route failed. This satisfied him, and he agreed to my

[1] Having in the interim ascended the Grandes Jorasses and crossed the Col Dolent with Croz, Almer and Biener; and ascended the Aiguille Verte and the Ruinette, and crossed the Col de Talèfre with Almer and Biener only. See *Scrambles amongst the Alps*, chaps. xvi-xx.

proposal. I then went up to Breuil, and discharged Almer and Biener —with much regret, for no two men ever served me more faithfully or more willingly. On the next day they crossed to Zermatt.

The 8th was occupied with preparations. The weather was stormy; and black, rainy vapours obscured the mountains. Towards evening a young man came from Val Tournanche, and reported that an Englishman was lying there, extremely ill; and on the morning of Sunday the 9th I went down the valley to look after the sick man. On my way I passed a foreign gentleman, with a mule and several porters laden with baggage. Amongst these men were Jean-Antoine and Cæsar, carrying some barometers. "Hullo!" I said, "what are you doing?" They explained that the foreigner had arrived just as they were setting out, and that they were assisting his porters. "Very well; go on to Breuil, and await me there; we start at midnight as agreed." Jean-Antoine then said that he should not be able to serve me after Tuesday the 11th, as he was engaged to travel "with a family of distinction" in the valley of Aosta. "And Cæsar?" "And Cæsar also." "Why did you not say this before?" "Because," said he, "it was not settled. The engagement is of long standing, but the *day* was not fixed. When I got back to Val Tournanche on Friday night, after leaving you, I found a letter naming the day." I could not object to the answer; still the prospect of being left guideless was provoking. They went up, and I down, the valley.

The sick man declared that he was better, though the exertion of saying as much tumbled him over on to the floor in a fainting fit. He was badly in want of medicine, and I tramped down to Châtillon to get it. It was late before I returned to Val Tournanche, for the weather was tempestuous, and rain fell in torrents. A figure passed me under the church-porch. "*Qui vive?*" "Jean-Antoine." "I thought you were at Breuil." "No, sir: when the storms came on I knew we should not start to-night, and so came down to sleep here." "Ha, Carrel!" I said; "this is a great bore. If to-morrow is not fine we shall not be able to do anything together. I have sent away my guides, relying on you; and now you are going to leave me to travel with a party of ladies. That work is not fit for *you* (he smiled, I supposed at the implied compliment); can't you send some one else instead?" "No, monsieur. I am sorry, but my word is pledged. I should like to accompany you, but I can't break my engagement." By this time we had arrived at the inn door. "Well, it is no fault of yours. Come presently with Cæsar, and have some wine." They came, and we sat up till midnight, recounting our old adventures, in the inn of Val Tournanche.

The weather continued bad upon the 10th, and I returned to Breuil. The two Carrels were again hovering about the above-mentioned châlet, and I bade them adieu. In the evening the sick man crawled up, a good deal better; but his was the only arrival. The Monday crowd[1] did not cross the Théodule, on account of the continued storms. The

[1] Tourists congregate at Zermatt upon Sundays, and large gangs and droves usually cross the Théodule pass on Mondays.

inn was lonely. I went to bed early, and was awoke the next morning by the invalid inquiring if I had "heard the news." "No; what news?" "Why," said he, "a large party of guides went off this morning to try the Matterhorn, taking with them a mule laden with provisions."

I went to the door, and with a telescope saw the party upon the lower slopes of the mountain. Favre, the landlord, stood by. "What is all this about?" I inquired, "Who is the leader of this party?" "Carrel." "What! Jean-Antoine?" "Yes; Jean-Antoine." "Is Cæsar there too?" "Yes, he is there." Then I saw in a moment that I had been bamboozled and humbugged; and learned, bit by bit, that the affair had been arranged long beforehand. The start on the 6th had been for a preliminary reconnaissance; the mule, that I passed, was conveying stores for the attack; the 'family of distinction' was Signor F. Giordano, who had just despatched the party to facilitate the way to the summit, and who, when the facilitation was completed, was to be taken to the top along with Signor Sella![1]

I was greatly mortified. My plans were upset; the Italians had clearly stolen a march upon me, and I saw that the astute Favre chuckled over my discomfiture, because the route by the eastern face, if successful, would not benefit his inn. What was to be done? I retired to my room, and soothed by tobacco, re-studied my plans, to see if it was not possible to outmanœuvre the Italians. "They have taken a mule's load of provisions." "That is *one* point in my favour, for they will take two or three days to get through the food, and, until that is done, no work will be accomplished." "How is the weather?" I went to the window. The mountain was smothered up in mist. "Another point in my favour." "They are to facilitate the way. Well, if they do that to any purpose, it will be a long job." Altogether, I reckoned that they could not possibly ascend the mountain and come back to Breuil in less than seven days. I got cooler, for it was evident that the wily ones might be outwitted after all. There was time enough to go to Zermatt, to try the eastern face, and, should it prove impracticable, to come back to Breuil before the men returned; and then, it seemed to me, as the mountain was not padlocked, one might start at the same time as the Messieurs, and yet get to the top before them.

The first thing to do was to go to Zermatt. Easier said than done. The seven men upon the mountain included the ablest mountaineers in the valley, and none of the ordinary muleteer-guides were at Breuil. Two men, at least, were wanted for my baggage, but not a soul could be found. I ran about, and sent about in all directions, but not a single porter could be obtained. One was with Carrel; another was ill; another was at Châtillon, and so forth. This, however, did not much trouble me, for it was evident that so long as the weather stopped traffic over the Théodule, it would hinder the men equally upon the Matterhorn; and I knew that directly it improved company would certainly arrive.

[1] The Italian Minister. Signor Giordano had undertaken the business arrangements for Signor Sella.

About mid-day on Tuesday the 11th a large party hove in sight from Zermatt, preceded by a nimble young Englishman, and one of old Peter Taugwalder's sons.[1] I went at once to this gentleman to learn if he could dispense with Taugwalder. He said that he could not, as they were going to recross to Zermatt on the morrow, but that the young man should assist in transporting my baggage, as he had nothing to carry. We naturally got into conversation. I told my story, and learned that the young Englishman was Lord Francis Douglas,[2] whose recent exploit—the ascent of the Gabelhorn—had excited my admiration. He brought good news. Old Peter had

LORD FRANCIS DOUGLAS.

lately been beyond the Hörnli, and had reported that he thought an ascent of the Matterhorn was possible upon that side. Almer had left Zermatt, and could not be recovered, so I determined to seek for old Peter. Lord Francis Douglas expressed a warm desire to ascend the mountain, and before long it was determined that he should take part in the expedition.

Favre could no longer hinder our departure, and lent us one of his men. We crossed the Col Théodule on Wednesday morning the 12th of July, rounded the foot of the Ober Théodulgletscher, traversed the Furggengletscher, and deposited tent, blankets, ropes,

[1] Peter Taugwalder, the father, was called *old* Peter, to distinguish him from his eldest son, *young* Peter. In 1865 the father's age was about 45.

[2] Brother of the present Marquis of Queensberry. An account of his ascent of the Gabelhorn, on July 7, 1865 (the first made on the Zinal side), was found after his death amongst his papers, and was published in the *Alpine Journal*, vol. ii, pp. 221-2.

and other matters in the little chapel at the Lac Noir.[1] All four were heavily laden, for we brought across the whole of my stores from Breuil: Of rope alone there was about 600 feet. There were three kinds. First, 200 feet of Mr. Buckingham's Manilla rope; second, 150 feet of a stouter, and possibly stronger rope than the first; and third, more than 200 feet of a lighter and weaker rope than the first, of a kind that I used formerly (stout sash-line).

We descended to Zermatt, sought and engaged old Peter, and gave him permission to choose another guide. When we returned

CHAPEL AT THE LAC NOIR (1865).

to the Monte Rosa Hotel, whom should we see sitting upon the wall in front but my old *guide chef*, Michel Croz. I supposed that he had come with Mr. B——, but I learned that that gentleman had arrived in ill-health, at Chamonix, and had returned to England. Croz, thus left free, had been immediately engaged by the Rev. Charles Hudson, and they had come to Zermatt with the same object as ourselves—namely, to attempt the ascent of the Matterhorn!

Lord Francis Douglas and I dined at the Monte Rosa Hotel, and had just finished when Mr. Hudson and a friend entered the *salle à manger*. They had returned from inspecting the mountain, and some idlers in the room demanded their intentions. We heard a confirma-

[1] For route, and the others mentioned in the subsequent chapters, see the Map of the Matterhorn and its Glaciers.

tion of Croz's statement, and learned that Mr. Hudson intended to set out on the morrow at the same hour as ourselves. We left the room to consult, and agreed it was undesirable that two independent parties should be on the mountain at the same time with the same object. Mr. Hudson was therefore invited to join us, and he accepted our proposal. Before admitting his friend—Mr. Hadow—I took the precaution to inquire what he had done in the Alps, and, as well as I remember, Mr. Hudson's reply was, "Mr. Hadow has done Mont Blanc in less time than most men."[1] He then mentioned several other excursions that were unknown to me, and added, in answer to a further question, "I consider he is a sufficiently good man to go with us." Mr. Hadow was admitted, and we then went into the matter of guides. Hudson thought that Croz and old Peter would be sufficient. The question was referred to the men themselves, and they made no objection.

[1] In the *Alpine Journal*, vol. iii, pp. 75-76, Mr. T. S. Kennedy, in speaking of this ascent (which was I believe made upon the 7th of July, 1865), says that Mr. Hadow went from the Grands Mulets to the summit of Mont Blanc in less than four hours and a half, and descended from the summit to Chamonix in five hours.

A STORE-HOUSE.

CHAPTER III.

THE FIRST ASCENT OF THE MATTERHORN.[1]

CHARLES HUDSON—CAMP ON THE EAST FACE—CROZ REPORTS FAVOURABLY—ASCENT OF THE EAST FACE—CROSS TO THE NORTHERN SIDE—ARRIVAL AT SUMMIT—DISCOMFITURE OF THE ITALIANS—ASTONISHMENT AT BREUIL—MARVELLOUS PANORAMA.

WE started from Zermatt on the 13th of July 1865, at half-past 5, on a brilliant and perfectly cloudless morning. We were eight in number—Croz, old Peter and his two sons,[2] Lord F. Douglas, Hadow, Hudson,[3] and I. To ensure steady motion, one tourist and one native walked together. The youngest Taugwalder fell to my share, and the lad marched well, proud to be on the expedition, and happy to shew his powers. The wine-bags also fell to my lot to carry, and throughout the day, after each drink, I replenished them secretly with water, so that at the next halt they were found fuller than before! This was considered a good omen, and little short of miraculous.

On the first day we did not intend to ascend to any great height, and we mounted, accordingly, very leisurely; picked up the things which were left in the chapel at the Schwarzsee at 8.20, and proceeded thence along the ridge connecting the Hörnli with the Matterhorn.[4] At half-past 11 we arrived at the base of the actual peak; then quitted the ridge, and clambered to the left round some ledges, on to the eastern face. We were now fairly upon the mountain, and were astonished to find that places which from the Riffel, or even from the Furggengletscher, looked entirely impracticable, were so easy that we could *run about*.

[1] Reprinted from the Fourth Edition of *Scrambles amongst the Alps*.

[2] The two young Taugwalders were taken as porters, by desire of their father, and carried provisions amply sufficient for three days, in case the ascent should prove more troublesome than we anticipated.

[3] Charles Hudson, Vicar of Skillington in Lincolnshire, was considered by the mountaineering fraternity to be the best amateur of his time. He was the organiser and leader of the party of Englishmen who ascended Mont Blanc by the Aiguille du Goûter, and descended by the Grands Mulets route, without guides, in 1855. His long practice made him surefooted, and in that respect he was not greatly inferior to a born mountaineer. His pupil Mr. Hadow was a young man of nineteen, who had the looks and manners of a greater age. He was a rapid walker, but 1865 was his first season in the Alps. Lord Francis Douglas was about the same age as Mr. Hadow. He had had the advantage of several seasons in the Alps. He was nimble as a deer, and was becoming an expert mountaineer. Just before our meeting he had ascended the Ober Gabelhorn (with old Peter Taugwalder and Jos. Viennin).

[4] Arrived at the chapel 7.30 A.M.; left it 8.20; halted to examine route 9.30; started again 10.25, and arrived at 11.20 at the cairn made by Mr. Kennedy in 1862 (see p. 27), marked 3298 mètres upon the map of the Matterhorn and its Glaciers. (This cairn has now disappeared.) Stopped 10 min. here. From the Hörnli to this point we kept, when possible, to the crest of the ridge. The greater part of the way was excessively easy, but there were a few places where the axe had to be used.

Before twelve o'clock we had found a good position for the tent, at a height of 11,000 feet.[1] Croz and young Peter went on to see what was above, in order to save time on the following morning. They cut across the heads of the snow-slopes which descended towards the Furggengletscher, and disappeared round a corner; but shortly afterwards we saw them high up on the face, moving quickly. We others made a solid platform for the tent in a well-protected spot, and then watched eagerly for the return of the men. The stones which they upset told us that they were very high, and we supposed that the way must be easy. At length, just before 3 P.M., we saw them coming down, evidently much excited. "What are they saying,

REV. CHARLES HUDSON.

Peter?" "Gentlemen, they say it is no good." But when they came near we heard a different story. "Nothing but what was good; not a difficulty, not a single difficulty! We could have gone to the summit and returned to-day easily!"

We passed the remaining hours of daylight—some basking in the sunshine, some sketching or collecting; and when the sun went down, giving, as it departed, a glorious promise for the morrow, we returned to the tent to arrange for the night. Hudson made tea, I coffee, and we then retired each one to his blanket bag; the Taugwalders, Lord Francis Douglas, and myself, occupying the tent, the others remain-

[1] Thus far the guides did not once go to the front. Hudson or I led, and when any cutting was required we did it ourselves. This was done to spare the guides, and to shew them that we were in earnest. The spot at which we camped was four hours' walking from Zermatt, and is marked upon the map—CAMP (1865). It was just upon a level with the Furggengrat, and its position is indicated upon the engraving on p. 20 by a little circular white spot, in a line with the word CAMP.

ing, by preference, outside. Long after dusk the cliffs above echoed with our laughter and with the songs of the guides, for we were happy that night in camp, and feared no evil.

We assembled together outside the tent before dawn on the morning of the 14th, and started directly it was light enough to move. Young Peter came on with us as a guide, and his brother returned to Zermatt.[1] We followed the route which had been taken on the previous day, and in a few minutes turned the rib which had intercepted the view of the eastern face from our tent platform. The whole of this great slope was now revealed, rising for 3000 feet like a huge natural staircase. Some parts were more, and others were less, easy; but we were not once brought to a halt by any serious impediment, for when an obstruction was met in front it could always be turned to the right or to the left. For the greater part of the way there was, indeed, no occasion for the rope, and sometimes Hudson led, sometimes myself. At 6.20 we had attained a height of 12,800 feet, and halted for half-an-hour; we then continued the ascent without a break until 9.55, when we stopped for fifty minutes at a height of 14,000 feet. Twice we struck the N.E. ridge and followed it for some little distance,[2]—to no advantage, for it was usually more rotten and steep, and always more difficult than the face. Still, we kept near to it, lest stones perchance might fall.[3]

We had now arrived at the foot of that part which, from the Riffelberg or from Zermatt, seems perpendicular or overhanging, and could no longer continue upon the eastern side. For a little distance we ascended by snow upon the arête[4]—that is, the crest of the ridge—descending towards Zermatt, and then, by common consent, turned over to the right, or to the northern side. Before doing so we made a change in the order of ascent. Croz went first, I followed, Hudson came third; Hadow and old Peter were last. "Now," said Croz, as he led off, "now for something altogether different." The work became difficult and required caution. In some places there was little to hold, and it was desirable that those should be in front who were least likely to slip. The general slope of the mountain at this part was *less* than 40°, and snow had accumulated in, and had filled up, the interstices of the rock face, leaving only occasional fragments projecting here

[1] It was originally intended to leave both of the young men behind. We found it difficult to divide the food, and so the new arrangement was made.

[2] For track, see the outline upon p. 69.

[3] Very few stones fell during the two days I was on the mountain, and none came near us. Others who have followed the same route have not been so fortunate; they may not, perhaps, have taken the same precautions. It is a noteworthy fact, that the lateral moraine of the left bank of the Furggengletscher is scarcely larger than that of the right bank, although the former receives all the débris that falls from the 4000 feet of cliffs which form the eastern side of the Matterhorn, whilst the latter is fed by perfectly insignificant slopes. Neither of these moraines is large. This is strong evidence that stones do *not* fall to any great extent from the eastern face. The inward dip of the beds retains the detritus in place. Hence the eastern face appears, when one is upon it, to be undergoing more rapid disintegration than the other sides: in reality, the mantle of ruin spares the mountain from farther waste. Upon the southern side, rocks fall as they are rent off; "each day's work is cleared away" every day; and hence the faces and ridges are left naked, and are exposed to fresh attacks.

[4] The snow seen in the engraving upon p. 20, half-an-inch below the summit, and a little to its right. It is now called 'the Shoulder.'

and there. These were at times covered with a thin film of ice, produced from the melting and refreezing of the snow. It was a place over which any fair mountaineer might pass in safety, and Mr. Hudson ascended this part, and, so far as I know, the entire mountain, without having the slightest assistance rendered to him upon any occasion. Sometimes, after I had taken a hand from Croz, or received a pull, I turned to offer the same to Hudson; but he invariably declined, saying it was not necessary. Mr. Hadow, however, was not accustomed to this kind of work, and required continual assistance. It is only fair to say that the difficulty which he found at this part arose simply and entirely from want of experience.

This solitary difficult part was of no great extent.[1] We bore away over it at first, nearly horizontally, for a distance of about 400 feet; then ascended directly towards the summit for about 60 feet; and then doubled back to the ridge which descends towards Zermatt. A long stride round a rather awkward corner brought us to snow once more. The last doubt vanished! The Matterhorn was ours! Nothing but 200 feet of easy snow remained to be surmounted!

You must now carry your thoughts back to the seven Italians who started from Breuil on the 11th of July. Four days had passed since their departure, and we were tormented with anxiety lest they should arrive on the top before us. All the way up we had talked of them, and many false alarms of "men on the summit" had been raised. The higher we rose, the more intense became the excitement. What if we should be beaten at the last moment? The slope eased off, at length we could be detached, and Croz and I, dashing away, ran a neck-and-neck race, which ended in a dead heat. At 1.40 P.M. the world was at our feet, and the Matterhorn was conquered. Hurrah! Not a footstep could be seen.

It was not yet certain that we had not been beaten. The summit of the Matterhorn was formed of a rudely level ridge, about 350 feet long,[2] and the Italians might have been at its farthest extremity. I hastened to the southern end, scanning the snow right and left eagerly. Hurrah! again; it was untrodden. "Where were the men?" I peered over the cliff, half doubting, half expectant, and saw them immediately—mere dots on the ridge, at a great distance below. Up went my arms and my hat. "Croz! Croz!! come here!" "Where are they, Monsieur?" "There, don't you see them, down there?" "Ah! the *coquins*, they are low down." "Croz, we must make those fellows hear us." We yelled until we were hoarse. The Italians seemed to regard us—we could not be certain. "Croz, we *must* make them hear us; they *shall* hear us!" I seized a block of rock and hurled it down, and called upon my companion, in the name of friend-

[1] I have no memorandum of the time that it occupied. It must have taken about an hour and a half.

[2] The highest points are towards the two ends. In 1865 the northern end was slightly higher than the southern one. In bygone years Carrel and I often suggested to each other that we might one day arrive upon the top, and find ourselves cut off from the very highest point by a notch in the summit-ridge which is seen from the Théodule and from Breuil (marked G on the outline on p. 43). This notch is very conspicuous from below, but when one is actually upon the summit it is hardly noticed, and it can be passed without the least difficulty.

ship, to do the same. We drove our sticks in, and prized away the crags, and soon a torrent of stones poured down the cliffs. There was no mistake about it this time. The Italians turned and fled.[1]

The others had arrived, so we went back to the northern end of the ridge. Croz now took the tent-pole,[2] and planted it in the highest snow. "Yes," we said, "there is the flag-staff, but where is the flag?" "Here it is," he answered, pulling off his blouse and fixing it to the stick. It made a poor flag, and there was no wind to float it out, yet it was seen all around. They saw it at Zermatt—at the Riffel—in the Val Tournanche. At Breuil, the watchers cried, "Victory is ours!" They raised 'bravos' for Carrel, and 'vivas' for Italy, and hastened to put themselves *en fête*. On the morrow they were undeceived. "All was changed; the explorers returned sad—cast down—disheartened—confounded—gloomy." "It is true," said the men. "We saw them ourselves—they hurled stones at us! The old traditions *are* true,—there are spirits on the top of the Matterhorn!"[3]

We returned to the southern end of the ridge to build a cairn, and then paid homage to the view.[4] The day was one of those superlatively calm and clear ones which usually precede bad weather. The atmosphere was perfectly still, and free from all clouds or vapours. Mountains fifty—nay a hundred—miles off, looked sharp and near. All their details—ridge and crag, snow and glacier—stood out with faultless definition. Pleasant thoughts of happy days in bygone years came up unbidden, as we recognised the old, familiar forms. All were revealed—not one of the principal peaks of the Alps was hidden. I see them clearly now—the great inner circles of

[1] I learnt afterwards from J.-A. Carrel that they heard our first cries. They were then upon the south-west ridge, close to the 'Cravate,' and *twelve hundred and fifty* feet below us; or, as the crow flies, at a distance of about one-third of a mile.

[2] At our departure the men were confident that the ascent would be made, and took one of the poles out of the tent. I protested that it was tempting Providence; they took the pole nevertheless.

[3] Signor Giordano was naturally disappointed at the result, and wished the men to start again. *They all refused to do so, with the exception of Jean-Antoine.* Upon the 16th of July he set out again with three others, and upon the 17th gained the summit by passing (at first) up the south-west ridge, and (afterwards) by turning over to the Z'Mutt, or north-western side. On the 18th he returned to Breuil.

Whilst we were upon the southern end of the summit-ridge, we paid some attention to the portion of the mountain which intervened between ourselves and the Italian guides. It seemed as if there would not be the least chance for them if they should attempt to storm the final peak directly from the end of the 'shoulder.' In that direction cliffs fell sheer down from the summit, and we were unable to see beyond a certain distance. There remained the route about which Carrel and I had often talked, namely, to ascend directly at first from the end of the 'shoulder,' and afterwards to swerve to the left—that is, to the Z'Mutt side—and to complete the ascent from the north-west. When we were upon the summit we laughed at this idea. Nevertheless, the summit was reached by that route by the undaunted Carrel. From knowing the final slope over which he passed, and from the account of Mr. F. C. Grove—who until 1895 was the only traveller by whom it had been traversed—I do not hesitate to term the ascent of Carrel and Bich in 1865 the most desperate piece of mountain-scrambling upon record. In 1869 I asked Carrel if he had ever done anything more difficult. His reply was, "Man cannot do anything much more difficult than that!"

[4] The summit-ridge was much shattered, although not so extensively as the south-west and north-east ridges. The highest rock, in 1865, was a block of mica-schist, and the fragment I broke off it not only possesses, in a remarkable degree, the *character* of the peak, but mimics, in an astonishing manner, the details of its form. [See illustration on page 63.]

giants, backed by the ranges, chains, and *massifs*. First came the Dent Blanche, hoary and grand; the Gabelhorn and pointed Rothhorn; and then the peerless Weisshorn: the towering Mischabelhörner, flanked by the Allaleinhorn, Strahlhorn, and Rimpfischhorn; then Monte Rosa—with its many Spitzes—the Lyskamm and the Breithorn. Behind were the Bernese Oberland, governed by the Finsteraarhorn; the Simplon and St. Gothard groups; the Disgrazia and the Orteler. Towards the south we looked down to Chivasso on the plain of Piedmont, and far beyond. The Viso—one hundred miles away—seemed close upon us; the Maritime Alps—one hundred and thirty miles distant—were free from haze. Then came my first love—the Pelvoux; the Ecrins and the Meije; the clusters of the Graians; and lastly, in the west, glowing in full sunlight, rose the monarch of all—Mont Blanc. Ten thousand feet beneath us were the green fields of Zermatt, dotted with châlets, from which blue smoke rose lazily. Eight thousand feet below, on the other side, were the pastures of Breuil. There were forests black and gloomy, and meadows bright and lively; bounding waterfalls and tranquil lakes; fertile lands and savage wastes; sunny plains and frigid *plateaux*. There were the most rugged forms, and the most graceful outlines—bold, perpendicular cliffs, and gentle, undulating slopes; rocky mountains and snowy mountains, sombre and solemn, or glittering and white, with walls—turrets—pinnacles—pyramids—domes—cones—and spires! There was every combination that the world can give, and every contrast that the heart could desire.

We remained on the summit for one hour—

"One crowded hour of glorious life."

It passed away too quickly, and we began to prepare for the descent.

THE ACTUAL SUMMIT OF THE MATTERHORN IN 1865.

CHAPTER IV.

DESCENT OF THE MATTERHORN.

ORDER OF THE DESCENT—A FRIGHTFUL AVALANCHE—HADOW SLIPS—DEATH OF CROZ, HADOW, HUDSON AND LORD F. DOUGLAS—TERROR OF THE TAUGWALDERS—AN APPARITION—AN INFAMOUS PROPOSITION—SURPRISED BY NIGHT—SEARCH FOR AND RECOVERY OF THE BODIES—OFFICIAL EXAMINATION—THEIR LAST RESTING-PLACE.

HUDSON and I again consulted as to the best and safest arrangement of the party. We agreed that it would be best for Croz to go first,[1] and Hadow second; Hudson, who was almost equal to a born mountaineer in sureness of foot, wished to be third; Lord Francis Douglas was placed next, and old Peter, the strongest of the remainder, after him. I suggested to Hudson that we should attach a rope to the rocks on our arrival at the difficult bit, and hold it as we descended, as an additional protection. He approved the idea, but it was not definitely settled that it should be done. The party was being arranged in the above order whilst I was sketching the summit, and they had finished, and were waiting for

[1] If the members of the party had been more equally efficient, Croz would have been placed *last*.

me to be tied in line, when some one remembered that our names had not been left in a bottle. They requested me to write them down, and moved off while it was being done.

A few minutes afterwards I tied myself to young Peter, ran down after the others, and caught them just as they were commencing the descent of the difficult part.[1] Great care was being taken. Only one man was moving at a time; when he was firmly planted the next advanced, and so on. They had not, however, attached the additional rope to rocks, and nothing was said about it. The suggestion was not made for my own sake, and I am not sure that it even occurred to me again. For some little distance we two followed the others, detached from them, and should have continued so had not Lord Francis Douglas asked me, about 3 P.M., to tie on to old Peter, as he feared, he said, that Taugwalder would not be able to hold his ground if a slip occurred.

A few minutes later, a sharp-eyed lad ran into the Monte Rosa hotel, to Seiler, saying that he had seen an avalanche fall from the summit of the Matterhorn on to the Matterhorngletscher. The boy was reproved for telling idle stories; he was right, nevertheless, and this was what he saw.

Michel Croz had laid aside his axe, and in order to give Mr. Hadow greater security, was absolutely taking hold of his legs, and putting his feet, one by one, into their proper positions.[2] So far as I know, no one was actually descending. I cannot speak with certainty, because the two leading men were partially hidden from my sight by an intervening mass of rock, but it is my belief, from the movements of their shoulders, that Croz, having done as I have said, was in the act of turning round, to go down a step or two himself; at this moment Mr. Hadow slipped, fell against him, and knocked him over. I heard one startled exclamation from Croz, then saw him and Mr. Hadow flying downwards; in another moment Hudson was dragged from his steps, and Lord F. Douglas immediately after him.[3] All

[1] Described upon pp. 59-60.

[2] Not at all an unusual proceeding, even between born mountaineers. I wish to convey the impression that Croz was using all pains, rather than to indicate inability on the part of Mr. Hadow. The insertion of the word 'absolutely' makes the passage, perhaps, rather ambiguous. I retain it now, in order to offer the above explanation.

[3] At the moment of the accident, Croz, Hadow, and Hudson, were close together. Between Hudson and Lord F. Douglas the rope was all but taut, and the same between all the others who were *above*. Croz was standing by the side of a rock which afforded good hold, and if he had been aware, or had suspected, that anything was about to occur, he might and would have gripped it, and would have prevented any mischief. He was taken totally by surprise. Mr. Hadow slipped off his feet on to his back, his feet struck Croz in the small of the back, and knocked him right over, head first. Croz's axe was out of his reach, and without it he managed to get his head uppermost before he disappeared from our sight. If it had been in his hand I have no doubt that he would have stopped himself and Mr. Hadow.

Mr. Hadow, at the moment of the slip, was not occupying a bad position. He could have moved either up or down, and could touch with his hand the rock of which I have spoken. Hudson was not so well placed, but he had liberty of motion. The rope was not taut from him to Hadow, and the two men fell ten or twelve feet before the jerk came upon him. Lord F. Douglas was not favourably placed, and could neither move up nor down. Old Peter was firmly planted, and stood just beneath a large rock which he hugged with both arms. I enter into these details to make it more apparent that the position occupied by the party at the moment of the accident was not by any means

this was the work of a moment. Immediately we heard Croz's exclamation, old Peter and I planted ourselves as firmly as the rocks would permit:[1] the rope was taut between us, and the jerk came on

us both as on one man. We held; but the rope broke midway between Taugwalder and Lord Francis Douglas. For a few seconds we saw

excessively trying. We were compelled to pass over the exact spot where the slip occurred, and we found—even with shaken nerves—that *it* was not a difficult place to pass. I have described the *slope generally* as difficult, and it is so undoubtedly to most persons; but it must be distinctly understood that Mr. Hadow slipped at a comparatively easy part.

[1] Or, more correctly, we held on as tightly as possible. There was no time to change our position.

our unfortunate companions sliding downwards on their backs, and spreading out their hands, endeavouring to save themselves. They passed from our sight uninjured, disappeared one by one, and then fell from precipice to precipice on to the Matterhorngletscher below, a distance of nearly 4000 feet in height. From the moment the rope broke it was impossible to help them.

So perished our comrades! For the space of half-an-hour we remained on the spot without moving a single step. The two men, paralysed by terror, cried like infants, and trembled in such a manner as to threaten us with the fate of the others. Old Peter rent the air with exclamations of "Chamonix! Oh, what will Chamonix say?" He meant, Who would believe that Croz could fall? The young man did nothing but scream or sob, "We are lost! we are lost!" Fixed between the two, I could neither move up nor down. I begged young Peter to descend, but he dared not. Unless he did, we could not advance. Old Peter became alive to the danger, and swelled the cry, "We are lost! we are lost!" The father's fear was natural—he trembled for his son; the young man's fear was cowardly—he thought of self alone. At last old Peter summoned up courage, and changed his position to a rock to which he could fix the rope; the young man then descended, and we all stood together. Immediately we did so, I asked for the rope which had given way, and found, to my surprise—indeed, to my horror—that it was the weakest of the three ropes. It was not brought, and should not have been employed, for the purpose for which it was used. It was old rope, and, compared with the others, was feeble. It was intended as a reserve, in case we had to leave much rope behind, attached to rocks. I saw at once that a serious question was involved, and made him give me the end. It had broken in mid-air, and it did not appear to have sustained previous injury.

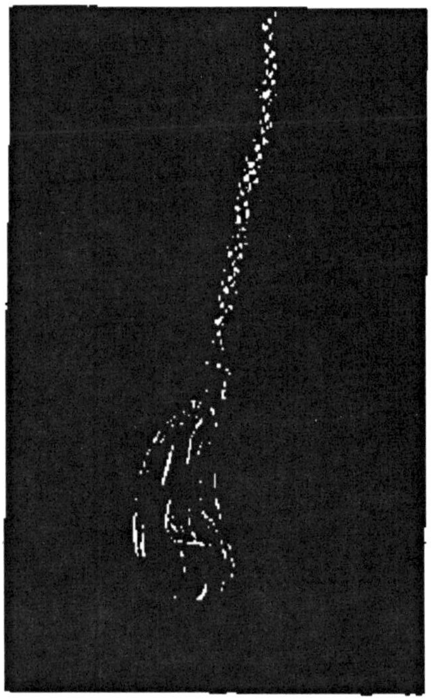

ROPE BROKEN ON THE MATTERHORN.

For more than two hours afterwards I thought almost every moment that the next would be my last; for the Taugwalders, utterly unnerved, were not only incapable of giving assistance, but were in such a state that a slip might have been expected from them at any moment. After a time, we were able to do that which should have been done at first, and fixed rope to firm rocks, in addition to being tied together. These ropes were cut from time to time, and were left behind.[1] Even with their assurance the men were afraid to proceed, and several times old Peter turned with ashy face and faltering limbs, and said, with terrible emphasis, "*I cannot!*"

About 6 P.M. we arrived at the snow upon the ridge descending towards Zermatt, and all peril was over. We frequently looked, but in vain, for traces of our unfortunate companions; we bent over the ridge and cried to them, but no sound returned. Convinced at last that they were neither within sight nor hearing, we ceased from our useless efforts; and, too cast down for speech, silently gathered up our things, and the little effects of those who were lost, preparatory to continuing the descent. When, lo! a mighty arch appeared, rising above the Lyskamm, high into the sky. Pale, colourless, and noiseless, but perfectly sharp and defined, except where it was lost in the clouds, this unearthly apparition seemed like a vision from another world; and, almost appalled, we watched with amazement the gradual development of two vast crosses, one on either side. If the Taugwalders had not been the first to perceive it, I should have doubted my senses. They thought it had some connection with the accident, and I, after a while, that it might bear some relation to ourselves. But our movements had no effect upon it. The spectral forms remained motionless. It was a fearful and wonderful sight; unique in my experience, and impressive beyond description, coming at such a moment.[2]

[1] These ends, for a long time, remained attached to the rocks, and marked our line of ascent and descent.

[2] I paid very little attention to this remarkable phenomenon, and was glad when it disappeared, as it distracted our attention. Under ordinary circumstances I should have felt vexed afterwards at not having observed with greater precision an occurrence so rare and so wonderful. I can add very little about it to that which is said above. The sun was directly at our backs; that is to say, the fog-bow was opposite to the sun. The time was 6.30 P.M. The forms were at once tender and sharp; neutral in tone; were developed gradually, and disappeared suddenly. The mists were light (that is, not dense), and were dissipated in the course of the evening.

It has been suggested that the crosses are incorrectly figured in the Frontispiece of *Scrambles amongst the Alps*, and that they were probably formed by the intersection of other circles or ellipses, as shewn in the annexed diagram. I think this suggestion is very likely correct; but in the Frontispiece I have preferred to follow my original memorandum.

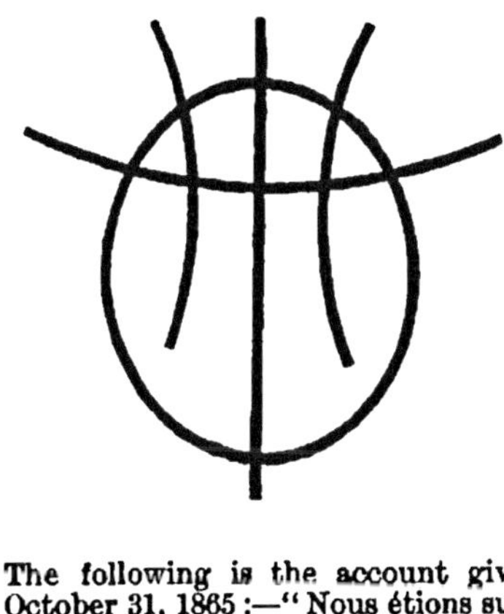

In Parry's *Narrative of an Attempt to reach the North Pole*, 4to, 1828, there is, at pp. 99-100, an account of the occurrence of a phenomenon analogous to the above-mentioned one. "At half-past five P.M. we witnessed a very beautiful natural phenomenon. A broad white fog-bow first appeared opposite to the sun, as was very commonly the case," etc. I follow Parry in using the term fog-bow.

It may be observed that, upon the descent of the Italian guides (whose expedition is noticed in the note upon pp. 73-4), upon July 17th, 1865, the phenomenon commonly termed the Brocken was observed. The following is the account given by the Abbé Amé Gorret in the *Feuille d'Aoste*, October 31, 1865:—"Nous étions sur l'épaule" (the 'shoulder') "quand nous remarquâmes un phénomène qui nous fit plaisir; le nuage était très-dense du côté de Valtornanche, c'était serein en Suisse; nous nous vîmes au milieu d'un cercle aux couleurs de l'arc-en-ciel; ce mirage nous formait à tous une couronne au milieu de laquelle nous voyions notre ombre." This occurred at about 6.30 to 7 P.M., and the Italians in mention were at about the same height as ourselves—namely, 14,000 feet.

I was ready to leave, and waiting for the others. They had recovered their appetites and the use of their tongues. They spoke in patois, which I did not understand. At length the son said in French, "Monsieur." "Yes." "We are poor men; we have lost our Herr; we shall not get paid; we can ill afford this."[1] "Stop!" I said, interrupting him, "that is nonsense; I shall pay you, of course, just as if your Herr were here." They talked together in their patois for a short time, and then the son spoke again. "We don't wish you to pay us. We wish you to write in the hotel-book at Zermatt, and to your journals, that we have not been paid." "What nonsense are you talking? I don't understand you. What do you mean?" He proceeded—"Why, next year there will be many travellers at Zermatt, and we shall get more *voyageurs*."[2]

Who would answer such a proposition? I made them no reply in words,[3] but they knew very well the indignation that I felt. They filled the cup of bitterness to overflowing, and I tore down the cliff, madly and recklessly, in a way that caused them, more than once, to inquire if I wished to kill them. Night fell; and for an hour the descent was continued in the darkness. At half-past 9 a resting-place was found, and upon a wretched slab, barely large enough to hold the three, we passed six miserable hours. At daybreak the descent was resumed, and from the Hörnli ridge we ran down to the châlets of Buhl, and on to Zermatt. Seiler met me at his door, and followed in silence to my room. "What is the matter?" "The Taugwalders and I have returned." He did not need more, and burst into tears; but lost no time in useless lamentations, and set to work to arouse the village. Ere long a score of men had started to ascend the Hohlicht heights, above Kalbermatt and Z'Mutt, which commanded the plateau of the Matterhorngletscher. They returned after six hours, and reported that they had seen the bodies lying motionless on the snow. This was on Saturday; and they proposed that we should leave on Sunday evening, so as to arrive upon the plateau at daybreak on Monday. Unwilling to lose the slightest chance, the Rev. J. M'Cormick and I resolved to start on Sunday morning. The Zermatt men, threatened with excommunication by their priests if they failed to attend the early mass, were unable to accompany us. To several of them, at least, this was a severe trial. Peter Perrn declared with tears that nothing else would have prevented him from joining in the search for his old comrades. Englishmen came to our aid. The Rev. J. Robertson[4] and Mr. J. Phillpotts[5] offered themselves, and their guide Franz Andermatten; another Englishman lent us Joseph Marie and Alexandre Lochmatter. Frédéric Payot, and Jean Tairraz, of Chamonix, also volunteered.

We started at 2 A.M. on Sunday the 16th, and followed the route

[1] They had been travelling with, and had been engaged by, Lord F. Douglas, and so considered him their employer, and responsible to them.

[2] Transcribed from the original memorandum.

[3] Nor did I speak to them afterwards, unless it was absolutely necessary, so long as we were together.

[4] Now Vicar of Whittlesford.

[5] The present Head Master of Bedford School.

that we had taken on the previous Thursday as far as the Hörnli. Thence we went down to the right of the ridge,[1] and mounted through the *séracs* of the Matterhorngletscher. By 8.30 we had got to the plateau at the top of the glacier, and within sight of the corner in which we knew my companions must be.[2] As we saw one weather-beaten man after another raise the telescope, turn deadly pale, and pass it on without a word to the next, we knew that all hope was gone. We approached. They had fallen below as they had fallen above—Croz a little in advance, Hadow near him, and

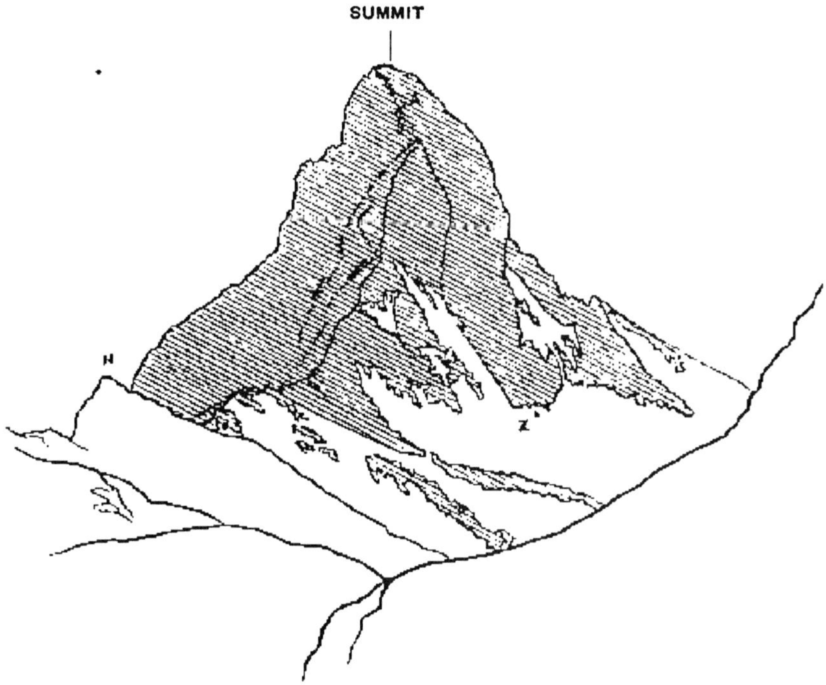

H. THE HORNLI. A. PLACE WHERE HADOW SLIPPED.
Z. PLACE WHERE THE BODIES WERE FOUND.

Hudson some distance behind; but of Lord Francis Douglas we could see nothing.[3] We left them where they fell: buried in snow at the base of the grandest cliff of the most majestic mountain of the Alps.

All those who had fallen had been tied with the Manilla, or with the second and equally strong rope, and, consequently, there had been only one link—that between old Peter and Lord Francis Douglas—where the weaker rope had been used. This had a very ugly look for Taugwalder, for it was not possible to suppose that the others would have sanctioned the employment of a rope so greatly inferior in strength when there were more than two hundred and fifty feet

[1] To the point marked Z on the map. [2] Marked with a cross on the map.

[3] A pair of gloves, a belt, and boot that had belonged to him were found. This, somehow, became publicly known, and gave rise to wild notions, which would not have been entertained had it been also known that the *whole* of the boots of those who had fallen *were off*, and were lying upon the snow near the bodies.

of the better qualities still remaining out of use.[1] For the sake of the old guide (who bore a good reputation), and upon all other accounts, it was desirable that this matter should be cleared up; and after my examination before the court of inquiry which was instituted by the Government was over, I handed in a number of questions which were framed so as to afford old Peter an opportunity of exculpating himself from the grave suspicions which at once fell upon him. The questions, I was told, were put and answered; but the answers, although promised, have never reached me.[2]

Meanwhile, the administration sent strict injunctions to recover the bodies, and upon the 19th of July, twenty-one men of Zermatt accomplished that sad and dangerous task.[3] Of the body of Lord Francis Douglas they, too, saw nothing; it was probably still arrested on the rocks above.[4] The remains of Hudson and Hadow were interred upon the north side of the Zermatt Church, in the presence of a reverent crowd of sympathising friends. The body of Michel Croz lies upon the other side, under a simpler tomb; whose inscription bears honourable testimony to his rectitude, to his courage, and to his devotion.[5]

So the traditional inaccessibility of the Matterhorn was vanquished, and was replaced by legends of a more real character. Others will essay to scale its proud cliffs, but to none will it be the mountain that it was to its early explorers. Others may tread its summit-snows, but none will ever know the feelings of those who first gazed

[1] I was one hundred feet or more from the others whilst they were being tied up, and am unable to throw any light on the matter. Croz and old Peter no doubt tied up the others.

[2] This was not the only occasion upon which M. Clemenz (who presided over the inquiry) failed to give up answers that he promised. It is greatly to be regretted that he did not feel that the suppression of the truth was equally against the interests of travellers and of the guides. If the men were untrustworthy, the public should have been warned of the fact; but if they were blameless, why allow them to remain under unmerited suspicion?

Old Peter Taugwalder laboured for a long time under an unjust accusation. Notwithstanding repeated denials, even his comrades and neighbours at Zermatt persisted in asserting or insinuating that he *cut* the rope which led from him to Lord Francis Douglas. In regard to this infamous charge, I say that he *could* not do so at the moment of the slip, and that the end of the rope in my possession shews that he did not do so beforehand. There remains, however, the suspicious fact that the rope which broke was the thinnest and weakest one that we had. It is suspicious, because it is unlikely that any of the four men in front would have selected an old and weak rope when there was abundance of new, and much stronger, rope to spare; and, on the other hand, because if Taugwalder thought that an accident was likely to happen, it was to his interest to have the weaker rope where it was placed.

I should rejoice to learn that his answers to the questions which were put to him were satisfactory. Not only was his act at the critical moment wonderful as a feat of strength, but it was admirable in its performance at the right time. He left Zermatt, and lived for several years in retirement in the United States; but ultimately returned to his native valley, and died suddenly on July 11, 1888, at the Lac Noir (Schwarzsee).

[3] They followed the route laid down upon the map, and on their descent were in great peril from the fall of a *serac*.

[4] This, or a subsequent, party discovered a sleeve. No other traces have been found.

[5] At the instance of Mr. Alfred (now Mr. Justice) Wills, a subscription list was opened for the benefit of the sisters of Michel Croz, who had been partly dependent upon his earnings. In a short time more than £280 were raised. This was considered sufficient, and the list was closed. The proceeds were invested in French Rentes (by Mr. William Mathews), at the recommendation of M. Dupui, at that time Maire of Chamonix.

upon its marvellous panorama; and none, I trust, will ever be compelled to tell of joy turned into grief, and of laughter into mourning. It proved to be a stubborn foe; it resisted long, and gave many a hard blow; it was defeated at last with an ease that none could have anticipated, but, like a relentless enemy—conquered but not crushed—it took terrible vengeance. The time may come when the Matterhorn shall have passed away, and nothing, save a heap of shapeless fragments, will mark the spot where the great mountain stood; for, atom by atom, inch by inch, and yard by yard, it yields to forces which nothing can withstand. That time is far distant; and, ages hence, generations unborn will gaze upon its awful precipices, and wonder at its unique form. However exalted may be their ideas, and however exaggerated their expectations, none will come to return disappointed!

THE GRAVE OF MICHEL CROZ.

CHAPTER V.

SUBSEQUENT HISTORY OF THE MATTERHORN.[1]

FIRST ASCENT ON THE ITALIAN SIDE—COMPARISON OF THE TWO ROUTES—HUT ON THE '*CRAVATE*'—MR. CRAUFURD GROVE'S ASCENT—CONSTRUCTION OF THE HUT ON THE EAST FACE—CABANE ON THE HÖRNLI RIDGE—ALTERATION IN THE FORM OF THE SUMMIT—DEATH OF JOSEPH BRANTSCHEN—DR. MOSELEY FALLS DOWN THE EAST FACE—ASCENTS FROM THE NORTH-WEST BY MESSRS. MUMMERY AND PENHALL—ABANDONMENT AND DEATH OF MR. BORCKHARDT—ANOTHER CATASTROPHE ON THE EAST FACE—DEATH OF JEAN-ANTOINE CARREL—LOSS OF ANDREAS SEILER AND JOSEPH BIENER.

THE Val Tournanche natives who started to facilitate the way up the south-west ridge of the Matterhorn for MM. Giordano and Sella, pitched their tent upon my third platform, at the foot of the Great Tower (12,992 feet), and enjoyed several days of bad weather under its shelter. On the first fine day (13th of July) they began their work, and about mid-day on the 14th got on to the 'shoulder,' and arrived at the base of the final peak (the point where Bennen stopped on July 28, 1862). The counsels of the party were then divided. Two—Jean-Antoine Carrel and J.-Joseph Maquignaz—wished to go on; the others were not eager about it. A discussion took place, and the result was they all commenced to descend, and whilst upon the 'cravate' (13,524) they heard our cries from the summit.[2] Upon the 15th they went down to Breuil and reported their ill-success to M. Giordano (see p. 61). That gentleman was naturally much disappointed, and pressed the men to set out again.[3] Said he, "Until now I have striven for the honour of making the first ascent,—fate has decided against me,—I am beaten. Patience! Now, if I go to any further expense, it will be on your account, for your honour, and for your interests. Will you start again to settle the question, or, at least, to let there be no more uncertainty?" The majority of the men (in fact the whole of them with the exception of Jean-Antoine) refused point-blank to have anything more to do with the mountain. Carrel, however, stepped forward, saying, "As for me, I have not given it up; if you (turning to the Abbé Gorret) or the

[1] We resume here the account of the proceedings of the Italians who started from Breuil on the 11th of July, 1865. See p. 53.

[2] The foregoing particulars were related to me by J.-A. Carrel.

[3] The following details are taken from the account of the Abbé Amé Gorret (published in the *Feuille d'Aoste*, Oct. 1865), who was at Breuil when the men returned.

others will come, I will start again immediately." "Not I!" said one. "No more for me," cried a second. "If you would give me a thousand francs I would not go back," said a third. The Abbé Gorret alone volunteered. This plucky priest was concerned in the very first attempts upon the mountain, and is an enthusiastic mountaineer. Carrel and the Abbé would have set out by themselves had not J. B. Bich and J.-A. Meynet (two men in the employ of Favre the innkeeper) come forward at the last moment. M. Giordano also wished to accompany them, but the men knew the nature of the work they had to undertake, and positively declined to be accompanied by an amateur.

These four men left Breuil at 6.30 A.M. on July 16, at 1 P.M. arrived at the third tent-platform, and there passed the night. At daybreak on the 17th they continued the ascent by the route which had been taken before; passed successively the Great Tower, the 'crête du coq,' the 'cravate,' and the 'shoulder,'[1] and at 10 A.M. gained the point at the foot of the final peak from which the explorers had turned back on the 14th. They had then about 800 feet to accomplish, and, says the Abbé, "nous allions entrer en pays inconnu, aucun n'étant jamais allé aussi loin."

The passage of the cleft which stopped Bennen was accomplished, and then the party proceeded directly towards the summit, over rocks which for some distance were not particularly difficult. The steep cliffs down which we had hurled stones (on the 14th) then stopped their way, and Carrel led round to the left or Z'Mutt side. The work at this part was of the very greatest difficulty, and stones and icicles which fell rendered the position of the party very precarious;[2] so much so that they preferred to turn up directly towards the summit, and climb by rocks that the Abbé termed "almost perpendicular." He added, "This part occupied the most time, and gave us the greatest trouble." At length they arrived at a fault in the rocks which formed a roughly horizontal gallery. They crept along this in the direction of a ridge that descended towards the north-west, or thereabouts, and when close to the ridge, found that they could not climb on to it; but they perceived that, by descending a gully with perpendicular sides, they could reach the ridge at a lower point. The bold Abbé was the heaviest and the strongest of the four, and he was sacrificed for the success of the expedition. He and Meynet remained behind, and lowered the others, one by one, into the gully. Carrel and Bich clambered up the other side, attained the ridge descending towards the north-west, shortly afterwards gained an "easy route,[3] they galloped," and in a few minutes reached the southern end of the summit-ridge.

[1] These terms, as well as the others, Great Staircase, Col du Lion, Tête du Lion, Chimney, and so forth, were applied by Carrel and myself to the various points, in consequence of real or supposed resemblances in the rocks to other things. A few of the terms originated with the author, but they were chiefly due to the inventive genius of J.-A. Carrel.

[2] I have seen icicles more than a hundred feet long hanging from the rocks near the summit of the Matterhorn.

[3] The words of the Abbé. I imagine that he meant *comparatively* easy.

The time of their arrival does not appear to have been noticed. It was late in the day, I believe about 3 P.M. Carrel and his comrade only waited long enough to plant a flag by the side of the cairn that we had built three days previously, then descended at once, rejoined the others, and all four hurried down as fast as possible to the tent. They were so pressed for time that they could not eat! and it was 9 P.M. before they arrived at their camp at the foot of the Great Tower. In descending they followed the gallery above mentioned throughout its entire length, and so avoided the very difficult rocks over which they had passed on the ascent. As they were traversing the length of the 'shoulder' they witnessed the phenomenon to which I have already adverted at the foot of p. 67.

J. B. BICH, IN 1892.

When Carrel and Bich were near the summit they saw our traces upon the Matterhorngletscher, and suspected that an accident had occurred; they did not, however, hear of the Matterhorn catastrophe until their return to Breuil, at 3 P.M. upon the 18th. The details of that sad event were in the mouths of all, and it was not unnaturally supposed, in the absence of correct information, that the accident was a proof that the northern side was frightfully dangerous. The safe return of the four Italians was regarded, on the other hand, as evidence that the Breuil route was the best. Those who were interested (either personally or otherwise) in the Val Tournanche made the most of the circumstances, and trumpeted the praises of the southern route. Some went farther, and instituted comparisons between the two routes to the disadvantage of the northern one, and were pleased to term our expedition on the 13-14th of July precipitate, and so forth. Considering the circumstances which caused us to leave the Val Tournanche on the 12th of July, these remarks were not in the best possible taste, but I have no feeling regarding them. There may be some, however, who may be interested in a comparison of the two routes, and for their sakes I will place the essential points in juxtaposition. We (that is the Taugwalders and myself) were absent from Zermatt 53 hours. Excluding halts and stoppages of one sort or another, the ascent and descent occupied us 23 hours. Zermatt is 5315 feet above the level of the sea, and the Matterhorn is 14,780; we had therefore to ascend 9465 feet. As far as the point marked 10,820 feet the way was known, so we had to find the way over only 3960 feet. The members of our party (I now include all) were very unequal in ability, and none of us could for a moment be compared as cragsmen with Jean-Antoine Carrel. The four Italians who started from Breuil on the 16th of July were absent during 56½ hours, and as far as I can gather from the published account, and from conversation with the men, excluding halts, they took for the ascent and descent 23¾ hours. The hotel at Gioment is 6890 feet above the sea, so they had to ascend 7890 feet. As far as the end of the 'shoulder' the way was known to Carrel, and he had to find the way over only about 800 feet. All four men were born mountaineers, good climbers, and they were led by the most expert cragsman I have seen. The weather in each instance was fine. It is seen, therefore, that these four nearly equally matched men took a *longer* time to ascend 1500 feet *less* height than ourselves, although we had to find the way over more than four times as much untrodden ground

CANON CARREL, OF AOSTA.

as they. This alone would lead any mountaineer to suppose that their route must have been more difficult than ours.[1] I know the greater part of the ground over which they passed, and from my knowledge, and from the account of Mr. Grove, which follows, I am sure that their route was not only more difficult, but that it was *much* more difficult, than ours.

This was not the opinion in the Val Tournanche at the end of 1865, and the natives confidently reckoned that tourists would flock to their side in preference to the other. It was, I believe, the late Canon Carrel of Aosta (who always took great interest in such matters) who first proposed the construction of a *cabane* upon the southern side of the Matterhorn. The project was taken up with spirit, and funds for its execution were speedily provided—principally by the members of the Italian Alpine Club, or by their friends. The indefatigable Jean-Antoine found a natural hole upon the ledge called the

[1] The pace of a party is ruled by that of its least efficient member.

'cravate' (13,524), and this, in course of time, was turned, under his direction, into a respectable little hut. Its position is superb, and gives a view of the most magnificent character.

Whilst this work was being carried out, my friend Mr. F. Craufurd Grove consulted me respecting the ascent of the Matterhorn. I recommended him to ascend by the *northern* route, and to place himself in the hands of Jean-Antoine Carrel. Mr. Grove found, however, that Carrel distinctly preferred the southern side, and they ascended accordingly by the Breuil route. Mr. Grove has been good enough to supply the following account of his expedition. He carries on my description of the southern route from the highest point I attained on that side (a little below the 'cravate') to the summit, and thus renders complete my descriptions of the two sides.

"In August 1867 I ascended the Matterhorn from Breuil, taking as guides three mountaineers of the Valtournanche—J.-A. Carrel, J. Bich, and S. Meynet,—Carrel being the leader. At that time the Matterhorn had not been scaled since the famous expedition of the Italian guides mentioned above.

"Our route was identical with that which they followed in their descent when, as will be seen, they struck out on one part of the mountain a different line from that which they had taken in ascending. After gaining the Col du Lion, we climbed the south-western or Breuil *arête* by the route which has been described in these pages, passing the night at the then unfinished hut constructed by the Italian Alpine Club on the 'cravate.' Starting from the hut at daylight, we reached at an early hour the summit of the 'shoulder,' and then traversed its *arête* to the final peak of the Matterhorn. The passage of this *arête* was perhaps the most enjoyable part of the whole expedition. The ridge, worn by slow irregular decay into monstrous and rugged battlements, and guarded on each side by tremendous precipices, is grand beyond all description, but does not, strange to say, present any remarkable difficulty to the climber, save that it is exceedingly trying to the head. Great care is of course necessary, but the scramble is by no means of so arduous a nature as entirely to absorb the attention; so that a fine climb, and rock scenery, of grandeur perhaps unparalleled in the Alps, can both be appreciated.

"It was near the end of this *arête*, close to the place where it abuts against the final peak, that Professor Tyndall's party turned in 1862,[1] arrested by a cleft in the ridge. From the point where they stopped the main tower of the Matterhorn rises in front of the climber, abrupt, magnificent, and apparently inaccessible. The summit is fully 750 feet in vertical height above this spot, and certainly, to my eye, appeared to be separated from me by a yet more considerable interval; for I remember, when at the end of the *arête*, looking upward at the crest of the mountain, and thinking that it must be a good 1000 feet above me.

"When the Italian guides made their splendid ascent, they traversed the *arête* of the shoulder to the main peak, passed the

[1] See pp. 44-5.

cleft which has been mentioned (p. 44), clambered on to the tremendous north-western face of the mountain (described by Mr. Whymper at pp. 59 and 61), and then endeavoured to cross this face so as to get on to the Z'Mutt *arête*.[1] The passage of this slope proved a work of great difficulty and danger. I saw it from very near the place where they traversed, and was unable to conceive how any human creatures managed to crawl over rocks so steep and so treacherous. After they had got about half-way across, they found the difficulties of the route and the danger from falling stones so great, that they struck straight up the mountain, in the hope of finding some safer way. They were to a certain extent successful, for they came presently to a small ledge, caused by a sort of fault in the rock, running horizontally across the north-western face of the mountain a little distance below the summit. Traversing this ledge, the Italians found themselves close to the Z'Mutt *arête*, but still separated from it by a barrier, to outflank which it was necessary to descend a perpendicular gully. Carrel and Bich were lowered down this, the other two men remaining at the top to haul up their companions on their return, as otherwise they could not have got up again. Passing on to the Z'Mutt *arête* without further difficulty, Carrel and Bich climbed by that ridge to the summit of the mountain. In returning, the Italians kept to the ledge for the whole distance across the north-western face, and descended to the place where the *arête* of the shoulder abuts against the main peak by a sort of rough ridge of rocks between the north-western and southern faces. When I ascended in 1867, we followed this route in the ascent and in the descent. I thought the ledge difficult, in some places decidedly dangerous, and should not care to set foot on it again; but assuredly it neither is so difficult nor so continuously dangerous as those gaunt and pitiless rock-slopes which the Italians crossed in their upward route.

"The credit of making the *Italian* ascent of the Matterhorn belongs undoubtedly to J.-A. Carrel and to the other mountaineers who accompanied him. Bennen led his party bravely and skilfully to a point some 750 feet below the top. From this point, however, good guide though he was, Bennen had to retire defeated; and it was reserved for the better mountain-craft of the Valtournanche guide to win the difficult way to the summit of the Matterhorn."

Mr. Craufurd Grove was the first traveller who ascended the Matterhorn after the accident, and the natives of Val Tournanche were, of course, greatly delighted that his ascent was made upon their side. Some of them, however, were by no means well pleased that J.-A. Carrel was so much regarded. They feared, perhaps, that he would acquire the monopoly of the mountain. Just a month after Mr. Grove's ascent, six Valtournanchians set out to see whether they could not learn the route, and so come in for a share of the good things which were expected to arrive. They were three Maquignaz's, Cæsar Carrel (my old guide), J.-B. Carrel, and a daughter of the last

[1] A ridge descending towards the Z'Muttgletscher.

named! They left Breuil at 5 A.M. on Sept. 12, and at 3 P.M. arrived at the hut, where they passed the night. At 7 A.M. the next day they started again (leaving J.-B. Carrel behind), and proceeded along the 'shoulder' to the final peak; passed the cleft which had stopped Bennen, and clambered up the comparatively easy rocks on the other side until they arrived at the base of the last precipice, down which we had hurled stones on July 14, 1865. They (young woman and all) were then about 350 feet from the summit! Then, instead of turning to the left, as Carrel and Mr. Grove had done, J.-Joseph and J.-Pierre Maquignaz paid attention to the cliff in front of them, and managed to find a means of passing up, by clefts, ledges, and gullies, to the summit. This was a shorter (and, though difficult, is a much easier) route than that taken by Carrel and Grove, and it has generally been followed by those who have since then ascended the mountain from the side of Breuil.[2] Subsequently, ropes were fixed over the most difficult portions of the final climb.

J.-JOSEPH MAQUIGNAZ.[1]

In the meantime they had not been idle upon the other side. A hut was constructed upon the eastern face, at a height of 12,526 feet above the sea, near to the crest of the ridge which descends towards Zermatt (north-east ridge).[3] The erection was undertaken by the Knubels, of St. Nicholas, at the expense of Monsieur Alex. Seiler and of the Swiss Alpine Club. This hut upon the east face is placed in an insecure position, and is now seldom used, as another hut or *cabane* has been built upon the Hörnli ridge,[4] a few yards to the east of, and slightly lower down than the spot where Mr. Kennedy put up his cairn in 1862 (see p. 27).

The second ascent of the Matterhorn on the northern side was

1 By permission, from a photograph by Signor Sella.

2 J.-Joseph and J.-Pierre Maquignaz alone ascended; the others had had enough and returned. It should be observed that ropes had been fixed, by J.-A. Carrel and others, over *all* the difficult parts of the mountain as high as the shoulder, *before* the ascent of these persons. This explains the facility with which they moved over ground which had been found very trying in earlier times. The young woman declared that the ascent (as far as she went) was a trifle, or used words to that effect; if she had tried to get to the same height before 1862, she would probably have been of a different opinion.

3 This is marked on the Map of the Matterhorn and its Glaciers (*Cab. S.A.C.*).

4 The position of the hut on the Hörnli ridge is marked by the word *Cabane* on the Map of the Matterhorn and its Glaciers.

THE CABANE ON THE EAST FACE OF THE MATTERHORN.

made by Mr. J. M. Elliot, on July 24-25, 1868, with the guides Joseph Marie Lochmatter and Peter Knubel. Down to the end of 1871, the ascents that were made were equally divided between the northern (or Zermatt) and the southern (or Breuil) route. Until that time, neither guides nor tourists had got clear of the idea that the Swiss route was more difficult and dangerous than the Italian one. In

THE HUT ON THE HÖRNLI RIDGE.

1872 (the year following the publication of *Scrambles amongst the Alps*) the Zermatt side found more favour, and it has continued to be the popular route to the present time (1897). In Appendix E of the 4th Edition of *Scrambles* the ascents have been tabulated down to the first which was made in 1880;[1] and, amongst the 194 which are enumerated, 136 were made on the Swiss side, against 23 upon the Italian side. On nine other occasions persons crossed the mountain from Zermatt to Breuil, and upon twenty-two more traversed it from Breuil to Zermatt.

Prof. Tyndall was the first to turn the summit of the Matterhorn into a pass. He went up the Breuil side and came down upon Zermatt. A few days later Messrs. Hoiler and Thioly crossed the mountain in the reverse direction.

After these, the first ascent which calls for notice is that by Signor F. Giordano. This gentleman came to Breuil several times after his visit in 1865, but he was always baffled by the weather. In July 1866, he got as high as the 'cravate' with Jean-Antoine Carrel and other men, and was detained there *five days and nights unable to move either up or down!* At last, on Sept. 3-5, 1868, he was able to

[1] It has not been possible to carry this list on to a later date. Ascents have multiplied, and are often made by persons whose names are unknown.

The *Geneva Telegraph* of Sept. 24, 1892, stated that on the previous Sunday there were twenty-three tourists upon the summit, one of whom was a Royal Prince.

gratify his desire, and accomplished the feat of ascending the mountain upon one side and descending it upon the other. Signor Giordano spent a considerable time in examining the structure of the Matterhorn, and became benighted upon its eastern face in consequence. I am indebted to him for the valuable note and the accompanying section which are given in Appendix H.[1]

Questions having been frequently put to me respecting the immediate summit of the Matterhorn, I made an ascent of the mountain in 1874, to photograph the summit, and to see what changes had occurred since our visit nine years before. The summits of all high mountains vary from time to time, and the Matterhorn is no exception to the general rule. It was sharper and narrower in 1874 than in 1865. Instead of being able 'to run about,' every step had to be cut with the axe; and the immediate summit, instead of being a blunt and rounded eminence, was a little cone of snow which went to a sharp point. In consequence of a strong north wind which was blowing at the time, we had to work down upon the edge of the cliff overlooking Breuil, to get protection for the camera, and eventually we gained a position which gave a good view of the summit; but our ledge was so small that we could not venture to unrope, and Jean-Antoine had to squat down whilst I photographed over his head. The engraving upon p. 82 has been made from the photograph which was taken on this occasion. The nearest of the lower peaks, on the left, is the summit of the Dent d'Hérens.

Carrel and I stopped a second night at the *cabane* on the east face, and whilst there we had the insecurity of its position forcibly impressed upon us by seeing a huge block break away from the rock at its side, and go crashing down over the very route which is commonly pursued by tourists. The view from this hut extends from the Bietschorn on the north to the Grand Tournalin in the south, and includes the Mischabel group, the Allaleinhorn, Alphubel, Rimpfischhorn and Strahlhorn, Monte Rosa, the Lyskamm and the Breithorn. The uppermost 800 feet of the Matterhorn can be seen from the hut, but the rest of the intervening part of the mountain is not visible, being hidden by a small ridge which projects from the face.

In 1879 two deaths occurred upon the Matterhorn, within a few hours of each other,—one in the hut on the 'cravate,' and the second upon the eastern face. On August 12, Dr. C. Lüscher and Prof. H. Schiess started from Breuil at a very early hour, accompanied by the guides Joseph Marie Lochmatter, Joseph Brantschen, and P. Beytrison. They gained the hut on the 'cravate' (13,524 feet) at 1.20 P.M., and stopped there for the night; and on the following day the party crossed the summit of the mountain, with the exception of Brantschen, who was left behind in the hut, some say only slightly ill, and others at

[1] Signor Giordano carried a mercurial barometer throughout the entire distance, and read it frequently. His observations enable me to determine the heights that were attained upon the different attempts which were made to ascend the mountain, and the various points upon it which have been so frequently mentioned. He left a minimum thermometer upon the summit in 1868. This was recovered by J.-A. Carrel in July 1869, and was found to register only 9° Fahrenheit below the freezing-point. It was supposed that it was protected from the winter cold by a deep covering of snow. The explanation is scarcely satisfactory.

THE SUMMIT OF THE MATTERHORN IN 1874.

the point of death. They sent back assistance to their sick comrade in a somewhat tardy fashion, and when the relief party arrived at the hut Brantschen was found dead. Dr. Lüscher and Prof. Schiess furnished an account of what happened to the Basel Section of the Swiss Alpine Club, and from this statement the following extracts are made.

"When we reached the 'cravate' it was already 1 P.M. Lochmatter told us we had still four hours' work to reach the top, and the question arose whether it would not be more prudent to spend the night in the Italian cabane. . . In the course of the afternoon we remarked that Brantschen was unwell; Lochmatter kept on pressing him to eat and drink. We took no great heed of the matter, and looked on it as mountain-sickness, or the result of drinking too much water during the ascent. On my asking Brantschen when he had first felt unwell, he answered, since he had slept in the sun. We observed no spitting of blood on his part during the ascent; had we noticed anything of the kind we should naturally not have taken him with us. Up to 5 P.M. he was sitting on the door-step, his gaze directed on Breuil. Later on, after he had lain down, he began to groan and throw himself about, in the night also to rattle in the throat. Being asked where he felt pain, he answered, he felt pains all over. There was altogether not much to be got out of him either by us or by Lochmatter. He was, however, in no high state of fever, he was not hot to the touch, and his pulse was not unusually rapid. There was no remarkable coughing. My guide acted as cook, and succeeded with the small stock of wood in making tea several times, and towards morning chocolate also. This tea was the only restorative we could offer to the sick man, and he seemed to take it gladly. Towards morning he at last became quieter, his breathing more regular, and he left off groaning and crying out."

"On the morning of August 13 the guides had given a hope that Brantschen might recover sufficiently to accompany us; for this reason the start was delayed to 6 o'clock. But it became evident that this was impossible. And now no discussion took place, neither was there any interchange of plans between the guides and Brantschen. It appeared best to all of us to wrap up Brantschen well, to furnish him with the necessary provisions, and to hurry over quickly to Zermatt and send him help. Had we remained with him it would have been no benefit to Brantschen; and I am also convinced that he himself thought our course of action perfectly natural, otherwise he would have made some remonstrance, which he did not do. We bade him keep up his courage and wished him farewell, in the hope that he would by degrees entirely recover. . . At 1.30 A.M. on August 14 we reached Zermatt. We had sent from the Swiss hut a message before us, and at 3 o'clock the relief party started over the Furgg-gletscher skirting the Matterhorn. It found Brantschen already dead and stiff; apparently a rupture of the heart or lungs had happened."[1]

[1] The above extracts are taken from the *Alpine Journal*, vol. ix, pp. 374-77. I entirely concur in the following remarks, which were appended by the Editor. "On the facts

At the time that this was taking place on the South side of the Matterhorn, Dr. William O. Moseley of Boston lost his life on the East Face. He left Zermatt at 10.30 P.M. on August 13, in company with Mr. A. E. Craven and the guides Peter Rubi and Christian Inabnit; and ascended the mountain by the usual northern route, without stopping at the hut. They reached the summit at 9 A.M. on the 14th, and had returned to within a short distance from the hut, when Dr. Moseley (who had found it irksome to be tied up, and had frequently wished to go unroped) untied himself from the rest, doing so entirely upon his own responsibility. A few minutes later the party had to cross a projecting piece of rock. Rubi went over first, and planted his axe in position to give firm footing to Dr. Moseley, who followed. But, unhappily, he declined assistance; placed his hand upon the rock, and endeavoured to vault over it. In doing so he slipped, lost hold of his axe, and fell with ever-accelerating velocity down the East Face for about 2000 feet, and of course was killed on the spot. His body was recovered three days later and was interred under the south wall of the English Church at Zermatt. "*I was shocked to find*," said a friend who examined his remains, "*that Dr. Moseley had hardly any nails in one of his boots.*"

Many persons have talked at different times about the possibility of finding a way up the Matterhorn from the side of the Z'Mutt Glacier; but it was not until the year 1879 that a way was discovered. On September 2-3, Mr. A. F. Mummery with the guides Alexander Burgener, Petrus, and Kentinetta succeeded in gaining the summit by first going up the long snow-buttress which runs out from the mountain towards the north-west, and then up the rocks above. When nearing the top, they joined the routes taken by Carrel and Mr. Grove upon the first ascents which were made on the Italian side.[1]

At the very time that Mr. Mummery was engaged in his expedition, Mr. W. Penhall, with the guides Ferdinand Imseng and Louis Zurbrucken, was occupied on a similar enterprise, and also ascended the Matterhorn from the direction of the Stockhi. Mr. Penhall, however, at first took a course slightly more to the south than Mr. Mummery, though he, at last, like the others, got on to the main Z'Mutt *arête*, and completed the ascent by following a portion of the old Italian route.[2]

of this account, but one judgment can be formed. In the face of the description given by Prof. Schiess of Brantschen's condition during the night, his excuses are altogether inadequate. The adoption of a route by which the nearest succour was (at the pace of the party) 19½ instead of 8 hours off, may have been simply a deplorable error of judgment; but the determination to leave the sick man alone showed unpardonable want of heart. It must ever be a matter of profound regret that any travellers or guides should, without the least pressure of necessity, have left a sick man, without firewood in a hut 13,000 feet above the sea, to over thirty hours of certain and absolute solitude. There can be no doubt that the desertion of Brantschen under such circumstances was a flagrant breach of the first tradition of all honourable mountaineering—the tradition, by virtue of which every member of a party, guide or mountaineer, has been accustomed in danger or distress to count on the support of his comrades."

[1] Mr. Mummery's description will be found in the *Alpine Journal*, vol. ix, pp. 458-62.

[2] See *Alpine Journal*, vol. ix, pp. 449-58.

Three days afterwards (Sept. 5-6), Mr. J. Baumann followed in Mr. Mummery's footsteps. "I found it," he said, "an interesting rock-climb, presenting no extraordinary difficulties. . . I am of opinion that this ascent by the Z'Mutt *arête* will in future become the favourite way of crossing the Matterhorn."[1] As yet, Mr. Baumann's anticipation has not been realised. Indeed, until 1894, I did not hear that *anyone* further had either ascended or descended by the routes of Messrs. Mummery and Penhall.[2]

On July 19, 1880, Mr. A. Mummery invented another way up the Matterhorn. With the guides Alexander Burgener and B. Venetz, he ascended *via* the Furgg Glacier and the East Face, keeping near the south-east ridge until reaching the level of the northern 'shoulder,' and then crossing the face to the 'shoulder.' Then the ascent was completed by the Zermatt route. See *Alpine Journal* vol. x, p. 96, and *My Climbs in the Alps and Caucasus*, chapter ii.

In 1886, another life was lost on the East Face. Two friends, named Borckhardt and Davies, resolved to climb the mountain. We knew, said the latter, that it had been done by ladies and youths. "It was the regular thing to go up the Matterhorn, and we accordingly determined to make the ascent."

Accompanied by Fridolin Kronig and Peter Aufdemblatten, they left Zermatt on Aug. 16, in fine weather; and at 3 A.M. on the 17th started from the hut on the Hörnli ridge, arriving on the summit at about 9 A.M. The comparative rapidity with which they *mounted* was probably due to the fact that they were closely following in the track of other parties of tourists. The weather changed during the early morning, and it began to hail while they were still on the top. They commenced to descend at 9.20 A.M., in the next *ten hours* came down scarcely 2000 feet, and were benighted some distance above the old hut on the East Face. All tracks on the mountain were obliterated by the hail and snow which fell. They remained on this spot from about 7 P.M. on the 17th of August until 1 P.M. on the 18th, and then Mr. Davies and the two guides continued the descent, leaving Mr. Borckhardt behind, upon the open face of the mountain, lying in a helpless condition, at the point of death! A few hours later he was found dead and stiff, partly covered by freshly-fallen snow.

The entire story exceeds in horror and incredibility the abandon-

[1] *Alpine Journal*, vol. ix, p. 366.

[2] The following paragraph is taken from the *Alpine Journal*, vol. xiii, pp. 399-400. On Aug. 3, 1887, Messrs. G. Lammer and A. Lorria "without guides, left the Stockje hut at 1.45 A.M. to attempt the ascent of the Matterhorn by Mr. Penhall's route. They reached a point not very far from the top, but were compelled at 1 P.M. to turn back, owing to iced rocks. At 5.30 or 6 P.M., while traversing Penhall's couloir, they were carried down by an avalanche. Herr Lorria received concussion of the brain, besides a fracture of the right leg above the ankle, had both feet frost-bitten, and became unconscious. Herr Lammer, with a badly-sprained ankle, pulled his friend on to a rock, stripped off his own coat to cover him, and then went for aid. He found no one at the Stockje hut, so had to crawl down to the Staffel Alp, whence he despatched a message to Zermatt. A relief party came up and reached Herr Lorria about 7.30 A.M. on Aug. 4. He was still unconscious, and in his delirium had stripped off his clothes." Further details of this mad adventure will be found in the *Alpine Journal*, vol. xiii, pp. 550-53.

ment of Brantschen, and is much too long to recount in these pages.[1] An inquiry into this miserable business was held by the Valaisan authorities, and in an official Report upon it by Prof. F. O. Wolf, which was published at Sion, it is said "that the sole causes of the accident were the sudden changes in the weather; the insufficient number of guides; and the facts that neither Mr. Davies nor Mr. Borckhardt were fit to climb such a peak, were insufficiently clad, and badly provisioned." A further cause might have been added, namely, the incapacity of the guides.

In 1890, there was yet another accident upon the East Face, which caused the loss of an entire party. A young man from Strasburg, Herr Goehrs, started from the hut on the Hörnli ridge at 3.30 A.M. on the 13th of September with two young guides, Alois Graven and Joseph Brantschen. They were shortly followed by several other persons. About 9 A.M., both parties encountered high wind when a thousand feet or so below the summit, and decided to return. Very soon afterwards, Fridolin Burgener (one of the guides of the lower party) heard a clatter, and saw Herr Goehrs and his guides flying through the air within a hundred yards of him. The three fell until they were brought up on the Furgg-gletscher, and of course were killed outright. Though the cause of this accident is unknown, the probability is that these three very young men (who could not have had adequate mountaineering experience) were killed through one or more of them slipping upon the easiest side of the mountain. Since this last lamentable affair the Zermatt face of the Matterhorn has been free from disaster, but there still remain to be mentioned two catastrophes which have occurred upon the Italian side.

When telegrams came in, at the beginning of September, 1890, stating that Jean-Antoine Carrel had died from fatigue on the south side of the Matterhorn, those who knew the man scarcely credited the report. It was not likely that this tough and hardy mountaineer would die from fatigue anywhere, still less that he would succumb upon 'his own mountain.' But it was true. Jean-Antoine perished from the combined effects of cold, hunger, and fatigue upon his own side of his own mountain, almost within sight of his own home. He started on the 23rd of August from Breuil, with an Italian gentleman and Charles Gorret (brother of the Abbé Gorret), with the intention of crossing the Matterhorn in one day. The weather at the time of their departure was the very best, and it changed in the course of the day to the very worst. They were shut up in the *cabane* at the foot of the Great Tower during the 24th, with scarcely any food, and on the 25th retreated to Breuil. Although Jean-Antoine (upon whom, as leading guide, the chief labour and responsibility naturally devolved) ultimately succeeded in getting his party safely off the mountain, he himself was so overcome by fatigue, cold, and want of food that he died on the spot.

Jean-Antoine Carrel entered his sixty-second year in January, 1890,[2]

[1] See the *Alpine Journal*, vol. xiii, pp. 95-110, and 166-171.

[2] The exact date of his birth does not seem to be known. He was christened at the Church of St. Antoine, Valtournanche, on January 17, 1829.

and was in the field throughout the summer. On 21st August, having just returned from an ascent of Mont Blanc, he was engaged at Courmayeur by Signor Leone Sinigaglia, of Turin, for an ascent of the Matterhorn. He proceeded to the Val Tournanche, and on the 23rd set out with him and Charles Gorret, for the last time, to ascend his own mountain by his own route. A long and clear account of what happened was communicated by Signor Sinigaglia to the Italian Alpine Club, and from this the following relation is condensed:—

"We started for the Cervin at 2.15 A.M. on the 23rd, in splendid weather, with the intention of descending the same night to the hut at the Hörnli on the Swiss side. We proceeded pretty well, but the glaze of ice on the rocks near the Col du Lion retarded our march somewhat, and when we arrived at the hut at the foot of the Great Tower, prudence counselled the postponement of the ascent until the next day, for the sky was becoming overcast. We decided upon this, and stopped.

"Here I ought to mention that both I and Gorret noticed with uneasiness that Carrel showed signs of fatigue upon leaving the Col du Lion. I attributed this to temporary weakness. As soon as we reached the hut he lay down and slept profoundly for two hours, and awoke much restored. In the meantime the weather was rapidly changing. Storm clouds coming from the direction of Mont Blanc hung over the Dent d'Hérens, but we regarded them as transitory, and trusted to the north wind, which was still continuing to blow. Meanwhile, three of the Maquignaz's and Edward Bich, whom we found at the hut, returning from looking after the ropes, started downwards for Breuil, at parting wishing us a happy ascent, and holding out hopes of a splendid day for the morrow.

"But, after their departure, the weather grew worse very rapidly; the wind changed, and towards evening there broke upon us a most violent hurricane of hail and snow, accompanied by frequent flashes of lightning. The air was so charged with electricity that for two consecutive hours in the night one could see in the hut as in broad daylight. The storm continued to rage all night, and the day and night following, continuously, with incredible violence. The temperature in the hut fell to − 3 degrees.

"The situation was becoming somewhat alarming, for the provisions were getting low, and we had already begun to use the seats of the hut as firewood. The rocks were in an extremely bad state, and we were afraid that if we stopped longer, and the storm continued, we should be blocked up in the hut for several days. This being the state of affairs, it was decided among the guides that if the wind should abate we should descend on the following morning; and, as the wind did abate somewhat, on the morning of the 25th (the weather, however, still remaining very bad), it was unanimously settled to make a retreat."

"At 9 A.M. we left the hut. I will not speak of the difficulties and dangers in descending the *arête* to the Col du Lion, which we reached at 2.30 P.M. The ropes were half frozen; the rocks were covered with a glaze of ice, and fresh snow hid all points of support.

Carrel Jean Antoine

Some spots were really as bad as could be, and I owe much to the prudence and coolness of the two guides that we got over them without mishap."

"At the Col du Lion, where we hoped the wind would moderate, a dreadful hurricane recommenced, and in crossing the snowy passages we were nearly *suffocated* by the wind and snow which attacked us on all sides.[1] Through the loss of a glove, Gorret, half an hour after leaving the hut, had already got a hand frost-bitten. The cold was terrible here. Every moment we had to remove the ice from our eyes, and it was with the utmost difficulty that we could speak so as to understand one another."

"Nevertheless, Carrel continued to direct the descent in a most admirable manner, with a coolness, ability, and energy above all praise. I was delighted to see the change, and Gorret assisted him splendidly. This part of the descent presented unexpected difficulties, and at several points great dangers, the more so because the *tourmente* prevented Carrel from being sure of the right direction, in spite of his consummate knowledge of the Matterhorn. At 11 P.M. (or thereabouts—it was impossible to look at our watches, as all our clothes were half frozen) we were still toiling down the rocks. The guides sometimes asked each other where they were; then we went forward again—to stop, indeed would have been impossible. Carrel at last, by marvellous instinct, discovered the passage up which we had come, and in a sort of grotto we stopped a minute to take some brandy."

"While crossing some snow we saw Carrel slacken his pace, and then fall two or three times to the ground. Gorret asked him what was the matter, and he said 'nothing,' but he went on with difficulty. Attributing this to fatigue through the excessive toil, Gorret put himself at the head of the caravan, and Carrel, after the change, seemed better, and walked well, though with more circumspection than usual. From this place a short and steep passage takes one down to the pastures, where there is safety. Gorret descended first, and I after him. We were nearly at the bottom when I felt the rope pulled. We stopped, awkwardly placed as we were, and cried out to Carrel several times to come down, but we received no answer. Alarmed, we went up a little way, and heard him say, in a faint voice, 'Come up and fetch me, I have no strength left.'"

"We went up and found that he was lying with his stomach to the ground, holding on to a rock, in a semi-conscious state, and unable to get up or to move a step. With extreme difficulty we carried him up to a safe place and asked him what was the matter. His only answer was, 'I know no longer where I am.' His hands were getting colder and colder, his speech weaker and more broken, and his body more still. We did all we could for him, putting with great difficulty the rest of the cognac into his mouth. He said something, and appeared to revive, but this did not last long. We tried rubbing him with snow, and shaking him, and calling to him continually; but he could only answer with moans.

[1] Signor Peraldo, the innkeeper at Breuil, stated that a relief party was in readiness during the whole of August 25 (the day on which the descent was made), and was prevented from starting by the violence of the tempest.

"We tried to lift him, but it was impossible—he was getting stiff. We stooped down, and asked in his ear if he wished to commend his soul to God. With a last effort he answered 'Yes,' and then fell on his back, dead, upon the snow."

Such was the end of Jean-Antoine Carrel,—a man who was possessed with a pure and genuine love of mountains; a man of originality and resource, courage and determination, who delighted in exploration. His special qualities marked him out as a fit person to take part in new enterprizes, and I preferred him to all others as a companion and assistant upon my journey amongst the Great Andes of the Equator. Going to a new country, on a new continent, he encountered much that was strange and unforeseen; yet when he turned his face homewards he had the satisfaction of knowing that he left no failures behind him.[1] After parting at Guayaquil in 1880, we did not meet again. In his latter years, I am told, he shewed signs of age, and from information which has been communicated to me it is clear that he had arrived at a time when it would have been prudent to retire—if he could have done so. It was not in his nature to spare himself, and he worked to the very last. The manner of his death strikes a chord in hearts he never knew. He recognized to the fullest extent the duties of his position, and in the closing act of his life set a brilliant example of fidelity and devotion. For it cannot be doubted that, enfeebled as he was, he could have saved himself had he given his attention to self-preservation. He took a nobler course; and, accepting his responsibility, devoted his whole soul to the welfare of his comrades, until, utterly exhausted, he fell staggering on the snow. He was already dying. Life was flickering, yet the brave spirit said '*It is nothing.*' They placed him in the rear to ease his work. He was no longer able even to support himself; he dropped to the ground, and in a few minutes expired.[2]

CARREL'S CROSS.

[1] See *Travels amongst the Great Andes of the Equator*, 1892.

[2] Signor Sinigaglia wrote in a letter to a friend, from which I am permitted to quote, "I don't try to tell you of my intense pain for Carrel's death. He fell after having saved me, and no guide could have done more than he did." Charles Gorret, through his brother the Abbé, wrote to me that he entirely endorsed what had been said by Sig. Sinigaglia, and added, "We would have given our own lives to have saved his."

Jean-Antoine died at the foot of the 'little staircase.' On the 26th of August his body was brought to Breuil, and upon the 29th it was interred at Valtournanche. At

I very much regret to have to mention yet another tragedy, which occurred more recently. On August 7, 1893, Andreas Seiler (one of the youngest members of the family of my old friend M. Alexandre Seiler) and Johann Biener of Zermatt lost their lives on the south side of the Matterhorn. Mr. Oscar Gysi, who was closely following them, has, at my request, furnished the following statement:—

"On August 7, shortly before 6 A.M., we left the Lac Noir Hotel, crossed the Furgg Joch, and on the Italian side joined the ordinary route from Breuil for the Matterhorn. There were five of us—Andreas Seiler, myself, and as guides Johann Biener (aged 24), Joseph Taugwalder (aged 27), and L. Moser of Taesch (aged 22). When about an hour below the Col du Lion we tied up,—Seiler insisting upon being roped to Biener, with whom he had been climbing all the summer. Biener and Seiler were in advance, but we kept well together. When we were considerably higher than the Tête du Lion, and within about thirty minutes of the hut at the foot of the Great Tower, we came to an almost perpendicular chimney, some twenty feet high, down which a stout knotted rope hung. Biener and Seiler passed up it. We followed, and on arriving at the top Moser took off his *sac* to tie up afresh the wood that he carried. Seiler and Biener were impatient to reach the hut, and wished to proceed without us; but Taugwalder and Moser asked them to wait. Their words were, however, useless. Moser, who had warned Seiler repeatedly during the last half-hour to be careful, and who did not like their over-confidence, prayed Seiler to let him tie himself to their rope. Seiler and Biener, however, only laughed at him for his concern, and started off. Moser finished tying up his wood, and we went on. The others were only five minutes ahead, and we had reached a difficult spot, and were standing in steps cut at the top of a small patch of ice, at an angle of 50°, and close to rock, when Moser called out, 'Beware of stones.' We pressed up close to the rock and listened, when the two" (Seiler and Biener) "shot past us. We were all three close together, and Moser could have touched them with his axe. . . I see them still—they were photographed in my mind. They were tied together. Seiler passed close to us, his back downwards, his head well bent up, as if he were preparing for a sudden shock. Biener flew far out against the blue sky, and the rope was stretched tightly between them." They fell on to the Glacier du Lion, and when the bodies were recovered they were still tied together. "With both, the crown of the head was cut away as though it had been done by a sharp instrument. . . Seiler's watch was crushed, and his left boot was missing, although the foot was uninjured. How the accident happened will never be known, as no one saw them slip. I am inclined to think that Seiler was climbing at the same time as Biener, instead of waiting until he had found firm hold, and that the former slipped, jerking Biener off his feet. I am strengthened in this belief by the position of the two as I saw them fly past."

the beginning of July, 1893, an iron cross was placed on the spot where he expired, at the expense of Sig. Sinigaglia, who went in person along with Charles Gorret to superintend its erection.

CHAPTER VI.

HOW TO GET TO ZERMATT.

ROUTE TO TAKE—TIMES, DISTANCES AND FARES—PONTARLIER—AT VALLORBES EVERYONE DESCENDS—LAUSANNE AND OUCHY—GIBBON AT LAUSANNE—*THE* LAKE—ST. MAURICE—THE RHONE VALLEY—MARTIGNY—SION—SIERRE—SOUSTE—VISP OR VIÈGE—ALL CHANGE HERE.

THE most direct way to Zermatt either from London or Paris is by the Paris, Lyons and Mediterranean Railway, *viâ* Dijon, Pontarlier, Vallorbes and Lausanne. The best train for those who wish to travel straight through leaves the Gare de Lyon at 8.40 p.m. If this is taken, you are landed at Zermatt in the following afternoon, in time to settle down before dinner. This train is supposed to arrive at Lausanne at 8.40 a.m. (central Europe time). As the corresponding train on the Jura-Simplon line [Lausanne to Visp] is fixed to leave at 9 a.m., there is apparently time to get something in the way of breakfast at Lausanne Buffet. It will be well to reckon that there will *not* be time.

The 8.40 p.m. train is first and second class to Pontarlier, but after that it takes third class. It stops 13 times between Paris—Lausanne (330 miles, 527 kils.), and does not remain anywhere long enough for a meal![1] Pay attention to the stomach before leaving Paris. The train in correspondence from Lausanne to Visp is a civilized one, with dining-cars (which were started in 1895). It is better to take advantage of these cars than to attempt a meal at Lausanne. They are not yet much patronized,—passengers probably being under the impression that extra charges are made for their use, and that prices are high. There is no extra charge, and the prices are fair. "Premier déjeuner (Café, Café au lait, Thé ou Chocolat, avec pain et beurre), 1.50. Diner, table d'hôte, 3.50." The *carte des vins* extends from Beer at 80 centimes a bottle to 'Pommery extra dry.' The 'Mont d'Or Johannisberg' is a good wine for the morning.

Try to sleep as far as Dôle. At Pontarlier look out for coffee. The high road which will be seen here near the line is memorable as that which was traversed by the retreating, demoralized Bourbaki Army, during the Franco-German war. At **Vallorbes** (2520 feet, **768** mètres;

[1] Lausanne deserves a better and more rapid train service from Paris. A step in the right direction will be made this year. From the 12th of July, 1897, twice a week during the season, the Paris, Lyons and Mediterranean Railway will run a new train in 11¾ hours from Paris to Lausanne *viâ* Pontarlier, composed exclusively of sleeping-cars (1st cl. only). These trains will leave Paris at 11.15 p.m. (Paris-Nord Stn.). Similar trains will leave Lausanne at 9.50 p.m. for Paris *viâ* Pontarlier, and will arrive in Paris Gare de Lyon) at 7.25 a.m. Make enquiry.

pop. 2147) there is the Swiss Custom-house. Everyone gets down. [This place is three miles from the eastern end of the Lac de Joux, a charming sheet of water 5½ miles long, in the heart of the Jura, not much known to English.] In the next 25 miles the line descends

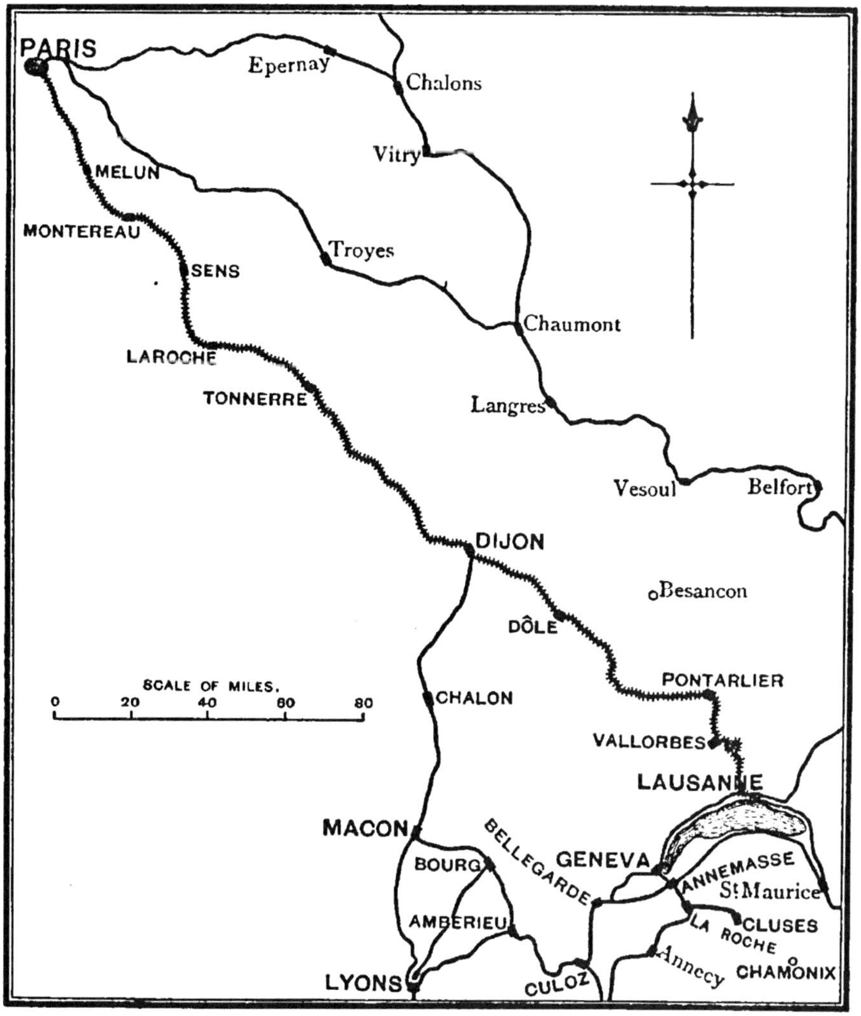

PARIS TO PONTARLIER, VALLORBES AND LAUSANNE.

1160 feet, with many windings, upon the Lake of Geneva, and passes a constant succession of beautiful views on each side. Six kils. before arriving at Lausanne it joins the railway coming from Geneva.

Lausanne Station[1] (1476 feet, 450 mètres) is situated between the town of Lausanne and Ouchy, its port on the Lake of Geneva. *Change here for Zermatt.* HOTEL TERMINUS ET BUFFET DE LA GARE (at the Station), 50 beds. **Lausanne.—Hotels**—HOTEL-PENSION BEAU-

[1] In the middle of the day, *during the height of the season*, this is a place to be shunned. There are too many travellers and too few porters.

Dist.	Stations.		Times.	1st Cl.	2nd Cl.	3rd Cl.
kils.	**Paris**	dep.	8.40 p.m.	fr. c.	fr. c.	fr. c.
155	,, to Laroche (B) .	arr.	11.3 ,,	17 35	11 60	7 65
315	,, **Dijon** (B) .	do.	1.33 a.m.	35 30	23 80	15 50
		dep.	1.38 ,,	Fares	from	Dijon
347	,, Auxonne .	arr.	2.11 ,,	3 60	2 40	1 60
362	,, Dole (B) .	do.	2.28 ,,	5 25	3 55	2 30
387	,, Arc-Senans .	do.	3.12 ,,	8 05	5 45	3 55
394	,, Mouchard (B)	do.	3.22 ,,	8 85	5 95	3 90
		dep.	3.30 ,,			
430	,, Boujeailles .	arr.	4.37 ,,	12 90	8 70	5 65
455	,, Pontarlier (B)	do.	5.9 ,,	14 80	10 00	6 50
		dep.	5.35 ,,	Fares	from	Pontarlier
472	,, Hopitaux-Jougne	arr.	6.4 ,,	1 90	1 30	0 85
481	,, **Vallorbes** .	do.	6.20 [1] ,,	2 95	2 00	1 30
		dep.	7.35 [2] ,,	Fares	from	Vallorbes
	,, La Sarraz .	arr.	8.10 ,,	..	...	...
	,, Cossonay .	do.	8.20 ,,	...	...	...
527	,, **Lausanne** (B)	do.	8.40 ,,	7 70	5 35	3 70
		dep.	9.0 ,,	Fares	from	Lausanne
546	,, Vevey . .	arr.	9.28 ,,	2 00	1 40	1 00
551	,, Clarens . .	do.	9.35 ,,	2 50	1 75	1 25
552	,, Montreux .	do.	9.40 ,,	2 60	1 85	1 30
554	,, Territet-Glion	do.	9.43 ,,	2 80	2 00	1 40
555	,, Veytaux-Chillon	do.	...	2 95	2 05	1 45
557	,, Villeneuve .	do.	9.51 ,,	3 15	2 20	1 60
567	,, Aigle . .	do.	10.6 ,,	4 20	2 95	2 10
575	,, Bex . .	do.	10.20 ,,	5 00	3 50	2 50
579	,, **St. Maurice** (B)	do.	10.28 ,,	5 40	3 80	2 70
		dep.	10.40 ,,	Fares	from	St. Maurice
586	,, Evionnaz .	arr.	...	0 75	0 55	0 40
589	,, Vernayaz-Salvan	do.	10.56 ,,	1 05	0 75	0 55
594	,, Martigny .	do.	11.5 ,,	1 60	1 10	0 80
599	,, Charrat-Fully	do.	...	2 10	1 50	1 05
603	,, Saxon . .	do.	11.17 ,,	2 50	1 75	1 25
608	,, Riddes . .	do.	...	3 05	2 15	1 50
613	,, Ardon . .	do.	...	3 55	2 50	1 80
620	,, **Sion** (B) .	do.	11.37 ,,	4 30	3 00	2 15
		dep.	11.40 ,,			
626	,, St. Léonard .	arr.	...	4 90	3 45	2 45
629	,, Granges .	do.	...	5 20	3 65	2 60
636	,, Sierre (Siders)	do.	12.1 p.m.	5 95	4 20	3 00
640	,, Salquenen .	do.	...	6 35	4 45	3 20
645	,, Louèche (Souste)	do.	12.20 ,,	6 90	4 85	3 45
650	,, Tourtemagne	do.	...	7 40	5 20	3 70
654	,, Gampel .	do.	...	7 80	5 50	3 90
658	,, Rarogne .	do.	...	8 25	5 80	4 10
665	,, **Viège** (Visp) (B)	do.	12.43 ,,	8 95	6 30	4 50
		dep.	1.5 ,,	Fares	from	Visp
700	,, **Zermatt** .	arr.	3.25 ,,	...	16 00	10 00

N.B.—Alterations may occur in the times of Arrival and Departure. Make enquiry.
(B) signifies Buffet. [1] Paris time. [2] Central Europe time.

SÉJOUR (near the Station), 100 beds; HOTEL NATIONAL ET PENSION GALLO (near the Station), 30 beds; HOTEL ET PENSION STE. LUCE (near the Station), 25 beds; HOTEL GIBBON (central), 100 beds; GRAND HOTEL RICHE-MONT (central), 100 beds; HOTEL DU GRAND-PONT (central), 75 beds; HOTEL BEAU-SITE ET DU BELVÉDÈRE (central), 40 beds; HOTEL DES MESSAGERIES (central), 50 beds; HOTEL DU FAUCON, 60 beds; HOTEL DU NORD, 40 beds; HOTEL ET PENSION BELLEVUE, 30 beds; HOTEL ET PENSION VICTORIA, 50 beds; PENSION CAMPART (on the road from Lausanne to Ouchy), 50 beds; PENSION GRANCY-VILLA, 45 beds.

Ouchy (1247 feet, 380 mètres).—HOTEL BEAU-RIVAGE, 200 beds; and HOTEL DU CHÂTEAU (picturesque building, close to the Lake), 80 beds. These two hotels, though separate buildings, are under the same management. HOTEL D'ANGLETERRE (close to the Lake), 40 beds; HOTEL DU PORT (small).

Lausanne is situated upon slopes facing the south, commanding admirable views of the Lake and of the mountains at its eastern end, and has long been a favourite place with English. The upper part of the town is several hundred feet above the railway station. Pop. in 1888, 34,049 (28,829 Protestant, 4793 Catholic), is said to have increased considerably of late. Those who have time to spare will do well to stop a while either at Ouchy or Lausanne, as, in addition to their own attractions, they are excellent centres for excursions. Steamers from Ouchy convey one to any part of the Lake. Besides the line to Vallorbes and Pontarlier by which we came, and the other around the eastern end of the Lake and up the Rhone Valley (by which we shall depart), there are railways to Geneva (one hour, by express) and to Bern *viâ* Fribourg (98 kils. in 2 hrs. 20 min.). On the former line there are many beautiful views of the Lake, and the latter passes through very picturesque country. Ouchy is connected by a rope tramway with Lausanne Railway Station and Lausanne. Trams run each way about every 15 min. Fares 40 and 20 centimes. It takes 20 min. to *walk* to Ouchy from Lausanne Station.

Although there has been a good deal of rebuilding at Lausanne, a considerable number of ancient houses remain clustered around the Cathedral, which is situated in the higher part of the town. Admittance to it can be obtained from 9 to 12, and from 1 to 4 free. At other times 50 centimes are charged. The tower can be ascended, and there is a superb view from it. The tower and west front are now undergoing restoration. An old staircase called *Escaliers du Marché* leads down from the Cathedral to the market-place, which is worth seeing at busy times. The *Musée Cantonal* (zoological and archæological) is close to the Cathedral. From the terrace in front of the *Tribunal Fédéral* there is a very fine view of the Lake and of the Alps on its farther side. The town of Evian-les-Bains lies almost immediately opposite. The most prominent mountain beyond the head of the Lake (a little to the right) is the Dent du Midi (10,777 feet, 3285 mètres). There are sometimes cheap excursions from Lausanne to Zermatt, at inclusive fares for rail and hotel. Enquire.

Gibbon the Historian had much to do with Lausanne and in making it known to his countrymen. He knew it in his youth, and lived there in his maturity. "You have often read," he said, "and heard the descriptions of this delightful Country, the banks of the lake of Geneva, and indeed it surpasses all description. A stranger is struck with surprise and admiration." After settling down there with the purpose of completing his "*Decline and Fall*," he wrote to Lord Sheffield in 1784—

"This place has in every respect exceeded my best and most sanguine hopes. How often have you said, as often as I expressed any ill-humour against the hurry, the expence, and the precarious condition of my London life, 'Ay, that is a nonsensical scheme of retiring to Lausanne that you have got into your head,—a pretty fancy; you remember how much you liked it in your youth, but you have now seen more of the World, and if you were to try it again, you would find yourself most woefully disappointed.' I had it in my head, in my heart; I have tryed it; I have not been disappointed."

And a little later, in a letter to his stepmother, he wrote—

"I have enjoyed a winter of the most perfect health that I have perhaps ever known, without any mixture of the little flying incommodities which in my best days have sometimes disturbed the tranquillity of my English life. . . I command a boundless prospect of vale, mountain, and water. . . A Terrace, one hundred yards long, extends beyond the front of the House, and leads to a close impenetrable shrubbery; and from thence the circuit of a long and various walk, carries me round a meadow and a vineyard. . . Few persons, either princes or philosophers, enjoy a more desirable residence."[1] *Private Letters of Edward Gibbon*, 3 vols. 8vo, London, 1897; vol. ii, pp. 89, 103-4.

On resuming the journey by the Jura-Simplon Railway, *secure a seat on the side of the Lake.* Points of view are very numerous, and we should not get to Zermatt this season if we stopped to look at half of them. The attractions of this corner of the Lake have caused the establishment of a multitude of Hotels and Pensions. The region is a Paradise for Pensionnaires. **Vevey**, pop. 8144, is about 12 miles from Lausanne, and **Clarens**, another favourite spot, is 2½ miles farther on. Then comes **Montreux**, and the next station is **Territet-Glion**, whence a very steep railway leads to the **Rochers-de-Naye** (6723 feet), a noted panoramic station, with a view extending Northwards to the Bernese Oberland and in the contrary direction to the Range of Mont Blanc. In less than a mile more the famous **Castle of Chillon** is passed. **Villeneuve**, pop. 1471, is the terminal point of the steamers. Two miles and a half away to the West the River Rhone falls into the Lake, and deposits there an enormous mass of matter brought down from the mountains.

The line now enters the Rhone Valley, and after passing **Aigle**, pop. 3555 (the station for Sepey, Ormont-dessous, and Ormont-dessus), and **Bex**, pop. 4420 (noted for its salt-mines and salt-baths), quits the Canton Vaud, and crossing to the left bank of the river, enters the **Canton Valais.** Shortly afterwards it passes through a small tunnel and arrives at

[1] Part of the grounds of the house in which Gibbon lived from 1783 to 1793 is now occupied by the Hotel Gibbon.

St. Maurice (St. Moritz), 1368 feet, 417 mètres; pop. 1666. Buffet good. HOTEL GRISOGONO (close to the Station). This is one of the oldest places in the Canton. The Abbey here is said to have been founded in the 4th century. The town lies about midway between the Dent du Midi (on its West) and the Dent de Morcles, 9639 feet, 2938 mètres (on its East). While in the Station, notice the Hermitage on the West, and the curious path to it, winding up the cliff.

[At St. Maurice the line from the N. shore of the Lake of Geneva meets that coming from Geneva round the S. side of the Lake, *viâ* Annemasse, Thonon, Evian and Bouveret. This latter line belongs to the Paris, Lyons and Mediterranean Railway. It is the best route to take if going from St. Maurice to Geneva, or to Chamonix. The first station upon this line is at **Monthey** (7 kils. from St. Maurice), at the entrance of the Val d'Illiez, famous for its remarkable assemblage of erratic blocks, some of which are 60 to 70 feet long. See *Essai sur les Glaciers et sur le terrain erratique du bassin du Rhone*, by Jean de Charpentier, 8vo, Lausanne, 1841; pp. 134-143.]

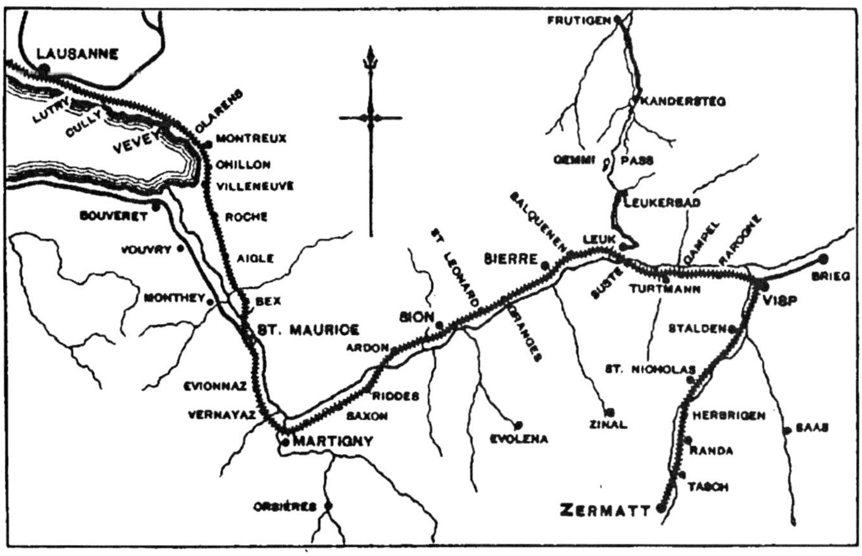

LAUSANNE TO VISP AND ZERMATT.

Soon after leaving St. Maurice the valley begins to open out again. Between the stations Evionnaz and Vernayaz the **Pissevache fall** is passed, and can be seen very well from the windows of the train. **Vernayaz** (HOTEL DE LA GARE, close to the station; simple place, civil people) is the station for those who wish to proceed to Chamonix *viâ* Salvan. For Plan, see my *Guide to Chamonix and the Range of Mont Blanc*, 8vo, London, 1897; chap. xiv. One can walk to Salvan in 70 min. from Vernayaz and return in 40 min. It is also the station for the **Gorges of Trient**, which are 12 min. walk distant. One of the finest ravines in the Alps; cool and comfortable on the hottest day, with good hotel GRAND HOTEL DES GORGES DU TRIENT two minutes from the entrance. The railway hereabouts runs close alongside the great Simplon Road. A round tower (la Batiaz) will be seen shortly before arriving at Martigny, which is a remnant of a *Château* that belonged to the early Bishops of Sion.

Martigny, 1539 feet, 475 mètres ; pop. 4731 ; is made up of Martigny-Ville, Martigny-Bourg, and Martigny-Combe. It is the station for the Great St. Bernard route, or for those going to Chamonix *viâ* the Col de Balme or the Tête Noire. **Hotels.**—HOTEL DU GRAND ST. BERNARD, and HOTEL-PENSION RESTAURANT DE LA GARE, both against the Station ; GRAND HOTEL DU MONT BLANC, HOTEL CLERC,

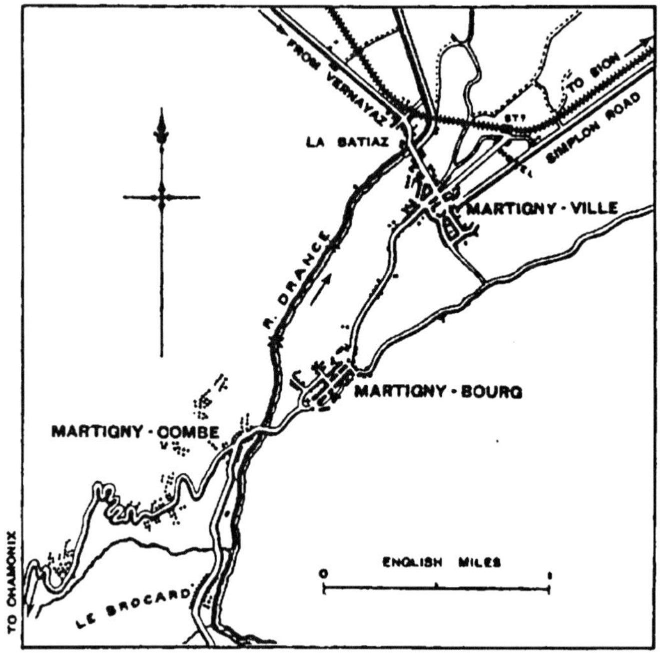

PLAN OF MARTIGNY.

HOTEL DE L'AIGLE, and HOTEL NATIONAL in Martigny-Ville. At Martigny the River Rhone makes a bend at right angles to its lower course, the valley broadens considerably, and one can see up it for a long distance. One of the most prominent natural features at this part (on the south side) is the small but rather striking peak called the **Pierre à Voir,** 8120 feet, 2476 mètres; which, though presenting sheer cliff on the side of Saxon and apparently inaccessible, can be ascended easily from several directions. Between the stations of Riddes and Ardon the base is passed of a mountain called the **Haut de Cry,** 9701 feet, 2956 mètres, on which the guide J. J. Bennen and others lost their lives on February 28, 1864, through disturbing unconsolidated snow. See *Scrambles amongst the Alps,* Appendix A. The railway crosses to the right bank of the Rhone at Riddes, and 12 kils. afterwards arrives at

Sion (Sitten), 1700 feet, pop. 5513, the capital of the Canton Valais. **Hotels.**—HOTEL DU MIDI; HOTEL DE LA POSTE. Get out here for the Val d'Hérens. In the Introduction to the fifth volume of his *Documents*, the Abbé Gremaud gives many details respecting the ecclesiastical and other buildings of Sion. He says that there was a Christian Church here *before* A.D. 377. The next station after Sion is at **St. Léonard**, where a fierce battle was fought in 1375 (in consequence of the assassination of Bishop Tavelli, see p. 8), which ended in the defeat and flight of the *Seigneurs.*

"At the news of this horrible crime, the patriots of Conches, Brigue, Louèche, Sierre and Sion swore that they would avenge the death of their Bishop. They flew to arms, and invaded the murderer's domains. After having taken the Château de Granges, they made for that of Ayent" [4 miles N.E. of Sion], "but near the bridge of St. Léonard they found themselves in the presence of the vassals and allies of Antoine de la Tour. The combat began; and here, as at Louèche, the *seigneurs* were conquered by the peasants. The armour glittering with gold, and the helmets with their floating plumes, were crushed under the avenging clubs. . . Pursuing their victory, they burnt the castles of Ayent and Conthey, and then laid siege to that of Châtillon."—*Hilaire Gay.*

Sierre (Siders), ten miles from Sion, 1765 feet, 538 mètres; pop. 1342. **Hotels.**—HOTEL BELLEVUE (good, English landlady) close to the station; HOTEL DE LA POSTE. "Perhaps the most ancient place in this part of the Valais, since it is mentioned in the act of foundation of the Abbey of St. Maurice, A.D. 516."—*Abbé Gremaud.* Those bound for the Val d'Anniviers (St. Luc and Zinal) get out here. Just before arriving at Souste the railway recrosses to the left bank of the Rhone.

Souste or Suste, 2044 feet, 623 mètres, is the station for Leuk or Louèche, pop. 1548. There is a decent little restaurant just outside the station. Those who are bound for Leukerbad (Louèche-les-Bains), and the Gemmi Pass, get out here.

[A good pedestrian can go on foot from Suste to Leukerbad as quickly as a carriage, as there are two places where much time can be saved by 'cutting zigzags,'—one just after crossing the railway, whence the path goes direct to the town of Leuk (which is 430 feet above the Rhone), and avoids a very long detour that the *road* makes towards the East. Enquire the way before leaving the Station. The second place where time can be saved by 'cutting' is just after crossing the large bridge over the R. Dala. Take the first footpath to the right, which leads direct to the village of Inden, where the road is again rejoined.]

After passing Souste, the railway runs closely alongside the Rhone for 18 kils. **Tourtemagne,** 2073 feet, 632 mètres, is the station for the Turtmannthal and Gruben, whence one can go by the Augstbord-pass to St. Nicholas in the Nicolaithal. The *village* of Turtmann, pop. 548 (two hotels), is on the Simplon Road, a kil. south of the railway-station. **Gampel,** 2087 feet, 636 mètres, is the station for the Lötschenthal. The village is ¾ mile away to the north, at the entrance to the valley. A little higher up the Rhone valley, on the same side, there is the small village of Bas-Châtillon or Niedergestelen, with the ruins of the castle (destroyed in 1379) which was the stronghold of the De la Tour family. See chap. i. There was a priory here in the 14th century. [Gremaud, vol. v, p. civ.]

The next station, **Rarogne (Raron)**, 2113 feet, 644 mètres, is not at that village, but lies about midway between it and the miserable hamlet Turtig (no inn), on the Simplon Road. The way to the Ginanzthal lies through Turtig. See chap. vii. The Rarogne family was one of the most important in the Valais. See chap. i. The Abbé Gremaud says that its origin "is very uncertain," and that the first Rarogne known was Henri, who was living in 1210, and was *vidomne* of Louèche and Rarogne. The Church of Rarogne, which will be seen perched on a rock, was built in 1512 on the site of a castle that was burnt in 1417.—*Abbé Rameau.*

About 4 kils. after passing Rarogne, the railway leaves the Rhone and makes for the entrance to the Vispthal. Get your small things together, for in a few minutes you will be at Visp (Buffet, good), where, as there is break of gauge, *all for Zermatt must change.*

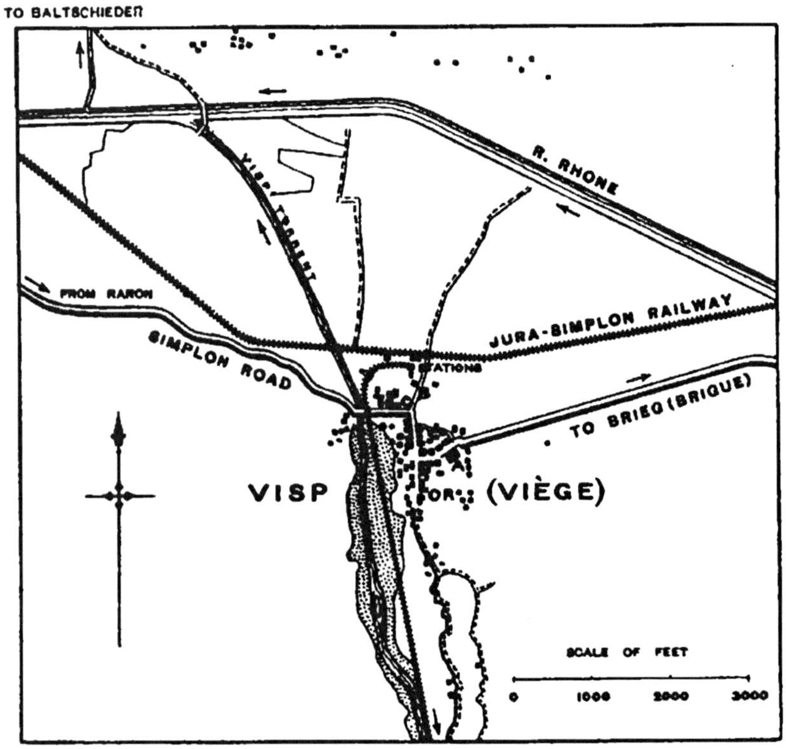

A. HOTEL DE LA POSTE. B. HOTEL DES ALPES. C. HOTEL DU SOLEIL.

CHAPTER VII.

UPON THE VALLEY OF ZERMATT (NICOLAI THAL).

VISP—THE ZERMATT RAILWAY AND THE ABT SYSTEM—NEUE BRUCKE—STALDEN—TÖRBEL—KALPETRAN—ST. NICHOLAS—ASCENTS FROM ST. NICHOLAS—PASSES FROM ST. NICHOLAS—BIRTHPLACE OF THOMAS PLATTER—HERBRIGGEN—RANDA—ASCENTS OF THE WEISSHORN, DOM, TÄSCHHORN, ETC.—PASSES FROM RANDA—TÄSCH—THE TÄSCH ALP AND VALLEY—ASCENTS OF THE ALLALIN, ALPHUBEL, AND RIMPFISCHHORN—PASSES FROM THE TÄSCH VALLEY—TÄSCH TO ZERMATT.

Visp, Viège or Vispach, 2165 feet, 660 mètres; 838 inhabitants; formerly called Vesbia, Vespia, or Vespie, is the chief town (*chef-lieu*) of a district in the Canton Valais,[1] to which it gives its name. The District de Viège (or Bezirk Visp) contains 21 Communes, namely—

Name.	Pop.	Name.	Pop.
Almagel (Almengell)	207	Randa (Randah)	229
Balen (Aballa)	172	St. Niklaus (St. Nicolas)	809
Baltschieder (Balschieder)	152	Stalden	409
Emd (Embd, Emdt)	206	Staldenried	241
Eisten (Eysten)	222	Täsch	231
Eyholz (Eiholz)	172	Törbel	551
Fée (Fee)	235	Visp (Vispach, Viège)	838
Grächen	336	Visperterbinen	605
Gründen	35	Zeneggen (Eggen)	240
Grund, im (Gruden, Saas)	386	Zermatt	525
Lalden	163	Total	6964

Several of these Communes [Baltschieder, Eyholz, Grunden and Lalden], though near Visp, are in the Rhone Valley.

Hotels.—HOTEL DES ALPES (close to the Railway Stations); HOTEL DE LA POSTE; HOTEL DU SOLEIL. Buffet at the Jura-Simplon Station good, prices reasonable; beer 25 centimes per glass. Post and Telegraph. Numerous general shops. Persons going by rail to Stalden, and intending to proceed to Saas, do well to arrange for mules or

[1] The Canton Valais (Kanton Wallis) had a population at the last (1888) census of 101,837 persons. Its area is 5247 square kilomètres, of which more than half are classed 'unproductive soil.' Of the unproductive soil, 971 sq. kils. are occupied by glaciers. In area the Valais is the third largest of the Swiss Cantons, but in population it stands twelfth. It has a smaller proportion of population to area than any of the Cantons, with the exception of Uri and Grisons. It is the most strictly Catholic Canton in the Confederation, there being nearly 117 Catholics to every Protestant. See *Nouvel Indicateur des Communes et de la population de la Suisse*, par Georges Lambelet, Zurich, 1889.

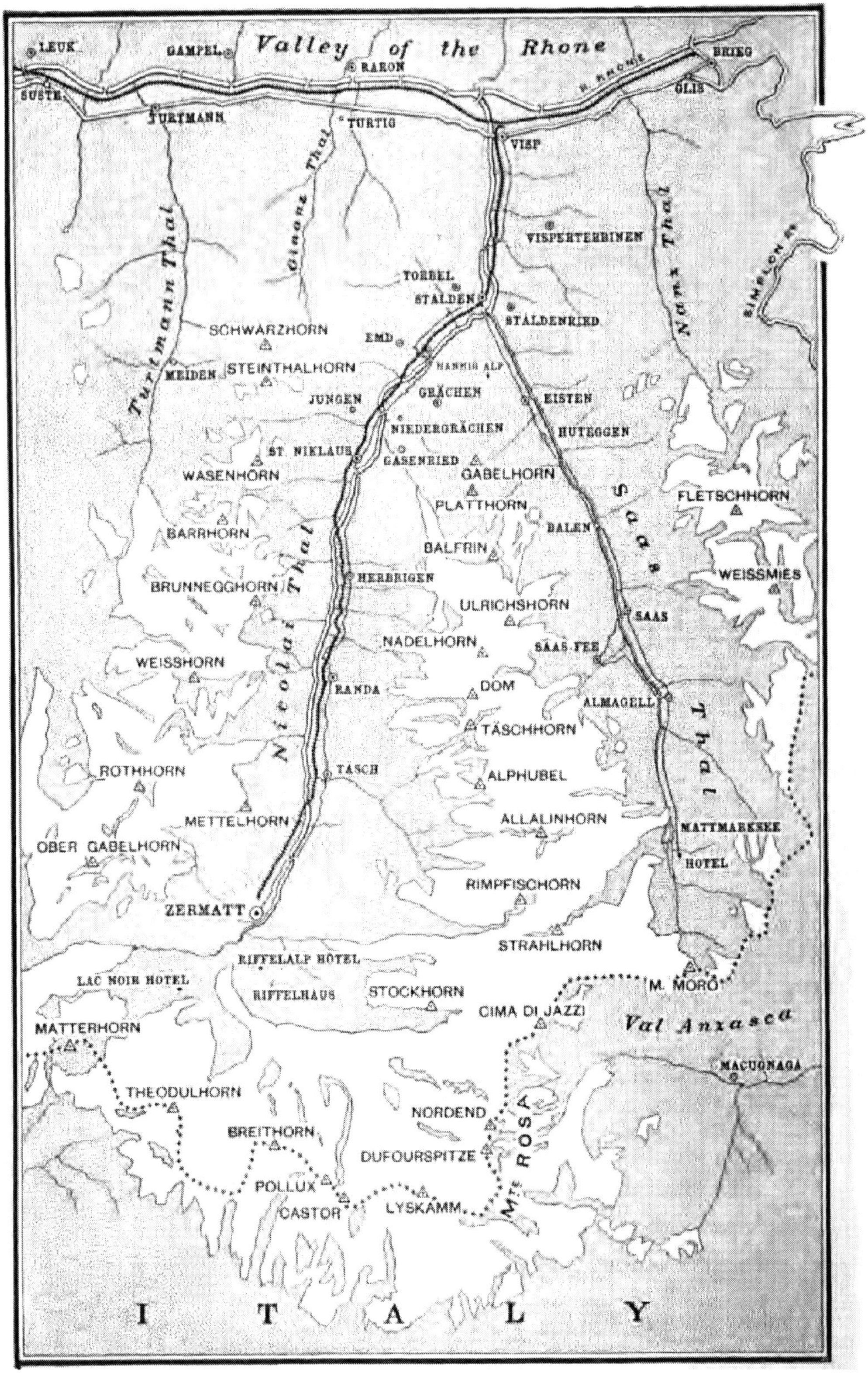

PLAN OF THE NICOLAI THAL, SAAS THAL, ETC.

SCALE, FIVE MILES TO ONE INCH.

porters before starting from Visp. This can be done either at the Hotel des Alpes or at the Hotel de la Poste.[1]

The **Station of the Zermatt Railway at Visp** is alongside that of the Jura-Simplon Railway. Tickets for Zermatt and intermediate stations are taken at the booking-office of the Jura-Simplon. The line is 35 kilomètres (or 22 miles nearly) in length. There are stations at Stalden, Kalpetran, St. Nicholas, Herbriggen, Randa and Täsch. The difference of level between Viège and Zermatt (3200 feet) might have been overcome by a ruling gradient of 1 in 36. If anything like this had been employed, very heavy and costly works would have been necessary; but they have been avoided by adopting the *système* Abt. Though short tunnels are numerous, there are no great cuttings or embankments on the Zermatt Railway. The principal bridge crosses a torrent (Muhlebach) which falls into the Vispbach about half-way between Stalden and Kalpetran. This is 220 feet long, and 144 feet above the bottom of the ravine.

THE "SYSTÈME ABT."

The Abt system aims at the avoidance of heavy works. Where the ground is flat the line skims the surface, and where there is an abrupt rise in the floor of the valley there are steep gradients upon which a third, cogged rail (*crémaillère*) is laid. The line presents therefore a succession of moderate inclines and very rapid ones. In some places the railway rises as much as one foot in eight. The third rail is not used when the gradients are less than one in forty, and is laid over only five miles. It is composed of two plates of steel which are bolted together in such a manner that the cogs alternate. The engines have two mechanisms—one for the ordinary rails and the other for the *crémaillère*. It is said that there are never less than four cogs or teeth biting at a time. In ascending the steep inclines the pace drops to four miles an hour and less. Great caution is used in *descending;* and, on the sections with the *crémaillère*, the trains

[1] Visp was formerly considered unhealthy, probably from its proximity to marshes. Dr. Schiner says (in his *Descrip. du Dép. du Simplon*), "it is undoubtedly these marshes . . . that produce in the lower part of Viège, in summer, the innumerable swarms of flies and gnats which destroy rest at this season, and disgust one by seeing the dishes covered with these tiresome insects." Since the embankment of the Rhone, there is much less marsh land in the Valais, and musquitoes have diminished at Visp.

seldom travel so fast as three miles an hour. There are several guardians to watch the line, who inspect the whole of it between the passage of each train. The early trains, during the season, are generally overfilled with passengers, eager to see the views. The evening ones are less crowded. The trains from Visp to Zermatt *wait* for those of the Jura-Simplon Railway, and sometimes wait a considerable length of time. Tickets from Visp to Zermatt, or from Zermatt to Visp permit the holders to descend at intermediate stations and resume the journey by a later train, but they are only good for the day on which they are issued. Return tickets are good for two days. The Fares are—

	Single Fares.		Return Tickets.	
	2nd Cl.	3rd Cl.	2nd Cl.	3rd Cl.
	fr. cts.	fr. cts.	fr. cts.	fr. cts.
Visp to Stalden . . .	3. 55	2. 25	6. 40	4. —
,, Kalpetran. . .	4. 90	3. 05	8. 80	5. 50
,, St. Nicholas . .	7. 55	4. 75	13. 60	8. 50
,, Herbriggen . .	9. 80	6. 10	17. 60	11. —
,, Randa . . .	11. 55	7. 25	20. 80	13. —
,, Täsch . . .	13. 35	8. 35	24. —	15. —
,, Zermatt . . .	16. —	10. —	28. 80	18. —

Visp is picturesquely situated on the left bank of the Rhone Valley, at the entrance to the Visp Thal. Five miles to the south this valley divides,—the western branch (the Valley of St. Nicholas or Nicolai Thal) leading to Zermatt, and the eastern one (Valley of Saas or Saas Thal) to the villages of Saas and Saas-Fée, and to the Monte Moro Pass.

There are a remarkable number of points of view in the Nicolai Thal (Valley of Zermatt), some of which are only seen from the *path*, and others only from the *railway*. A tourist who wishes to obtain a comprehensive idea of the valley should go one way by the path. The hotels on the route are at convenient distances apart. Some of the points of view are indicated by arrows upon the four little plans which accompany the text. The walking times between the several villages are about these—

Ascending.	h.	min.	Descending.	h.	min.
Visp to Stalden . . .	1	30	Zermatt to Täsch . . .		55
Stalden to St. Nicholas. .	1	55	Täsch to Randa . . .		35
St. Nicholas to Randa . .	1	45	Randa to St. Nicholas . .	1	30
Randa to Täsch . . .		40	St. Nicholas to Stalden . .	1	45
Täsch to Zermatt . . .	1	5	Stalden to Visp . . .	1	15
Total . . .	6	55	Total . . .	6	

The path to Zermatt turns rather sharply to the right at the southern end of Visp [the other path leading straight on goes to Visperterbinen, 4396 feet, 1340 mètres, pop. 605, a village seldom visited by tourists. A church was built there in 1256], and soon gets near the Visp torrent. So far as Stalden it is a fairly good mule-path, but it has scarcely been improved during the last forty years. When the largely increasing number of visitors rendered a *road* from Visp to Zermatt desirable, it was not found possible to carry one right through. Though some support was rendered by the natives at the southern end of the valley, the objections of the northern communes could not be overcome; and, at the present time, while there is a carriage *road* in the southern and upper end of the valley, at the northern end [Visp to St. Nicholas] the mule-*path* retains its primitive simplicity.

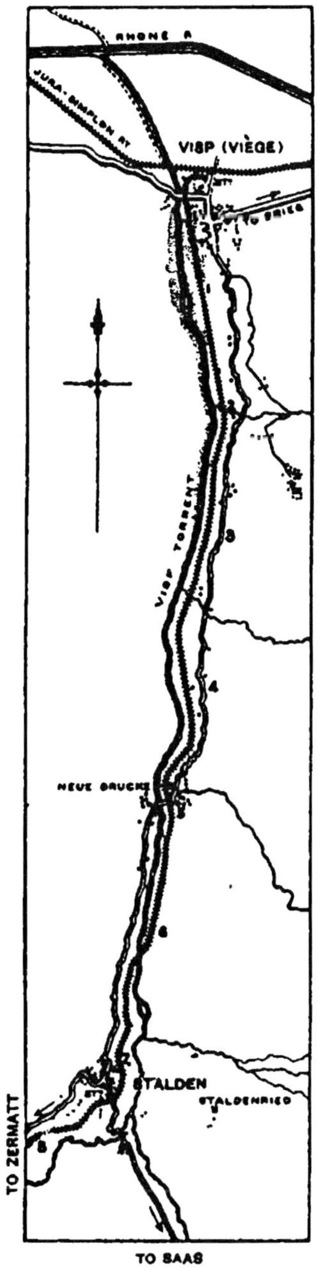

VISP TO STALDEN.

For the first five kils.[1] from Visp the road and railway keep close together. Numerous vineyards hereabouts. But at **Neue Brucke** (2280 feet, 695 mètres) the path crosses to the left bank of the stream by a bold single-arch bridge. The mountains seen in front when coming up this part of the valley are at the Northern end of the Saas Grat or range of the Mischabelhörner (separating the Nicolai Thal from the Saas Thal). The snow peak is the **Balfrin (Balenfirn)**, 12,473 feet, and the tooth of rock a little to its right is the Gabelhorn, 10,276 feet, hitherto unascended. At 6 kils. from Visp the railway also crosses the torrent, and commences the ascent of the first of the steep inclines, upon which the third, cogged rail is laid.

Stalden, 2608 feet, 795 mètres; pop. 409; is 7½ kils. from Visp and 27½ kils. from Zermatt. Travellers by rail *change here for Saas.* Post and Telegraph. **Hotel.**—HOTEL STALDEN (kept by the Proprietors of the Hotel de la Poste at Visp, who are also Proprietors of three hotels at Saas-Fée). The path to the Saas Thal leads past the Railway Station. See Chapter on the Valley of Saas.

"Stalden, says a Latin Chronicle, had its own particular lords, but they sold their property to the natives, and went over to the Valley of Aosta. Their tower is still in existence, but the inhabitants are free."—*Abbé Rameau.* A good deal of Muscat wine is made in this neighbourhood. It used to be procurable at 70 to 80 centimes a bottle. Prices have risen.

A pleasant excursion can be made from Stalden to **Törbel**, one of the oldest villages in the valley, pop. 551, which, though not far

[1] The distances marked upon the accompanying Plans in the text (Visp to Stalden, Stalden to St. Nicholas, etc.) are according to the kilomètre posts on the *Railway*. They give also a fair idea of the distances by road.

away, is out of sight. About 1½ hs. going up; 30 min. descending. Törbel is situated on a slope facing the south; and, although 4892 feet high, is warmer and more sunny than the villages lower down, which for a large part of the day are shut out from the sun. Red currants ripen there. Törbel has a reputation for cheese. Anyone who expects to stand a long siege should buy it, for it is said that it will keep for fifty years![1] The Church of Törbel was considerably damaged by the earthquake of 1855, and its roof fell in.

NEUE BRUCKE.

"I had an opportunity at Stalden," said Prof. J. D. Forbes, "of witnessing here a remarkable scene on my last visit."

"A comedy was to be acted by peasants dressed in costume, who were to perform on a stage erected in the open air. There were not less than forty actors, the female parts being performed by men, and the costumes were elaborately and ingeniously devised—in some cases not without propriety and taste. I was able to remain long enough to see only the opening of the piece named *Rosa von Tannenburg*, which was preluded by a procession of the actors, amongst the most conspicuous of whom were three devils attired in tight suits of black, with horns and tails, the senior wearing goat's horns and the subordinates those of the chamois. The entertainment was under the immediate patronage, and even direction of the clergy. The morning mass at Saas was said that day at four, instead of five o'clock, in order to allow the pastor and his flock to reach Stalden in good time, and one of the *vicaires* of Stalden (who

[1] Lord Minto, when at St. Nicholas in 1830, was struck by the cheese that was set before him by the Curé. "I had coveted," he said, "the remains of a delightful piece of old cheese upon which we had feasted . . . and he presented it to me. . . The prize which I carried off was about twenty years old, perfectly fresh and pungent, like a fine old ewe-milk cheese in Scotland. . . We had one cheese put before us which we were told was thirty years old; it was perfectly fresh and good."

correspond to our curates) seemed to be the master of ceremonies, for he was frequently seen in earnest conversation with the junior devil with the chamois

STALDEN.

horns. I must add, that the scene was one of the most romantic which can be conceived. Behind the village was a truly natural theatre, with a green meadow for the pit, while a range of low cliffs, with a concave front festooned with ivy and brushwood, represented the boxes and gallery."—*Travels through the Alps of Savoy*, pp. 354-5.

The Fares from Stalden are—

	Single Fares. 2nd Cl. fr. cts.	3rd Cl. fr. cts.	Return Tickets. 2nd Cl. fr. cts.	3rd Cl. fr. cts.
Stalden to Visp (Viège) . . .	3. 55	2. 50	6. 40	4. —
,, Kalpetran	1. 80	1. 15	3. 20	2. —
,, St. Nicholas . . .	4. —	2. 50	7. 20	4. 50
,, Herbriggen . . .	6. 70	4. 20	12. —	7. 50
,, Randa	8. 45	5. 30	15. 20	9. 50
,, Täsch	10. 25	6. 40	18. 40	11. 50
,, Zermatt . . .	12. 45	7. 80	22. 40	14. —

A pedestrian bound for Zermatt, on leaving Stalden, will save time by taking the path *which leads away in front of the Hotel.* Between Stalden and Kalpetran, the prominent peak seen to the south (*i.e.* looking up the valley) is the **Brunnegghorn,** 12,619 feet, 3846 mètres. The summit of the Weisshorn, 14,803 feet, 4512 mètres, can also be seen behind the Brunnegghorn (a little to its right), from Stalden *nearly* up to Kalpetran. The large bridge over the Muhlebach is passed just before kil. 9, and shortly afterwards the path for a kilomètre and a half is of a superior order, and is carried along a shelf cut out of the slopes, nearly at a level. The Mattervisp torrent, at this part, runs through a deep gorge or defile, which is *better seen from the railway than from the path.*

Kalpetran, 10·9 kils. from Visp, 24·1 kils. from Zermatt; 2907 feet, 886 mètres. This is only a small group of châlets, no inn.[1] The path crosses here to the right bank of the torrent, and the railway does the same at kil. 12. The Fares from Kalpetran are—

	Single Fares.		Return Tickets.	
	2nd Cl.	3rd Cl.	2nd Cl.	3rd Cl.
	fr. cts.	fr. cts.	fr. cts.	fr. cts.
Kalpetran to Visp (Viège) .	4. 90	3. 05	8. 80	5. 50
,, Stalden . .	1. 80	1. 15	3. 20	2. 00
,, St. Nicholas .	2. 70	1. 70	4. 80	3. 00
,, Herbriggen .	4. 90	3. 05	8. 80	5. 50
,, Randa . .	6. 70	4. 20	12. 00	7. 50
,, Täsch . .	8. 45	5. 30	15. 20	9. 50
,, Zermatt . .	11. 15	6. 95	20. 00	12. 50

BRIDGE OVER THE MUHLEBACH.

From kil. 12 to kil. 14 the railway runs immediately alongside the torrent, and gives excellent views of its tumultuous eddyings. This is one of the most interesting parts of the line. *Keep on the side of the water.* These views cannot be seen from the path, which mounts high above the stream, and at this part becomes undulatory. At kil. 14 the railway recrosses to the left bank, and mounts to St. Nicholas (Niklaus or Nicolas). The ascending and descending trains frequently pass here, and a long halt is usually made. There is a Buffet, with little to eat. Beer 30 centimes per glass.

[1] It is mentioned under the name Kalpotran in a document of 1339 [Gremaud, No. 1788].

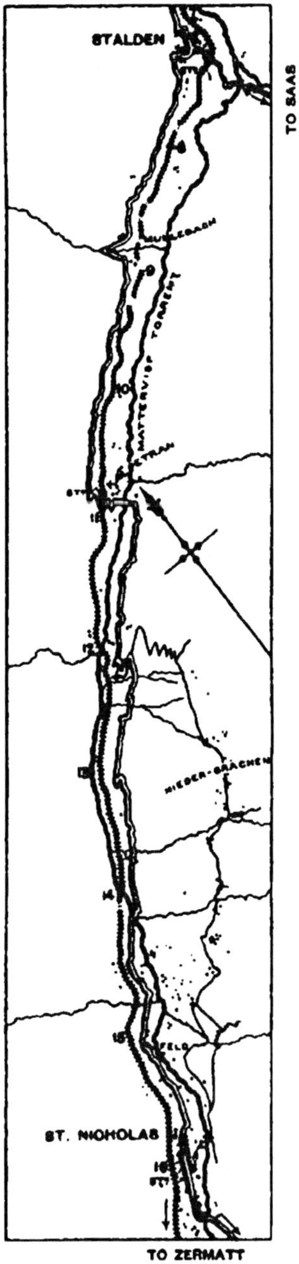

St. Niklaus (Nicolas), 3678 feet, 1121 mètres; pop. 809; 16 kils. from Visp, 19 kils. from Zermatt. Post and Telegraph. Barber (shaving 20 centimes), Tailor, Baker, Shoemaker, Watchmaker and general shop. **Hotels**: GRAND HOTEL-PENSION ST. NICOLAS (in middle of village); HOTEL-PENSION LOCHMATTER[1] (southern end of village). English Church Service (C.C.C.S.) is held on Sundays in the School Room.

St. Nicholas is the largest Commune in the Valley. The Village is in an agreeable position, on the left bank of and close to the Mattervisp torrent. It is warmer than Zermatt, and cooler than Visp. In winter there is not ordinarily at any time more than a mètre of snow on the ground. In July and August temperature seldom sinks so low as 45° F. at night, or rises above 72° F. in the day; and, as a number of small and easy excursions can be made from it, it is one of the most eligible places in the Valley.[2] There is a carriage-road to Zermatt, and *voitures* can be had at a somewhat lower cost (for three or more persons) than third-class railway fares.

The principal mountains visible from the village are the Brunnegghorn, 12,619 feet, 3846 mètres; the Petit Cervin, 12,750 feet, 3866 mètres; and the Breithorn, 13,685 feet, 4171 mètres. Slightly S. of E. of St. Nicholas there is a mountain called the **Gabelhorn** (not to be confounded with the Ober and Unter Gabelhorns at Zermatt), which has not been ascended, and is reputed to be inaccessible. The height given for it on the Siegfried Map is 3135 mètres (10,276 feet), and seen from St. Nicholas it is apparently higher than the Platthorn, lying a little to its south, to which the height of 3249 mètres (10,660 feet) is assigned. The true summit of the Platthorn, however, is not seen from St. Nicholas. At the top of the Gabelhorn there are two rocky towers,—the northern is the loftier, and is the culminating point of

[1] Kept by Mons. Alexandre Lochmatter, formerly Guide [see page 68], who is well acquainted with the Zermatt district, and has much information for those who are interested in the mountaineering history of the Valley.

[2] It appears to be healthy. I was informed by M. the Curé in 1894 that he had recently buried one of his parishioners who had attained the age of 90, and another shortly before who had got to 96; and that there were then about 20 persons living of the age of 70 and upwards.

the mountain. It is an appetizing morsel for a mountaineer. This peak can be seen from Visp (to the right of the Balfrin), and upon part of the way between Visp and Stalden.

The village of St. Nicholas was much damaged by the earthquake of 1855, and was not thoroughly restored several years afterwards. The Church suffered considerably. This edifice has also been twice nearly destroyed by avalanches from the Sparrhorn, which descend

ST. NICHOLAS.

through a ravine on the west of the village. An avalanche in 1618 wrecked the tower and choir, and another in 1750 destroyed the remainder. Avalanches fall not unfrequently through this ravine, but they are sometimes deflected towards the north, and do no harm. The three brothers Knubel who perished on the Lyskamm in 1877 (see chap. x), and Joseph-Marie Lochmatter who was killed on the Dent Blanche in 1882 (see chap. ix) were buried in the churchyard, on the east side of the church.

Excursions from St. Nicholas.—**Ascents** of the **Grabenhorn,** 11,072 feet, 3375 mètres (12-13 hs.); **Gabelhorn,** lower peak, and **Platthorn,** 10,660 feet, 3249 mètres (10-11 hs.); **Ulrichshorn,** 12,891 feet, 3929 mètres (12-13 hs.); **Hohberghorn,** 13,865 feet, 4226 mètres (13-

14 hs.); **Balfrin (Balenfirn or Balfrinhorn),** 12,473 feet, 3802 mètres (9-10 hs.; or it can be crossed to Saas-Fée in about 15 hs.); **Brunnegghorn,** 12,619 feet, 3846 mètres (12-13 hs.); **Sparrhorn (Sparrenhorn),** 9810 feet, 2990 mètres; **Festihorn,** 10,660 feet, 3249 mètres; **Wasenhorn,** 10,958 feet, 3340 mètres; **Rothhorn,** 10,702 feet, 3262 mètres; **Stellihorn,** 11,204 feet, 3415 mètres; **Schwarzhorn,** 10,512 feet, 3204 mètres; and **Barrhorn,** 11,880 feet, 3621 mètres (from 8 up to 10-11 hours).

Passes.—The Ried Pass, about 11,800 feet, from St. Niklaus to Saas-Fée, between the Balfrin and Ulrichshorn (10-12 hs.). This is one of the oldest passes between the Nicolai Thal and the Saas Thal. **The Ferrichjoch or Ferrichlücke,** 9479 feet, 2889 mètres, between the Platthorn and Ferrichhorn is another pass between the two valleys; and leads either through the village of Gasenried, or that of Hellenen, to the south of the Platthorn, and descends either to Saas, or to Huteggen in the Saas Thal (9-10 hs.). **The Gabelhorn Pass.**—I made another pass with Alexandre Lochmatter, in 1895, between St. Niklaus and Huteggen, by going over the Gabelhorn just below and to the south of the towers at the summit. Excluding halts, the time occupied was 11 hs. This pass is about 690 feet higher than the Ferrichjoch. Neither pass can be recommended. In each case, a great part of the way near the summit is over loose stones and boulders, which are unpleasant to traverse. There is a fourth way of getting into the Valley of Saas by passing through the village of Grächen and across the **Hannig Alp.** The top of the Hannig Alp is a good place for a pic-nic. Châlets, milk. This is a route rather than a pass. The path upon the Saas Thal side descends on the village of Eisten (5-6 hs.),[1] or one can go down through forest from the top of the Alp to Stalden. Steep way.

To the West of St. Niklaus the **Jungpass,** 9823 feet, 2994 mètres, and the **Augstbordpass,** 9492 feet, 2893 mètres, lead to Gruben in the Turtmannthal. Both of these routes go through the village of Jungen, 6391 feet, 1948 mètres, but they separate shortly afterwards,—the former passing between the Furggwanghorn, 10,377 feet, 3163 mètres, and the Rothhorn, and the latter between the Steinthalhorn, 10,213 feet, 3113 mètres, and the Schwarzhorn. In 1896, with Alois Pollinger, I found a way of getting to St. Niklaus from Turtig in the Rhone Valley in 9 hs. 25 min., *viâ* the Ginanzthal, and this route, should it become known, would I think find favour, as it passes through a delightful valley (hitherto quite unvisited) which affords very pleasant walks.

The path for the Ginanzthal Pass commences at Turtig, 2123 feet, 647 mètres, and rises steeply towards the south by zigzags through forest. Interesting view over the Valley of the Rhone and of the mountains on the farther side. In 1½ hs. it arrives at **Unterbach,** situated on open ground, 4036 feet, 1230 mètres; pop. 336; Church; no regular inn, but food can be obtained. [Two kils. to the East there is the village of **Birchen,** 4751 feet, 1448 mètres; pop. 418; Church. This is a separate Commune.] The ground here is

[1] This route across the Hannig Alp has been known for a long time. In 1818, Ebel said it was frequented by botanists.

moderately flat (dotted all over with châlets), and cannot be seen from the Rhone Valley. Paths in various directions. Enquire the way. In 1½ hs. from Unterbach there are the **châlets of Waldmatten**, 5246 feet, 1599 mètres. Milk can be had. The path then approaches the stream flowing down the Ginanzthal, and keeps near it (on its right bank), up to the head of the valley; passing at first through forest, and in 1½ hs. a group of seven buildings at the **Obere Ginanzalp**, 7441 feet, 2268 mètres. End of paths. After the beginning of September there is no one either here or higher up the valley. Steer slightly East of South towards the nameless peak marked 2962 mètres (9718 feet) on the Siegfried Map; and go to the E. of the little lake called the **Ginanzsee**, 8452 feet, 2576 mètres. Grass ends there. Take advantage of the snow beds under peak 2962, and steer S.W. across them to the nearest depression on the E. of the Dreizehnenhorn. The summit of **the Col** is 2 hs. from the Obere Ginanz châlets, and 50 mètres or thereabouts lower than peak 2962,—*i.e.* about 9550 feet above the sea. The ridge that is crossed runs almost precisely due East and West. The lake and the upper part of the Ginanzthal are well seen from the Col. To the N., Altels, the Balmhorn, and the Bietschhorn are prominent; towards the E. the view includes the Fletschhorn, Laquinhorn, and Weissmies, and the entire range of the Mischabel; and turning round to the S. and W. there is first Monte Rosa and all between it and the Breithorn, the Brunnegghorn and Weisshorn, Schwarzhorn and Dreizehnenhorn. On the southern side of the Col there is the (nameless) *vallon* leading to the Augstbordpass. Descend over stony slopes to the bottom of it, turn to the left (*i.e.* east), and go through Jungen to St. Nicholas. Time, Col to Jungen, 1 h. 40 min.; Jungen to St. Nicholas, about 1 h. 15 min.

Minor excursions and quiet walks can be taken on the West of St. Nicholas to the villages of Jungen, Emd, and Törbel. **The path to Jungen**, 6391 feet, 1948 mètres, is in shade most of the way. It starts at the Railway Station. Time ascending, about 1 h. 50 min.; descending, 1 h. is quick time. To get to the village of **Emd**,[1] go from St. Nicholas by the ordinary path as far as the railway bridge at kil. 14. On the western side of this bridge there is a small and rather rough path leading in about 2 hs. to Emd (4450 feet, 1356 mètres, pop. 206), which is situated upon a steep slope of the Emderberg,—a prolongation of the lower slopes of the Augstbordhorn. [I have been unable to find the fowls 'shod with iron to enable them to keep on their legs,' which are referred to in Baedeker's *Switzerland.*] From Emd one can either descend to Kalpetran Railway Station, or get in 1 h. 20 min. by a fair path to **Törbel.** Descend thence to Stalden, and return home by train.

Upon the East of St. Nicholas, perhaps the most agreeable little excursion that can be made is to the lower **Ried Glacier.** This can be done either by passing through the village of Gasenried, or, by a more direct route, *viâ* the village of Hellenen and the Schallbett Alp. The latter way is preferable, as the path passes almost entirely through forest, and is in shade. Path good. Time from St. Nicholas to the Schallbett Alp, 6916 feet, 2108 mètres, 3 hs. The lower glacier can be crossed easily. The 'ice-falls' from the upper glacier are well seen from it, but to view the upper plateau of the Ried Glacier, and the peaks which encircle it, a considerably greater

[1] This village is mentioned under the names of Embda, Embsa, Emda, and Empda in documents of 1324, 1330, 1339 and later. [Gremaud, Nos. 1504, 1590, 1788, etc.] In those times it was embraced in the Parish of Visp.

elevation must be gained. No part of the Ried Glacier can be seen from the bottom of the Nicolai Thal. Return home through Gasenreid.

The villages of **Niedergrächen**, 4807 feet, 1465 mètres, and **Grächen**, 5305 feet, 1617 mètres, may also be made the subject of an agreeable excursion. They lie N.E. of St. Nicholas, on the way to the Hannig Alp. There is a house at the former village in which Thomas Platter the Reformer is said to have been born,—an ordinary châlet, which does not look nearly 400 years old. If it is actually the case (as they aver on the spot) that it is the original house and has not been renovated, one can readily credit the opinion of people in the valley that there are châlets in the Zermatt district which are 700 years old, and even more. This opinion, it seems to me, however, is not based on any firmer foundation than the knowledge that there are records which carry the history of the valley back to the 13th century.

THE PATRON SAINT (ST. NICHOLAS).

Thomas Platter was born at the little village Niedergrächen in 1499.[1] My mother, he says, was a Summermatter,[2] and her "father was one hundred and twenty-six years old. Six years before his death, I talked with him myself, and he told me that he knew ten men in the parish of Visp who were all older than he then was. When he was a hundred years old he married a woman of thirty and had a son by her."[3] Platter's father died so early in his life that he could not remember having seen him. His mother married again, and "almost all my brothers and sisters," he says, "had to go out to service as soon as they were able. Because I was the youngest, my aunts each had me in turn."

[1] An account of his early life, written by himself, was printed at Basle in 1840. A curtailed translation of this was contributed by Sir W. M. Conway to the *Alpine Journal*, vol. xii, pp. 380-90. The following extracts are taken from this very interesting article.

[2] There are various Summermatters now living at Randa.

[3] In Schiner's *Description du Département du Simplon*, at p. 226, when speaking of the Valley of Saas, there is the following remarkable statement.—"Les gens dans cette vallée parviennent beaucoup à un grand âge; il n'est point rare d'y compter plusieurs centenaires. On se souvient encore, que, lorsque la vallée s'assemblait pour prévenir de grands maux, on formait un cercle sur la place, qui n'était composé que de nonage-

"When I was about six years old I was taken to Eisten" [Saas Thal] "a valley within Stalden, where my mother's sister was married to a man by name Thomas an Riedijn, who lived in a farm called Imboden. The first year I had to tend the kids for him near the house. There I remember once sticking fast in the snow, so that I could scarcely get out. I had to leave my shoes in it and come home barefoot. The same peasant owned about eighty goats, which I had to tend in my seventh and eighth years. I was still so small that, when I opened the goat-pen, if I did not spring quickly behind the door, the goats knocked me down and trod upon my head, ears, and back. When I drove the goats across the Visp over the bridge, those in front ran into the corn-fields, and when I drove them out the rest ran in, so I wept and cried, for I knew well that I should be beaten at night. However, the goatherds of other peasants came to me and helped me, one big boy especially, Thomas of the Leidenbach. He pitied me and did me much kindness. So when we drove the goats up into the high and terrible mountains, we all sat and ate together. Each one had a shepherd's wallet fastened on his back, with cheese and rye bread in it.

. . . . . .

Perhaps about half a year afterwards, I drove my goats again early one morning before the other goatherds (for I was the nearest) up over a spur, called the Wysseggen. There my goats went to the right hand up a little rock, a good stride broad, below which was a terrible precipice, certainly more than a thousand feet high—sheer rock. From the little rock one goat went after another up a steep place, their little hoofs clinging to the bunches of grass growing among the rocks. When they had all gone up I wanted to follow them, but I had not taken more than one step upon the grass before I could go no farther, nor could I step back upon the steep place, and I dared still less jump backwards, for I feared, if I did so, I should roll down and fall over the terrible precipice. So I remained a long while standing and waited for the help of God, being no longer able to help myself, except by holding on with both hands to a tuft of grass and standing with my great toe upon another tuft. When I was tired I raised myself off the tuft and put my other toe there. In this plight I was most afraid of the great lammergeiers, which were flying in the air below me; for I feared they would carry me off, as sometimes happens in the Alps. While I was standing thus, the wind blowing my jacket about behind, for I had no breeches on, my comrade Thomas saw me from afar but knew not what it was, for as he saw my coat blowing he thought it was a bird. When however he saw me plainly he grew pale with fright, and called out to me, 'Now, little Tommy, stand still!' and then he climbed up the little rock, took me by the arm and drew me up to where we could climb up to the goats."

Little Platter was shifted about to various masters, one, he says, "beat me terribly, and often lifted me by the ears from the ground"; and another "taught me absolutely nothing, and flogged me merci-

naires et de centenaires, avec de grandes barbes blanches: là ne s'approchait point la jeunesse, et les femmes n'osaient point y paraître, l'âge et l'expérience seuls y géraient les affaires, et la jeunesse n'y comptait pour rien."

I have enquired for centenarians in the Valleys of Zermatt and Saas, but have not heard of one, or learnt that one has been known in recent times. In 1895 I asked M. le Curé of Grächen if he knew or had known of people in his parish who had attained such a patriarchal age, and he told me that he had buried a man of 96, six years before, who had taken part in the Russian campaign of Napoleon I, in 1812. Since then he had buried one of 93, and several of 80 to 84, but he thought that in 1895 there was no one living so old as 70.

The result of enquiry at St. Nicholas is mentioned at p. 109. At Zermatt, the oldest man in 1896 was aged 92. At Täsch (1896) oldest man was 87. Saw him returning from work carrying a hay-rake—apparently had been haymaking. At Randa (1896) there was a man and woman each aged 84. Saw the former carrying a basket of dung on his back. The oldest man at St. Nicholas was (in 1896) aged 86. It was said that there was a man (in 1896) at Emd over 90, and still working in the fields. At Stalden (in 1896) the oldest man was 84, and at Saas the oldest man was 83.

lessly." So that he began to wish to fly in the air, to "fly away over the mountains out of that country into Germany"; and at last he went away with a cousin to Lucerne, Zurich, Nuremberg and many other places, returning home from time to time to see his mother. After one of these visits, he says,

"I went away from the country again with two of my brothers. When we went to bid my mother farewell, she wept and said, 'God pity me, who have to see three of my sons go forth to misery.' That was the only time I ever saw my mother weep; for she was a brave, manly woman, but hard. When her third husband died she remained a widow and did all work like a man, so that she might the better bring up her youngest children. She hewed and threshed and did other work rather belonging to men than women. Three children also she buried with her own hands when they died in a terrible pestilence; for in the pestilence it costs much to employ a gravedigger. She was very hard towards us, her first children, so that we seldom came to her house. At one time, as I remember, I was not with her for five years, but wandered far in foreign parts. When I came to her, the first word she said to me was, 'Has the devil brought you here then?' 'No, mother,' I answered, 'the devil has not brought me here, but my feet. I shall not burden you long.' 'You don't burden me,' she said, 'only it vexes me that you go thus roving hither and thither, and doubtless are learning nothing. Learn to work as your father did. You will never be a priest. I am not so blessed as to be the mother of a priest.'"

St. Nicholas is suitable for persons who do not wish to spend much, and for those who prefer picturesque scenery or quiet to high mountain ascents or a crowd. The village has produced in the past a number of the best guides of the Zermatt district, and it is at the present time the home of capable men. During the season, however, they are seldom at home, and will more likely be found at Zermatt than at their own village. For names of **Guides of St. Nicholas** see Appendix G. The published **Tarif of Excursions** is given in Appendix A. It includes only a few of those above mentioned.

The Railway Fares from St. Nicholas are—

		Single Fares.		Return Tickets.	
		2nd Cl.	3rd Cl.	2nd Cl.	3rd Cl.
		fr. cts.	fr. cts.	fr. cts.	fr. cts.
St. Nicholas to	Herbriggen .	2. 70	1. 70	4. 80	3. 00
,,	Randa . .	4. 45	2. 80	8. 00	5. 00
,,	Täsch . . .	6. 25	3. 90	11. 20	7. 00
,,	Zermatt . .	8. 90	5. 55	16. 00	10. 00
,,	Kalpetran . .	2. 70	1. 70	4. 80	3. 00
,,	Stalden . .	4. 00	2. 50	7. 20	4. 50
,,	Visp . . .	7. 55	4. 75	13. 60	8. 50

The carriage-road to Zermatt begins at the southern end of St. Nicholas, and in 3 min. crosses to the right bank. There is a fine view looking *down* the valley between kils. 17·18. On the east side of the road hereabouts a former village of St. Nicholas is said to lie buried under a great rock-fall. The cluster of châlets at Mattsand, 4042 feet, 1232 mètres, is passed just before kil. 20, and a mile and a quarter farther on one comes to Herbriggen. No inn here, nor anywhere on the road between St. Nicholas—Randa.

After leaving St. Nicholas, the **railway** continues for a time on the left bank, and between kils. 18-19 makes another steep ascent by means of the cogged rails. At this part the views both up and down the valley are very striking. At the 19th kil. it crosses to the right bank, and runs closely alongside the road for a considerable distance. A brief halt only is made at

Herbriggen (Herbrigen), 4134 feet, 1260 mètres; 21·6 kils. from Visp, 13·4 kils. from Zermatt. This hamlet is situated on the right bank of the Mattervisp torrent, about a quarter of a mile from the Railway Station. Few people get in or out here. The Fares from Herbriggen are—

	Single Fares. 2nd Cl. fr. cts.	Single Fares. 3rd Cl. fr. cts.	Return Tickets. 2nd Cl. fr. cts.	Return Tickets. 3rd Cl. fr. cts.
St. Nicholas .	2. 70	1. 70	4. 80	3. —
Kalpetran .	4. 90	3. 05	8. 80	5. 50
Stalden . .	6. 70	4. 20	12. —	7. 50
Visp (Viège) .	9. 80	6. 10	17. 60	11. —
Randa . .	2. 25	1. 40	4. —	2. 50
Täsch . .	3. 50	2. 25	6. 40	4. —
Zermatt . .	6. 25	3. 90	11. 20	7. —

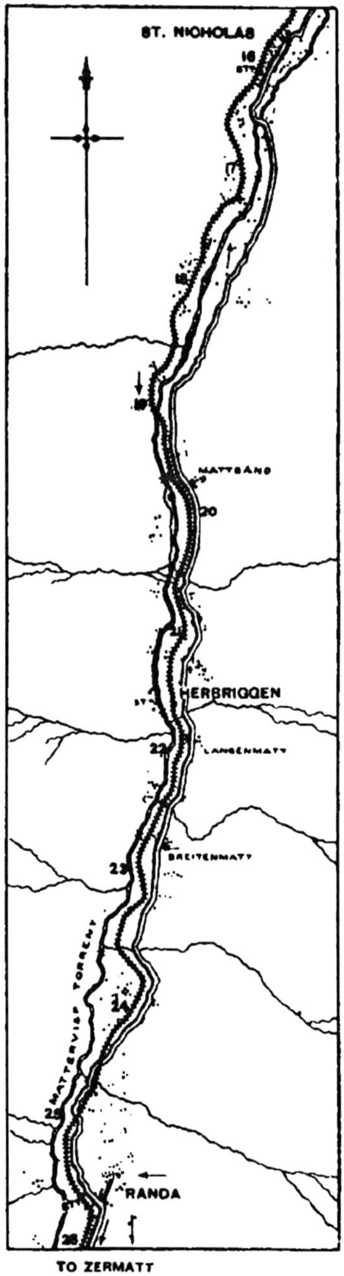

ST. NICHOLAS TO RANDA.

The road from Herbriggen to Randa skirts lower slopes of the Mischabelhörner. The streams descending these slopes have often cut the road, and sometimes have interrupted the railway. At kil. 22 the hamlet of Langenmatt is passed, and that of Breitenmatt, 4186 feet, 1276 mètres, about half a mile farther on. Small chapel. Grand views here of the cliffs of the Brunnegghorn, and of the Bies Glacier descending between the Brunnegghorn and the Weisshorn, on the opposite side of the valley. The numerous châlets seen hereabouts are storehouses and are not tenanted, but afford convenient shelters in case of bad weather. Though passing close under the peaks of the Mischabel very little can be seen of the upper part of this fine range. There is another steep incline on the railway from kil. 23·7 to k. 24·7, alongside the road, where a pedestrian can amuse himself by *outwalking the train.* Half a mile farther on, upon turning a corner, one comes in sight of

Randa, 4741 feet, 1445 mètres; pop. 229; 25·7 kils. from Visp, 9.3 kils. from Zermatt. Post and Telegraph. **Hotel.**—HOTEL AND

HOTEL AND PENSION WEISSHORN, RANDA.

PENSION WEISSHORN, a little to the south of the village, about 3 min. from the Railway Station. Good; much visited by Swiss, French, and Germans. The Railway Fares are—

		Single Fares.		Return Tickets.	
		2nd Cl.	3rd Cl.	2nd Cl.	3rd Cl.
		fr. cts.	fr. cts.	fr. cts.	fr. cts.
Randa to	Herbriggen . .	2. 25	1. 40	4. —	2. 50
,,	St. Nicholas . .	4. 45	2. 80	8. —	5. —
,,	Kalpetran . .	6. 70	4. 20	12. —	7. 50
,,	Stalden . . .	8. 45	5. 30	15. 20	9. 50
,,	Visp (Viège) . .	11. 55	7. 25	20. 80	13. —
,,	Täsch . . .	1. 80	1. 15	3. 20	2. —
,,	Zermatt. . .	4. 45	2. 80	8. —	5. —

The Hotel is well situated, and there are admirable views from its windows, particularly from those facing the south. For the **Guides of Randa** see Appendix G, and Appendix B for **Tarif of Excursions.** This 'tarif' by no means includes all the excursions that can be made. It addresses itself solely to those who are concerned with snow-peaks and passes. There are many minor excursions, suited to all sorts and conditions of persons; and, as both railway and road go in two directions, there is liberty of movement. The principal **ascents** made from Randa are those of the Weisshorn, the Dom, and the Täschhorn.

The Ascent of the Weisshorn, 14,803 feet, 4512 mètres, is the most considerable one to be made from Randa. This mountain is not so happily placed as the Matterhorn and other peaks which might be mentioned, and it cannot anywhere be seen to advantage *from a low level.* But from moderate and from the higher elevations it always appears a grand mountain. It can be seen well 3000 feet or so above Randa on the route to the Dom; or, more easily, from the Täsch Valley. "Of all mountain tops that I know, that of the Weisshorn is, I think, the most beautiful, with perhaps the one exception of the Wetterhorn. It is formed by three of those firm and delicate edges which can only be modelled in the mountain snow, uniting to meet in a mathematical point."—*Leslie Stephen.* The first ascent was made on Aug. 18-19, 1861, by the guides J. J. Bennen and Ulrich Wenger (an Oberlander) with Dr. John Tyndall.

The summit of the Weisshorn lies due W. of Randa, but it is not approached in a direct manner. The usual course when making an ascent is to round the Schallenberg (Schalliberg) towards the south and west, until about S.E. of the summit; then to go northwards, and strike the great eastern ridge of the mountain, and follow its *arête* to the top. This long eastern ridge is well seen from the Riffelberg, the Mettelhorn, and various other points. When a good way up it, "the *arête* narrowed," says Tyndall, "to a mere wall, which, however, as rock would present no serious difficulty. But upon the wall of rock is placed a second wall of snow, which dwindles to a knife-edge at the top. It is white and pure, of very fine grain, and a little moist. . . I had no idea of a human foot trusting itself upon so frail a support. Bennen's practical sagacity was, however, greater than mine. He tried the snow by squeezing it with his foot, and to my astonishment commenced to cross. Even after the pressure of his feet the space he had to stand on did not exceed a handbreadth. I followed him, exactly as a boy walking along a horizontal pole, with toes turned outwards. Right and left the precipices were appalling; but the sense of power on such occasions is exceedingly sweet. . .

. . We had been ten hours climbing from our bivouac to the summit, and it was now necessary that we should clear the mountain before the close of the day. . . We once fancied that the descent would be rapid, but it was far from it. . . Our muscles are sorely tried by the twisting round the splintered turrets of the *arête*, and we resolve to escape from it when we can; but a long, long stretch of the ridge must be passed before we dare to swerve from it. . . The face of the pyramid is here scarred by *couloirs*, of which the deeper and narrower ones are filled with ice, while the others are highways to the bottom of the mountain for the rocks quarried by the weather above. Steps must be cut in the ice. . . No word of warning was uttered here as we ascended, but now Bennen's admonitions were frequent and emphatic,—'Take care not to slip.' . . I imagined, however, that even if a man slipped he would be able to arrest his descent; but Bennen's response when I stated this opinion was very prompt, 'No! it would be utterly impossible. If it were snow you might do it, but it is pure ice, and if you fall you will lose your senses before you can use your axe.'

A deep and confused roar attracted our attention. From a point near the summit of the Weisshorn, a rock had been discharged; it plumped down a dry *couloir*, raising a cloud of dust at each bump against the mountain. A hundred similar ones were immediately in motion, while the spaces between the larger masses were filled by an innumerable flight of smaller stones. The clatter of this devil's cavalry was stunning. Black masses of rock emerged here and there from the cloud, and sped through the air like flying fiends. . . They whizzed and vibrated in their flight as if urged by wings. The clang of echoes resounded from side to side, from the Schallenberg to the Weisshorn and back, until finally the whole troop came to rest, after many a deep-sounding thud in the snow, at the bottom of the mountain. This stone avalanche was one of the most extraordinary things I had ever witnessed, and in connection with it I would draw the attention of future climbers to the danger which would infallibly beset any attempt to ascend the Weisshorn from this side, except by one of its *arêtes*. At any moment the mountain side may be raked by a fire as deadly as that of cannon."—*Mountaineering in* 1861, by John Tyndall, 8vo, London, 1862.

The Randa **Tarif** for the Weisshorn is 80 francs per guide and 45 francs per porter. The route generally followed is substantially that which was taken on the first ascent. A night is usually passed at a *cabane*, 9380 feet, 2859 mètres, which is S.E. of the summit, not far from the place where Tyndall bivouacked. The condition of this *cabane* is lamentable, and tourists sometimes prefer to camp outside.

Ascents have been made from several other directions. From the Bies Glacier by the N.E. face, by Mr. J. H. Kitson, with Christian and Ulrich Almer, on Aug. 10-11, 1871 (see *Alpine Journal*, vol. v, p. 274). From the Schalliberg Glacier by the S. face and S.S.W. ridge, by Messrs. W. E. Davidson, Hartley, and Hoare, with Pollinger, Rubi, and Jaun, on Sept. 5-6, 1877 (*A. J.*, vol. viii, p. 419). From the W., by Mr. G. A. Passingham, with Ferdinand Imseng and Louis Zurbrücken, on Aug. 12-13, 1879 (*A. J.*, vol. ix, pp. 428-31). By the Schalliberg Glacier, *viâ* the Schallijoch, and the S.S.W. ridge, by Mr. E. A. Broome, with J.-M. Biener, and A. Imboden, on Sept. 1-2, 1895 (*A. J.*, vol. xviii, p. 145). Variations on these routes have also been made.

In 1888, a young man of Munich, named Winkler, disappeared on the Weisshorn. He started from Zinal on Aug. 16 to attempt to climb it alone, and on the 29th his cap was found in the remains of an avalanche, which it is supposed had overwhelmed him.

After the Weisshorn, the principal ascents to be made from Randa are those of the Dom and the Täschhorn.

The first ascent of the **Dom**, 14,941 feet, 4554 mètres, was made on Sept. 11, 1858, by the Rev. J. Llewelyn Davies, with Johann zum Taugwald[1] (who had previously made some unsuccessful attempts on the mountain), — Kronig, and a volunteer from Randa. They left that village at 2.10 a.m., reached the summit at 11 a.m., returned to Randa at 4.20 p.m., and then walked up to Zermatt in time for the *table d'hôte!* The route that is now usually followed is marked on the Map of the Valley of Zermatt; and, so far as I can learn, does not differ much from that which was taken on the first ascent. It leads through the village of Randa, and then turns E., and mounts by the side of the Randaierbach, at first on the left bank, and afterwards by the right bank to the Festi *cabane*, 9400 feet, 2865 mètres. A night is commonly passed there, and the ascent effected on the following day. There are magnificent views of the Weisshorn and the Bies Glacier from this path, 2000 to 3000 feet above Randa. Guides so far are unnecessary. **Tarif** for the ascent, 60 francs per guide, 40 frs. per porter. More than 20 ascents were made in 1895.

The Dom is the highest of the Mischabelhörner, and is the loftiest mountain that is completely in Switzerland; for, although the *summit* of Monte Rosa is Swiss, that mountain is partly in Italy. The Dom has also been ascended,— 1. From the eastern side, *viâ* the Eggfluh and the Nadeljoch, by Rev. C. Taylor, Mr. R. Pendlebury, and Mr. G. E. Foster, with Hans Baumann and Gab. Spectenhauser, July 22-23, 1874 (*A. J.*, vol. vii, p. 105). 2. From the south, *viâ* the northern branch of the Kien Glacier and the Domjoch, by Messrs. Penhall and Conway, with F. Imseng and P. J. Truffer, Aug. 18-19

[1] Both Mr. Davies and Johann zum Taugwald are living. The latter is the oldest man at Zermatt who has acted as Guide.

1878. 3. From the west, partly by the Domjoch route, and then by the W. ridge of the mountain, by Dr. P. Güssfeldt, with Alex. Burgener and B. Venetz, July 27-8, 1882 (*A. J.*, vol. xi, p. 117). Several variations have been made on these routes. The Dom has been ascended in winter (Jan. 1894). Three days were occupied on this excursion (*A. J.*, vol. xvii, pp. 67, 384, etc.).

A direct ascent of the Dom from Saas is not to be recommended. Mr. Mich. Carteighe, who went that way in 1885, says, "Having heard on all sides that falling stones and ice usually enliven all expeditions in the Mischabel range undertaken on the Saas side, we decided to start early. . . Our progress was barred by an inverted pyramid of stones perched on the face. This could not be turned, and it was obviously necessary to pass over with caution. Accordingly Gabriel (Taugwalder) went over first with about 60 feet of rope that he might 'prospect.' Imseng was roped next, and was on one side of the pyramid, while I was last and lower down on the other side of the stones. When the rope was tight between Gabriel and Imseng[1] the latter began to move. Instead of crawling in a loving manner over the group, he thoughtlessly made a spring, seized a large boulder-shaped stone, which he pulled upon himself, and then, turning head over heels backwards, freed himself from the stone and regained his foothold, the rope being 'ganz fest.' The stone then bounded over to the right towards me. I managed to avoid a direct collision, but one end caught me on the mouth and jaw, removing, as the dentists say, two teeth, and then as the stone rebounded to the left, the opposite end struck the palm of my left hand, gashed up the flesh, and then sped its way down to the glacier below."—*A. J.*, vol. xv, p. 102.[2]

The **Täschhorn**, 14,757 feet, 4498 mètres, is the second highest of the Mischabelhörner. It was first ascended by the Rev. J. Llewelyn Davies and the late Rev. J. W. Hayward, with the brothers Johann and Stephan zum Taugwald,[3] on July 31, 1862. No account of this expedition has been preserved, and I am unable to say whether the original route is that which is now taken. The latter is marked on the Map of the Valley of Zermatt. After leaving the Hotel at Randa, it leads diagonally across the Tschuggen Alp towards the Kien Glacier. At about 9180 feet, there is a sleeping-place, 3 hs. above Randa.

Several other ways have been found up the mountain. 1. From Saas-Fée, at first by the Mischabeljoch route and subsequently up the E. face of the mountain [Mr. P. Watson and Rev. F. T. Wethered, with Alex. Burgener, B. Venetz, and L. Proment, Aug. 7, 1875.—*A. J.*, vol. viii, p. 108]. 2. From the top of the Mischabeljoch, *vià* the S.E. ridge of the peak [Mr. J. Jackson, with Christian and Ulrich Almer, Aug. 15, 1876.—*A. J.*, vol. viii, pp. 345-6]. 3. From the N., *vià* the Domjoch [Mr. F. Cullinan and Mr. Gerald Fitz Gerald, with Peter Knubel and Joseph Moser, Sept. 1-2, 1878.—*A. J.*, vol. ix, pp. 109-110]. 4. By the W.S.W. ridge. See *My Climbs in the Alps and Caucasus*, by A. F. Mummery, London, 1895.

In 1893, a fatal accident occurred on the lower slopes of the Täschhorn, not far from Randa. On Aug. 15, Messrs. Williamson and Lucas (the latter an Oxford undergraduate) passed the night on some rocks on the east side of the peak, and at 11 a.m. on the next day reached the summit, intending to arrive that night at Randa. At 10 p.m. they had not got clear of the forest below the Kien Glacier! and as "the guides considered that it would be unwise to attempt to descend further, as their lanterns were burnt out, they selected a smooth piece of grass on which to pass the night." One of the guides awoke about 1 a.m., and missed Mr. Lucas; and at 4 a.m. he was found dead a short distance away, at the foot of a rock 60 mètres in height. His watch had stopped at 12.20. See *Alpine Journal*, vol. xvi, p. 503, and vol. xvii, pp. 39-40. The guides were Adolph Andenmatten (of Almagell) and Franz Zurbriggen (of Saas).

[1] Xavier Imseng, of Saas-Fée.

[2] It may be well to point out that several fatal or very serious accidents have occurred in recent years in this district through *guides* dislodging stones or boulders. Both ascending and descending, it is impossible to exercise too much caution to avoid dislodging rocks when anyone is *below*.

[3] Stephan zum Taugwald became Curé of Täsch.

Both Dom and Täschhorn have of late years, on more than one occasion, been ascended by the same party within the compass of a long day; and, in 1895, Mr. W. E. Davidson, with Christian Klucker and Daniel Maquignaz, starting from above Saas-Fée, ascended the Täschhorn from the Mischabeljoch, crossed over the summit and descended on the Domjoch, thence ascended the Dom and descended on its northern side, reaching Randa the same evening.

The Randa **Tarif** for the Täschhorn is the same as for the Dom.

The other peaks included in the Randa *Tarif* are the Bieshorn, Dürrenhorn, Hohberghorn, and Süd-Lenzspitze. The **Bieshorn** is the peak to the N. of the Weisshorn marked 4161 (without name) on the V. of Zermatt Map. It can be reached from the Biesjoch (marked on Map 3549) in about 2½ hs. The **Dürrenhorn** is just outside the range of the V. of Zermatt Map, to the N.W. of the Nadelhorn, and can be got at *viâ* a little valley running E. from Breitenmatt. The **Hohberghorn** is the peak 4226, to the N.W. of the Nadelhorn. It can be ascended by more than one route. The **Süd-Lenzspitze** is the point 4300, to the S.E. of the Nadelhorn. Upon more than one occasion the three peaks Süd-Lenzspitze, Nadelhorn, and Ulrichshorn have been ascended in one day.[1] There are, besides, several other ascents which can be made from Randa that are not on the *Tarif;* namely, the **Nadelhorn** (the highest point of the Saas Grat N. of the Dom), the **Galenhorn, Grabenhorn, Strahlbett** (12,320 feet, 3755 mètres, W.S.W. of the Täschhorn), and **Leiterspitz.** The **Mettelhorn,** also, is sometimes ascended from Randa. For the elevations and positions of these peaks see Appendix E.

There are several lofty and fine **Passes from Randa** over the Saas Grat to Saas-Fée, which have, however, small claim to practical utility, or to the attention of the general public, and they are mostly ignored by the *Tarif;* namely, the **Mischabeljoch, Domjoch, Nadeljoch, Lenzjoch** (between the Süd-Lenzspitze and the Nadelhorn), and **Hohbergpass.** On the Western side of the valley, the **Biesjoch** leads to the Turtmann Thal, and the **Schallijoch** to Zinal. For positions and elevations of these Passes see Appendix F.

The **road from Randa to Zermatt** runs closely alongside the railway for ¾ mile, and at this part there are especially good views of the Breithorn and Petit Mont Cervin (right in front). The prominent mountain on the right is the Mettelhorn. After passing the hamlet Wildi (small chapel) there are few houses against the road, which in about 40 min. arrives at—

Täsch (Taesch or Tæsch), 4777 feet, 1456 mètres; pop. 231; 29½ kils. from Visp, 5½ kils. from Zermatt. No hotel. Wine can be obtained. The village is situated on the right bank of the Mattervisp torrent, about a quarter of a mile from the Railway Station. The Fares are—

	Single Fares.		Return Tickets.	
	2nd Cl.	3rd Cl.	2nd Cl.	3rd Cl.
	fr. cts.	fr. cts.	fr. cts.	fr. cts.
Täsch to Randa	1. 80	1. 15	3. 50	2. —
,, Herbriggen	3. 55	2. 25	6. 40	4. —
,, St. Nicholas	6. 25	3. 90	11. 20	7. —
,, Kalpetran	8. 45	5. 30	15. 20	9. 50
,, Stalden	10. 25	6. 40	18. 40	11. 50
,, Visp (Viège) . . .	13. 35	8. 35	24. —	15. —
,, Zermatt	2. 70	1. 70	4. 80	3. —

[1] It is possible to go along the top of the entire range of the Saas Grat without descending to the valleys at all. The directions are simple. Commencing at the Schwarzberg Weissthor, go over the summit of the Strahlhorn and descend on the Adler Pass; then go over the Rimpfischhorn and come down on the Allalin Pass; next walk up the Allalinhorn and descend to the Alphubeljoch, whence you cross over the

The torrent (Täschbach) from the Täsch Valley flows through Täsch, and is now embanked. It was formerly a source of trouble, and frequently rendered the road to Zermatt nearly or quite impassable. In the village itself there is little to be seen except the collection of skulls and bones which is preserved in a small building (*beinhaus*) attached to the Church. At Täsch, and various other places, they do not allow one to remain peaceably in his grave in perpetuity. You are disinterred and your bones are stacked away in this fashion. There are similar collections at St. Nicholas and at Visp. For names of **Guides** of Täsch see Appendix G.

CHARNEL-HOUSE ('BEINHAUS') AT TÄSCH.

[From the village of Täsch, a good path starts at the upper bridge over the Täschbach for the **Täsch Alp**. The name Täsch Alp is sometimes applied to a small **Inn** situated in a valley which leads at first a little S. of E. and afterwards about S.E., and sometimes to the *Valley itself*. In this volume the valley is called the Täsch Valley, and the ground round about the inn is termed the Täsch Alp.

The path gets into forest soon after leaving the bridge, and is steep for about 1500 feet. When it begins to enter the Täsch Valley the inclination becomes moderate, and it so continues to the Inn (about 7000 feet) which can

Alphubel to the Mischabeljoch, and go successively over the Täschhorn, Dom, Süd-Lenzspitze, Nadelhorn, Ulrichshorn and Balfrin. The whole route has been traversed in sections upon one or another occasion.

be reached easily in 1 h. 50 min. from Täsch. This inn is now often used as a starting-point for the ascents of the Allalinhorn, Alphubel, and Rimpfischhorn, and for the passages of the Mischabeljoch, Alphubeljoch, Féejoch, Allalinpass, etc. It is sometimes closed early in the season, and enquiry

TÄSCH.

should be made before leaving Täsch, to avoid disappointment. In the event of the Täsch Alp inn being closed, Randa can be used as a starting-point for these excursions. It is nearer than Zermatt.

A promenade on foot or mule-back can be taken by anyone, alone, to the foot of the Mellichen, Hubel, and Langenfluh Glaciers at the head of the Täsch Valley (about 8000 feet). They can be reached in a leisurely fashion in 1¼ to 1½ hs. Fair path. This is good grazing-ground, and there are often many cattle about, some of whom are uncivilized. Carry a stick. Admirable views of the Weisshorn will be seen in front, when returning.

The first ascent of the **Allalinhorn,** 13,235 feet, 4034 mètres, was made on Aug. 28, 1856, by Mr. E. L. Ames, with the guides Franz Andermatten and — Imseng of Saas. They started from the Mattmark Inn, and after getting to the top of the Allalinpass followed the ridge which leads thence N.E. by N. to the summit of the mountain. The ascent from the Col and back occupied them about 4 hs. From the Col they descended to Zermatt, *viâ* Täsch. From place to place 14 hs. were taken. The mountain was crossed from N. to S. (Saas to Zermatt) by Mr. L. Stephen and Rev. W. Short, with Franz Andermatten and Moritz Anthonmatten (?) on Aug. 1, 1860. Sixteen hours were occupied from place to place.

The **Alphubel**, 13,803 feet, 4207 mètres, was first ascended on Aug. 9, 1860, by Mr. Leslie Stephen, *viâ* the Täsch Valley. No account of this ascent has been preserved, and I am unable to indicate the route that was taken. The summit can be attained in 1½ hs. from the Alphubeljoch, and in even less time from the Mischabeljoch, and it is also accessible from the West.

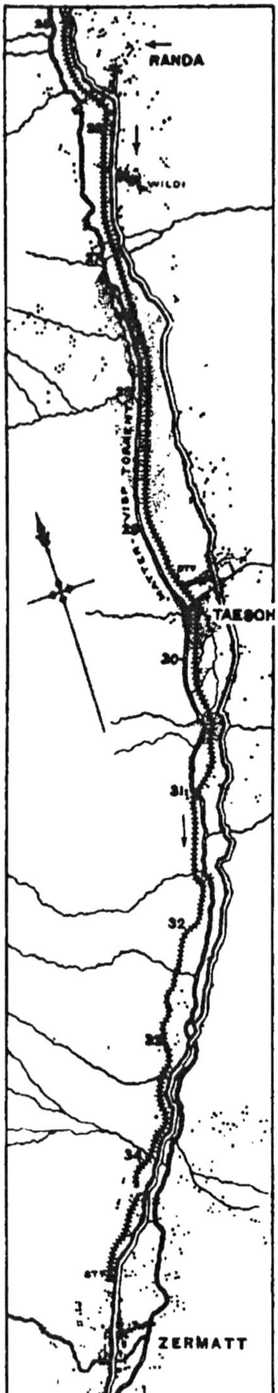

RANDA TO ZERMATT.

The first ascent of the **Rimpfischhorn**, 13,790 feet, 4203 mètres, was made by Dr. R. Liveing and Mr. Leslie Stephen in 1859, with the guides Melchior Anderegg and Johann zum Taugwald, from Zermatt, *viâ* the long ridge called the Rimpfischwänge. Twelve hours of actual going seem to have been occupied on the ascent and descent. This mountain has also been ascended from the Allalinpass (5 hs. from the Pass to the top), but the route which is probably the shortest and easiest is that marked on the Map of the Valley of Zermatt, from the Täsch Valley, crossing the Hubel Glacier near its foot, mounting the buttress between it and the Langenfluh Glacier, and crossing the latter to a point high up on the Rimpfischwänge, which is then followed to the summit. The Rimpfischhorn is a more appetizing morsel for a mountaineer than the Allalin and Alphubel, which also, as points of view, are inferior to a number of positions in this district which can be gained more easily.

The passes out of the Täsch Valley, leading to the Saas Thal, are all moderately easy; though, as they are lofty, they are, under any circumstances, somewhat laborious. The **Mischabeljoch**, 12,651 feet, 3856 mètres, between the Täschhorn and the Alphubel, was first traversed by Messrs. Coutts and William Trotter, the Rev. H. B. George and the Rev. W. S. Thomason, with the guides Peter Bohren, Christian Almer, and two Saas men, on July 30, 1862, from Saas (im Grund) to Zermatt. Fifteen hours were taken going right through. The route now usually followed for this pass is marked on the Map of the Valley of Zermatt.

The **Alphubeljoch**, 12,474 feet, 3802 mètres, between the Alphubel and Allalinhorn is easy; but with new snow may be very laborious. The ordinary route for it is marked. Time from Saas-Fée to Täsch Alp in 9 to 10 hs., actual going. In 1889, a French lady and gentleman fell, "*with their guide*, into a crevasse on this pass, and were only saved by the arrival of another party."—*Alpine Journal*, vol. xiv, p. 475.

The **Féejoch**, 12,507 feet, 3812 mètres, is not shewn upon the Map of the Valley of Zermatt. It lies between the point marked 3912 and the Allalinhorn. That peak can be ascended from the Col. It is a circuitous route from the Täsch Valley to Saas-Fée; but, being easy, is as quick as the more direct ones.

The **Allalinpass**, the next one to the south, 11,713 feet, 3570 mètres, between the Allalinhorn and Rimpfischhorn, is known to have been crossed in 1847, and possibly was in use long before. This is a very circuitous way of getting from the Täsch Valley to Saas, but the time occupied is not more than upon the above-mentioned passes. Deducting the 4 hs. taken on the first ascent of the Allalin from the Col to the Summit and back, Mr. Ames' party went through from Mattmark to Zermatt in 10 hs.

There remains to be mentioned a little pass at the head of the Täsch Valley, the **Langenfluh Pass,** leading from it into the Findelen Valley, across the western end of the long ridge called the Rimpfischwänge. This has not yet been recognized on the Official Maps of Switzerland. It goes between the points marked 3258 and 3314, by the track laid down on the Valley of Zermatt Map, and is, approximately, 10,500 feet high. One can get by it easily in 5 to 6 hs. from the Täsch Alp Inn to the Fluhberg Hotel (by the side of the Findelen Glacier).

In descending from the Täsch Valley with the intention of proceeding to Zermatt, the *quickest* way is to return by the path to the village of Täsch, and thence by train. If *time* is not an object, another way may be taken. When about 20 min. down, a rough path will be noticed leading away to the left (about S.S.W.) by the side of an old, disused watercourse. Baedeker's *Switzerland* terms this "a direct but disagreeable forest-path." I have found it very serpentine and highly agreeable.]

South of Täsch, the **road** to Zermatt does not rise much for 3 kils. It then crosses to the left bank of the Mattervisp (5023 feet, 1531 mètres), and becomes steeper on the next two kils. The last bit, just before entering Zermatt, is flat.

A kilomètre and a half to the south of Täsch, the **railway** crosses to the left bank for the last time, and rises rapidly, in 1 kil., high above the torrent and road, by the last of the inclines with cogged rails. At this part it skirts the base of the Mettelhorn. There is a grand view, between kils. 31-32, of a gorge through which the Mattervisp runs. Get on the side of the stream. The Matterhorn first shews itself, to those in the train, about the 34th kil., and after passing through a little tunnel Zermatt comes in sight, with Mont Cervin towering above. At the Terminus there is a good Buffet, and Omnibuses from the Hotels will be found in the Station Yard. The Railway Fares from Zermatt are—

		Single Fares.		Return Tickets.	
		2nd Cl.	3rd Cl.	2nd Cl.	3rd Cl.
		fr. cts.	fr. cts.	fr. cts.	fr. cts.
Zermatt to	Täsch . . .	2. 70	1. 70	4. 80	3. —
,,	Randa . . .	4. 45	2. 80	8. —	5. —
,,	Herbriggen . .	6. 25	3. 90	11. 20	7. —
,,	St. Nicholas . .	8. 90	5. 55	16. —	10. —
,,	Kalpetran . .	11. 15	6. 95	20. —	12. 50
,,	Stalden . . .	12. 45	7. 80	22. 40	14. —
,,	Visp (Viège) . .	16. —	10. —	28. 80	18. —
,,	Lausanne . . .	26. —	17. 15	44. 80	29. 40

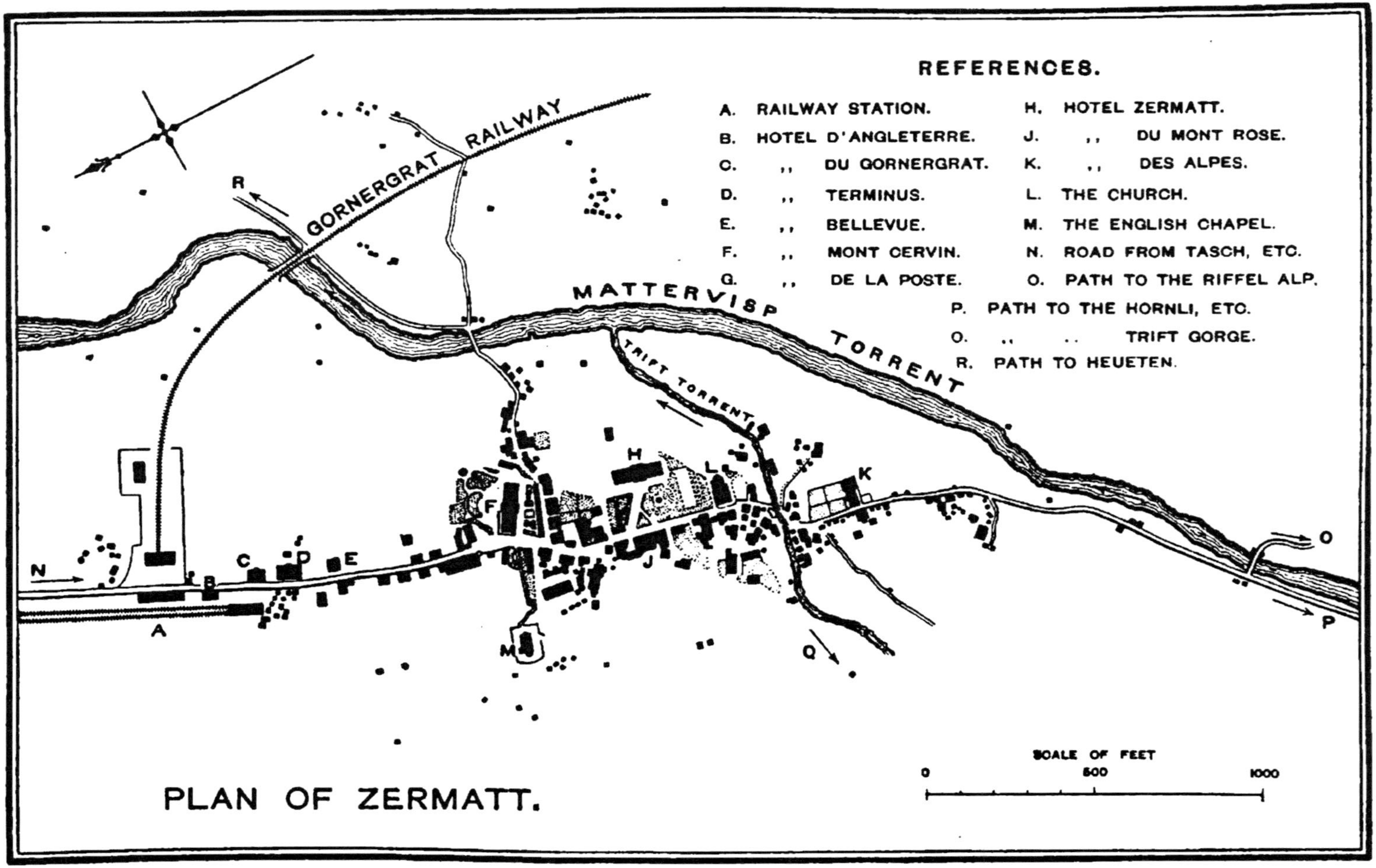

PLAN OF ZERMATT.

CHAPTER VIII.

UPON THE VILLAGE OF ZERMATT.

ZERMATT—ITS POPULATION—AUTHORITIES—REPARATION OF PATHS—COMMUNAL FORESTS—HOTELS—THE STREET—SHOPS—MANNERS AND CUSTOMS—THE CHURCH—INSCRIPTIONS IN GRAVEYARD—ENGLISH CHURCH AND INSCRIPTIONS IN ITS GRAVEYARD—AN ALPINE GARDEN!—ZOOLOGICAL GARDENS—POST OFFICE—TEMPERATURES—GLACIERS—EARTHQUAKES—BRIDGES—GUIDES AND MULES—THE GORNERGRAT RAILWAY.

THE **Village of Zermatt**,[1] 35 kils. from Visp, is situated in a basin at the head of the Nicolai Thal, upon nearly level ground, on the left bank of the Mattervisp torrent. It is in the *District de Viège* (or *Bezirk Visp*). See p. 101. **Altitude**, 5315 feet (1620 mètres). Post and Telegraph.

The permanent **Population** at the last Census was 525, and it is now estimated at 600. During the season, the residents are largely augmented by the persons employed in the Hotels, and by shopkeepers and others who come from various parts of Switzerland. For Zermatters in early times, see p. 9. The **Authorities** comprise the President of the Commune (with a Council of five), a *Juge*, and *sous-Juge de Commune.*

The whole of the upper parts of the surrounding *Alps* and mountains, up to the limits of pasturage, are the property of the Commune. On the lower ground, many little patches and plots are private property. The Zermatters set a high value on their **land**, and ask prices equivalent to those which are obtainable in the City of London. The Commune derives a considerable revenue from rents.

Reparation of Roads and Paths.—The Commune determines what shall be done in this matter, and assesses the amount that shall be contributed by each person, according to his means. I am told that very little in the way of reparation is carried out. The condition of the paths has scarcely improved since I have known them.

Forests.—Although the Forests around Zermatt (in consequence of the high average elevation of the soil) are not so extensive as those belonging to some of the Communes lower down the Valley, they

[1] The name Zermatt is of comparatively modern origin. See chap. i. I have remarked the following variations in spelling. Zermatten (Bourrit, 1781); Zer-Matt (De Saussure, 1796); Zur-Matt (Ebel, 1804); Zermat (Schiner, 1812); Matt (Ebel, 1818); and Zurmatt (Marc Viridet, 1833).

form a large and valuable property. Every member of the Commune has right to wood to build a house, if he has not already got one, but he has to pay for its transport.

The most picturesque tree in this neighbourhood is the Arolla Pine, and it is also one of the most serviceable for its timber, but it is not considered so valuable as the Larch. The greater part of the châlets are built of the latter wood. Furniture and floors are made from the Arolla Pine.

Hotels.—GRAND HOTEL DU MONT CERVIN (300 beds; Pension, 7-16 francs; *Bierhalle;* Lift). HOTEL MONTE ROSA (100 beds; Pension, 7-14 frs.; open all the year). HOTEL ZERMATT (180 beds; Pension, 7-15 frs.). These are the three largest and oldest established Hotels (see pp. 15, 17). They are all central, and are favourites with English and Americans.

Pension includes '*déjeuner du matin*' (*café, thé, ou chocolat complet*), '*déjeuner à la fourchette*' (lunch), dinner, rooms, and attendance. It must be for a week, at least, reckoning from the day the arrangement is made. For a supplementary payment of 50 centimes per head, pensionnaires in the three above (Seiler) hotels at Zermatt can lunch at the RIFFELALP HOTEL, at the RIFFELBERG HOTEL (RIFFELHAUS), or at the LAC NOIR (SCHWARZSEE). At all these six establishments the price of *Pension* is reduced *until* July 1, and *after* September 1.

HOTEL GORNERGRAT; GRAND HOTEL TERMINUS; HOTEL D'ANGLETERRE (small). These three are nearest to the Railway Station. HOTEL BELLEVUE; HOTEL DE LA POSTE (central, but not well-situated); HOTEL DES ALPES (at the southern end of the village). The positions of all the Hotels are indicated upon the Plan of Zermatt. They have the Electric Light; and omnibuses from them leave for the Railway Station before the departure of each train. *The Trains start punctually.*

In the Street.—Zermatt has one street, which runs through the whole length of the village. The side alleys and lanes leading off it are *not* recommended. The **Shops** are in 'the street,' and include one kept by the renowned guide **Melchior Anderegg** of Meyringen, for the sale of Carvings, Photographs, etc. The **bookseller Pfister** has a large stock of light literature, Maps, and Photographs. There are a dozen or more general shops, a Baker, Bank, half-a-dozen Bootmakers, Confectioner, Doctor, Florist and Fruiterer, Forwarding Agents, Hairdresser (shaving 60 centimes), Jeweller, and Photographer. J. Lauber deals in minerals. At the general shops, bread, cheese, tobacco and tourists' requisites are sold. 'Long John,' Liebig's Extract, Chlorodyne and Photo. Chemicals can be obtained at the Chemist's, opposite the Mont Cervin Hotel. A Newspaper, the *Journal et Liste des Etrangers de Zermatt*, is published once a week during the Season. *Réclames* (puffs) may be inserted in it at 2 francs per line.

Manners and customs at Zermatt.—The *Journal de Zermatt*, Aug. 18, 1895, contained the following paragraph.—

"**Mœurs et coutumes de Zermatt.**—On connait les beautés de la contrée, mais on ignore les mœurs du pays. Par exemple, sait-on qu'à Zermatt il n'a

THE GRAND HOTEL MONT CERVIN, ZERMATT.

jamais été constaté de délit, vol ou rixe. Le casier judiciaire de la contrée est immaculé. Les magasins n'ont pas de volet, les étalages restent dehors la nuit, les portes des châlets n'ont pas de serrure ; il arrive souvent que des étrangers, inconnus des négociants, emportent, manquant de monnaie, des marchandises qu'ils viennent religieusement solder le lendemain ; le cas contraire, de mémoire d'homme, ne s'est jamais produit. Les guides jouissent d'une réputation de probité sans tache ; nombre de touristes leur confient les fonds dont ils sont porteurs et il ne s'est jamais élevé même de contestation. Détail typique, le banquier du pays dort avec la fenêtre ouverte. A minuit, dans tous les cafés de Zermatt, l'obscurité se fait, par suite de l'extinction de la lumière électrique et chacun se retire, sans murmurer. Le seul gendarme du village semble plutôt préposé à la surveillance de la vertu qu'à la répression du vice."

ZERMATT CHURCH.

Zermatt Church, dedicated to St. Maurice, is a plain structure externally, and is less ornate internally than most of the churches in this district. Admission can be had at all reasonable times. According to Ruden's *Familien-Statistik*, it is not known when it was erected. The sacristy is dated 1587, and stands, it is said, on the site of a charnel-house (*beinhaus*). On Sundays, First Mass at 5.30 a.m. ; Second Mass, 7 a.m. ; High Mass, 9 a.m. On week-days, Mass at 6.30 and 7.30 a.m. The **parsonage** is on the S.E. side of the Church, and is the house where visitors lodged before the first Hotel was opened. See p. 14. The **Parish of Zermatt** extends on the S. up to the Italian frontier, and on the N. is bounded by the Parish of Täsch. Like all the rest of the Valley, it is in the Diocese of Sion.

In the centre of the **Churchyard**, on the S. side of the Church, there is the monument to Michel Croz (see p. 71), bearing this inscription, on the side facing the street.—

"à la memoire de Michel Auguste Croz né au Tour vallée de Chamounix, en temoignage de regrets de la perte d'un homme brave et dévoué, aimé de ses compagnons estimé de voyageurs, il périt non loin d'ici en homme de cœur et guide fidéle."

Upon the N. and S. sides respectively of the monument there are the dates of his birth and death [Avril 22me, 1830 ; Juillet 14me, 1865].

On the north of the Church there are the graves of the Rev.

Charles Hudson and Mr. Hadow (see p. 70), and at their side there is that of Mr. W. K. Wilson of Rugby School, with these inscriptions.—

"Douglas Robert, eldest son of Patrick Douglas and Emma Hadow, who perished in descending the Matterhorn, July 14, 1865, aged 19 years. Even so Father, for so it seemed good in thy sight. S. Matt. xi.—26.

"Charles Hudson, Vicar of Skillington, Lincolnshire, killed in descending the Matterhorn, July 14, 1865, aged 36 years. Be ye therefore also ready. S. Luke xii. 40."

" + William Knyvet Wilson, M.A. Fellow of Trin. Coll. Cambridge. + Born Nov. 2. 1838. + Killed by a fall on the Riffelhorn, July 18. 1865. + "It is I be not afraid." St. John vi. 10."

By their side there is the tomb of Mr. E. von Grote, inscribed "Eduard von Grote xiii August MDCCCLIX semper idem" and close by there is the grave of Mr. Goehrs (see p. 86), bearing this inscription.—

"Edouard Goehrs né a Strassbourg le 23 Oktober 1863 Mort au Cervin le 11 September 1890 Mes pensèes ne sont pas vos pensèes et mes voies ne sont pas vos Voies a dit l'Eternel. E.S.S.S."

And alongside there is the grave of Mr. Chester (see chap. x) inscribed "Henry Chester of Poyle Surrey who died on the Lyskamm."

The English Church is placed upon an eminence opposite to the Hotel du Mont Cervin. The keys are kept at the Hotel du Mont Rose. Upon its S. side there are the graves of Mr. Gabbett (see chap. ix), Mr. Borckhardt (see pp. 85-6), Mr. Lewis (see chap. x), and Miss Sampson (see chap. ix) with the following inscriptions.—

"W. E. Gabbett aged 32 fell from the Dent Blanche August 12th 1882 In the midst of life we are in death. I am the resurrection and the life."

THE GRAVES OF HUDSON, HADOW, AND WILSON.

"In memory of Frederick C. Borckhardt St. Albans, Herts who perished on the Matterhorn during a terrible snowstorm 18 August 1886 Aged 48."

"In loving memory of my beloved husband William Arnold Lewis barrister at law of the Middle Temple and 29 Elsham Road, Kensington, son of the late W. D. Lewis Q.C. who lost his life on September 6TH 1877 by a fall from the Lyskamm Aged 30. Thy will be done."

"In Memory of Ellen Emma Sampson of Hendon, Middlesex, killed by falling stones on the Triftjock 30th August 1895."

In front of the English Church there is what is termed an '**Alpine Garden**'! which affords more wonder than delight. At the entrance to it, it is stated that it is "Propriété de l'Etat." The plants do not flourish under State Patronage, and they seem to exercise a depressing influence upon the **Eagles** which are confined in an enclosure alongside.

[A list of **Plants** that are found in the neighbourhood of Zermatt is given at the end of Ruden's *Familien-Statistik*, embracing more than 500 species. The following *genera* are amongst those which are most strongly represented. —*Anemone* (6), *Arenaria* (8), *Artemisia* (7), *Campanula* (8), *Carex* (23), *Cerastium* (6), *Draba* (7), *Gentiana* (13), *Geranium* (4), *Gnaphalium* (5), *Hieracium* (19), *Myosotis* (4), *Potentilla* (14), *Ranunculus* (9), *Saxifraga* (14), *Silene* (5), *Trifolium* (9), *Veronica* (9), *Viola* (7).

Digging up plants by their roots.—The following notification was printed in the *Journal de Zermatt*, Aug. 11, 1895.

"**Expéditions de fleurs avec leurs racines.**—Pour arracher et expédier des fleurs destinées à être transplantées, une autorisation du maire de Zermatt, M. Pierre-Louis Perren, est indispensable. De plus ces fleurs devront acquitter un droit municipal de 5 fr. le kilo pour les edelweiss et 3 fr. pour les autres fleurs."

It is impossible to collect the tax, and the 'indispensable authorisation' is, I think, very generally ignored.]

The **Gardens** of the Mont Cervin Hotel, close at hand, are **Zoological** in their tendencies. In 1896, they contained four Marmots, an Owl and a forlorn Eagle, and two very young Bouquetin (supposed not to be more than two months old). Pay attention to the Marmots. In going to them from the English Church you will pass the **Post Office**, which is open on week-days from 7 a.m. to 8 p.m., and on Sundays from 8 to 10 a.m. and 1—3 p.m. **Telegraph Office** is always open. For **the Swiss Post** see p. iv of Introduction.

Temperature.—The *maximum* temperature in the shade at Zermatt is seldom higher than 24° C. (75°·2 Fah.). The highest recorded temperature in recent years occurred, I believe, on Aug. 16-17, 1892, when the thermometer rose to 76°·1 Fah. In the sun, however, the heat (both on high and low ground) is often sufficient to make one wish for shade, and an umbrella is not to be despised. In Winter, the *minimum* may be as low as −6° Fah. (38° below freezing-point).

Glaciers.—Since 1860, most if not all of the glaciers in this district have diminished and retreated. In the Report on the periodical variations of glaciers in the *Jahrbuch* of the Swiss Alpine Club, 1897, it is stated that in 1896 the Gorner, Findelen and

Zmutt glaciers all shewed a slight shrinkage. The Findelen in 1894, however, *advanced* 60 mètres.

Earthquakes.—The Nicolai Thal has experienced earthquake shocks several times in the course of the 19th century, but Zermatt itself has taken scarcely any harm. The last occurred on Aug. 21, 1895, at 9.15 a.m. It was a single, moderately strong shock, accompanied by loud noise. Many persons rushed out of the Hotels in alarm. There was a second, feebler shock at 1 p.m. on the same day, attended by a very loud noise, resembling that made on the fall of

THE MATTERHORN BRIDGE.

a great avalanche. I could not learn that damage was done in any part of the Valley.

At the end of July, 1855, the earthquakes were more severe. Canon J. G. Smyth, who was at Zermatt at the time, says, "we were assembled a little before dinner and suddenly heard a rumbling, and presently felt the floor shaking, just as if all the people in the Hotel had taken to dancing about the different rooms. On looking out of the window we perceived some large stones tumbling down into the valley. The shocks were repeated two or three times at intervals. . . No damage was done at Zermatt. . . At St. Nicholas the whole side of one of the Hotels was thrown down, so that people outside could see into the bed-rooms." The damage done on this occasion at St. Nicholas and other places lower down the valley was very extensive.

Bridges.—Those who desire to make Excursions alone will do well to acquaint themselves with the Bridges. 1. There is first the Village Bridge, called *Schwebsteg*, which is reached by the lane (usually in a filthy condition) on the southern side of the Mont Cervin Hotel, or by a path at the back of the Hotel Zermatt. The way over it leads to Haueten, etc. 2. The next bridge higher up the Mattervisp is called the Riffel Bridge (*Pont du Riffel*). This is the bridge for the Riffelberg, Gornergrat, etc. These two are marked on the Plan of Zermatt. 3. The next one higher up, called *zum Waldsteg*, is over the Zmutt torrent, just above its junction with the Mattervisp. Go over it to the Gorges of the Gorner. 4. Half a kil. higher up the Zmutt torrent there is the bridge for the Lac Noir, Hörnli, etc., called the Matterhorn Bridge (*Pont du Mont Cervin*). The little bridge in the middle of the village crosses the Triftbach, coming from the Trift Gorge.

Guides and Mules.—Guides are in demand at Zermatt, yet there is not a *Bureau* or any place where a would-be employer can learn what Guides are available. He has first to occupy his time in searching for men out of work, and then to enquire whether those he proposes to select are fit to employ on the contemplated excursion. This is wasteful of the time of the employer; and many persons quit Zermatt, without making excursions they wish to make, from inability to meet with the right men,—although there may be at the moment a dozen or a score of competent guides available, who, in consequence, lose business.

Zermatt is a meeting-place for Guides. Besides the men of the district, whose names are given in Appendix G, and other Valaisan guides, one often finds there some of the best men from the Oberland, the Engadine, Chamonix, Courmayeur and the Val Tournanche; and it would be a convenience to tourists, and would put annually many thousands of francs in the pockets of those who want them, if an Office could be opened for the registration of Guides out of employment, where employers might call and make enquiries.[1] **Mules and drivers** can be engaged at the Hotels.

The Gornergrat Railway, from Zermatt to the Gornergrat, is well-advanced towards completion, and it is intended that it shall be opened early in the season of 1898. The terminus at Zermatt is opposite to the Station of the Zermatt—Visp line. It will always be necessary to change trains.

The line is one mètre gauge. The first 300 mètres over the meadows are level. It then crosses the Mattervisp by an iron bridge of 24 mètres span, and after that no more is level.

At the commencement, the gradients are not steeper than the steepest ones on the Viège—Zermatt line,—that is to say 12 in 100; but after passing the

[1] In the *Jahrbuch des Schweizer Alpenclub*, 1897, p. 402, there are the following remarks, "Le Comité central a constaté avec peine que les deux guides victimes de la catastrophe au Lyskamm ne figuraient pas sur nos tableaux d'assurance. La répugnance ou la négligence des guides valaisans à se faire assurer contre les accidents disparaîtraient certainement dans une grande mesure si les guides étaient organisés en corporation par vallée ou par région. Le Comité central discutera s'il ne convient pas que le Club Alpin Suisse fasse des démarches pour provoquer cette organization *qui offrirait encore d'autres avantages.*"

THE HOTEL ZERMATT IN 1895.

bridge at the entrance to the Findelen Valley they are almost always 20 in 100. The line at this part is already a considerable elevation above Zermatt and the mule-path to the Riffel, and gives fine views of the Gabelhorn and Zinal Rothhorn. After passing through three small rock tunnels of ordinary character, it arrives (at kil. 3) at a fourth tunnel, 200 mètres long, which makes a complete semi-circle, and mounts 1 in 5 all the way through! The upper

THE BUFFET AT THE RAILWAY-STATION.

end of the tunnel, which is quite a short distance from the lower entrance, is thus 131 feet above it! Shortly afterwards, the line makes a great sweep round to the right, and at kil. 5 approaches the Riffelalp Hotel, where there is the first station. There are then several curves, and at kil. 6·6 one reaches the second station, Riffelhaus, close to the Hotel. So far, the railway has not touched the mule-path, but after this line and path are close together. The little lakes at the foot of the Riffelhorn are passed at kil. 8, and the line terminates at a sort of plateau, 9908 feet, 3020 mètres, to the W. of the Gornergrat, at kil. 9·2. In this distance it rises 4593 feet (1400 mètres).

This is an adhesion railway, and it will be worked by electricity. As it would be impossible to obtain sufficient adhesion on an ordinary pair of rails, the line will have, throughout its entire length, a third, central, cogged-rail, on the Abt system. The most important works upon it are the semi-circular tunnel, and the great bridge over the Findelenbach. This is in three spans, and from the level of the torrent, which it crosses, to the rails, is a height of 164 feet (50 mètres), or 16 feet more than the bridge at Fribourg (on the Lausanne—Berne line), which until now has been the loftiest in Switzerland. The estimated cost of the line (including an electric installation capable of developing 1500 h.p.) is 3,500,000 francs.

CHAPTER IX.

EXCURSIONS FROM ZERMATT.

TO THE RIFFELALP—LAC NOIR (SCHWARZSEE)—ZMUTT AND STAFFEL—GORGES OF THE GORNER—THE FINDELEN VALLEY—TRIFT GORGE—HÖHBALM—TÄSCH ALP AND VALLEY—HEUETEN—TO THE RIFFELHAUS AND GORNERGRAT—GUGEL—THE HÖRNLI RIDGE AND THE MATTERHORN CABANE—THE ZMUTT GLACIER AND STOCKJE—ASCENT OF THE GORNER GLACIER TO THE RIFFELHORN—THE FLUH ALP AND UPPER FINDELEN GLACIER—TRIFT HOTEL AND TRIFT-KUMMEN—TUFTEREN ALP TO EGGEN—THE RIFFELHORN—A ROUND *VIA* STAFFEL, THE LAC NOIR, ETC.—THE STOCKHORN PASS—METTELHORN AND PLATTENHÖRNER—UNTER AND OBER ROTHHORN—UNTER GABELHORN, TRIFTHORN AND WELLENKUPPE—ZINAL ROTHHORN—OBER GABELHORN—DENT BLANCHE—TÊTE BLANCHE—TÊTE DE VALPELLINE—THÉODULE PASS—ASCENT OF THE BREITHORN—PETIT MONT CERVIN—COL DE TOURNANCHE—TIEFENMATTENJOCH—COL DE VALPELLINE—COL D'HÉRENS—COL DE LA DENT BLANCHE—COL DURAND—ARBENJOCH—TRIFTJOCH—MOMING PASS.

EXCURSIONS from Zermatt are divided in this chapter into **A.** simple *Walks.* **B.** *Extensions of excursions* 1—9. **C.** *Ascents.* **D.** *Passes.* Those which come under **A** are within the capacity of all; but the majority of those which are included in sections **C, D** are only suitable for persons who have at least an elementary acquaintance with the art of the mountaineer. An unlimited number of variations can be made upon the excursions which are enumerated, the central position of Zermatt giving it unique advantages, and permitting an almost infinite variety of combinations. For **Tarif** see Appendix D.

A. Walks around Zermatt.

§ 1. To the **Riffelalp Hotel**, by the ordinary path, returning by the Hotel-Pension du Glacier de Findelen and the Findelen Valley.

Go past the Church to the S. end of the Village, and cross the Riffel Bridge (see p. 134).[1] The way then rises to the hamlet of Winkelmatten, 5499 feet, 1676 mètres. At its Chapel the path divides. Take that on the

[1] There has been for several years a deceitful iron plate affixed to a post close to this Bridge, a few feet beyond it, bearing this inscription—

AUX GORGES DU GORNER RIFFELALP ET RIFFEL.

Persons are liable to be deceived by being led to suppose that the path *beyond* the bridge is *the* way. One *can* get to the Riffelalp *viâ* the Gorges of the Gorner, just as one can get from London to Dover *viâ* Brighton, but it is not *the* way (the regular way), which, as I have said, leads over the bridge.

LOWER SLOPES OF THE HORNLI
ZMUTT VALLEY
HOHBALM
ENTRANCE TO THE TRIFT GORGE
RAILWAY STATION
THE MATTERVISP
WHYMPER

right, which descends to a bridge over the torrent (Findelenbach) coming from the Findelen Valley. The path then remounts, and crosses a piece of flat meadow. After that it rises continuously to the Riffelalp Hotel. In 30 min. from Zermatt there is the first drinking-shed. The second one, 15 min. farther on, is near the lower end of the semi-circular tunnel on the Gornergrat Railway (see p. 136), and in the immediate vicinity there are some of the finest and most picturesque views of the Matterhorn that can be had from this direction. So far, a good deal of the way is in shade. The path here turns sharply to the left, and in the middle of the day this is a hot piece. At the top of the twists and turns time can be saved by shaping a direct course towards the Riffelalp Hotel, across open ground, instead of following the regular path past the châlets of Augstkummen (where there is a third drinking-place, with elastic prices). After the open ground, the path again turns to the left, and then doubles back to the

Riffelalp Hotel, 7307 feet, 2227 mètres; one of the Seiler Hotels, very popular from its excellence and position. Full and unimpeded view of the Matterhorn from its southern windows. Open from June 1 to October 15; 250 beds; Pension 10 to 16 francs per day; Catholic and English Chapels; Post and Telegraph. In the middle of the season this Hotel is usually full and overflowing, and those who propose to take up residence there should make inquiry at one of the Seiler Hotels, before leaving Zermatt, to learn if there is room.

Instead of returning the same way (which would take about 40 min., anything less is quick time) continue the walk to the Findelen Valley, by the path which starts *at the back of the Hotel.* Good path, partly in shade; slightly undulating; with excellent views of the Matterhorn, Dent Blanche, Gabelhorn, Rothhorn (Moming) and Weisshorn. In 40 min. it arrives at the HOTEL-PENSION DU GLACIER DE FINDELEN, situated a few hundred feet above the ice, on the left bank of the valley. Descend from it to the bridge over the Findelenbach (a short distance below the end of the glacier) in 20 min.; remount to the Village of Findelen, and take the path back, down the right bank of the valley, that joins the route by which you came at the Chapel of Winkelmatten.

In ascending to the Riffelalp something can be saved by 'cutting' the path at several places. Look ahead. The following will be about the times occupied on the excursion.

Monte Rosa Hotel to Riffel Bridge	5 min.
Riffel Bridge to first drinking-shed	25 ,,
First to second drinking-shed	15 ,,
Second drinking-shed to Riffelalp Hotel	45 ,,
Riffelalp Hotel to Hotel du Glacier de Findelen . .	40 ,,
Hotel du Glacier de Findelen to Findelen . . .	25 ,,
Findelen to Monte Rosa Hotel	40 ,,
Total . .	3 hs. 15 min.

§ 2. To **the Lac Noir (Schwarzsee)**, ascending by the old path and descending by the new one, or *vice versâ.*

Go to the S. end of the village, and follow the path marked P on the Plan of Zermatt. The path divides 9 or 10 min. after passing the Riffel Bridge. Take the one on the right [the other goes to the Gorges of the Gorner], which rises, and continues on the left bank of the stream until it comes to the Matterhorn Bridge (Pont du Mont Cervin). See p. 133. After crossing the bridge, it bears round to the right, and passes through the hamlet of Zum See. Shortly afterwards it commences to rise steeply, and in about 20 min. divides again. Here there is a shed, inscribed

VINS et BIERE LIMONADE LAIT.

Take the path on the left [the other one goes up the Zmutt Valley to the châlets of Staffel], and in 20 min. or so more you arrive at another drinking-place, overlooking the Gorner Glacier. Thence the way mounts directly towards the Hörnli, and in about 25 min. divides again. It is immaterial which way is taken, as both lead to the Lac Noir. The right hand one (the old path) has fine views of the Rothhorn, Ober Gabelhorn and Dent Blanche; and the left hand or new path (rather the steeper of the two ways) has a magnificent prospect over the Gorner Glacier up to Monte Rosa. In 2¼ to 2½ hours from Zermatt you come to the

Hotel du Lac Noir (Schwarzsee), 8494 feet, 2589 mètres; one of the Seiler Hotels; near the lakelet from which it takes its name; 50 beds; Pension 9 to 12 francs. The view from this place is very extensive, and embraces nearly all the peaks in the Zermatt district. At the Chapel against the Lake (see Illustration on p. 55), Mass on Sundays at 8 a.m. Descent can be made to Zermatt by either of the two ways in 50 min., moving briskly; or by a more circuitous path *viâ* the châlets of Staffel and the Zmutt Valley.

§ 3. To the Châlets of **Staffel and the end of the Zmutt Glacier,** *viâ* the Village of Zmutt, returning by the right bank.

Follow the route for the Lac Noir nearly to the Matterhorn Bridge. A little short of it, a path goes away on the right, to the **Village of Zmutt,** 6365 feet, 1940 mètres. Chapel. Old châlets. Time from Zermatt, 1 hour. In the middle of the day, this place is often completely deserted, everyone being at work out of doors. Descend in 5 min. to a bridge over the Zmuttbach (romantic position), a few hundred yards away, on the W. of the Village. Cross it and turn to the right, up the valley. The way to Staffel lies almost entirely through forest (many Arolla pines), picturesque, and well-shaded. On getting clear of the trees there is a remarkable view of the Matterhorn, which will be a surprise to those who have only seen the mountain from the Riffelalp (see p. 49). "There are precipices, apparent, but not actual; there are precipices absolutely perpendicular; there are precipices overhanging, there are glaciers and hanging glaciers; there are glaciers which tumble great *séracs* over greater cliffs, whose débris, subsequently consolidated, becomes glacier again."—*Scrambles amongst the Alps.* The châlets of Staffel, 7021 feet, 2140 mètres, are close to the end of the Zmutt Glacier, and a rough path or track continues for some distance up its right bank. Several spots in the vicinity of the châlets are well-adapted for picnics. Good water. Bring food,—prices are high at the small inn at Staffel. For returning home down the right bank of the valley (good path all the way), and through Zum See and across the Matterhorn Bridge, allow 80 to 90 minutes. I strongly recommend this Excursion.

§ 4. To the **Gorges of the Gorner** and the end of the **Gorner Glacier,** going by the zum Waldsteg Bridge (see p. 134), and returning by the Matterhorn Bridge.

Take the path marked P on the Plan of Zermatt to the zum Waldsteg Bridge, which crosses the Zmuttbach, 10 to 12 min. above the Riffel Bridge. On its farther side the path divides. That on the right leads through the hamlet of Platten; that on the left gets in 7 min. to the northern end of **the Gorges.** Admittance 1 franc. At the entrance there is a small erection called 'Travellers rest,' where refreshments can be obtained. "This gorge seems to have been made chiefly by the torrent, and to have been excavated subsequently to the retreat of the glacier. It seems so because not merely upon its walls are there the marks of running water, but even upon the rounded rocks at the top of its walls, at a height of seventy or eighty feet above the present level of the torrent, there are some of those queer concavities which rapid streams alone are known to produce on rocks."—*Scrambles amongst the Alps.* The plank path through the Gorges emerges not far from the end of the **Gorner Glacier.** This glacier has retreated at least ¼ mile since 1860, and it has now no ice-cavern at its extremity. To get to it, cross the bridge which will be seen. Return home *viâ* Zum See and the Matterhorn Bridge in about 35 min. The round, allowing for halts, can be made comfortably in 3 hours.

§ 5. To the **Village of Findelen,** and end of the **Findelen Glacier.**

Cross the Riffel Bridge; pass the Chapel at Winkelmatten (take the path going straight on, and leave the Riffel path on the right). A few minutes afterwards the way commences to mount, and rises steeply through forest, on the right bank of the valley (passing châlets at Zum Stein, 6204 feet, 1891

GORGE OF THE GORNER.

mètres), and arrives at the **Village of Findelen,** 6808 feet, 2075 mètres, in little more than an hour from Zermatt. Chapel. No inn. At this village the path divides. The upper (left hand) one goes to the Fluh Alp on the right bank of the valley, and the other descends to a little bridge and remounts on the left bank to the Hotel-Pension du Glacier de Findelen. See § 1. This Hotel can be seen from Findelen Village. After passing it, go a little higher up the left bank, cross the glacier to the other side, and return home through Findelen Village. The excursion can be made in an afternoon.

§ 6. To the **Trift Gorge,** and Tea House.

The Trift Gorge is immediately to the W. of Zermatt. A path to it starts at the English Church, and at first leads away from the Gorge, and apparently goes in the wrong direction. When it has risen to a good height, and opposite to the Hotel Terminus, it doubles back. Another more direct path starts at the passage on the S. side of the Monte Rosa Hotel, turns first to the left and then to the right, and leads in the direction of the arrow marked Q on the Plan of Zermatt. These two paths meet at the entrance to the gorge, just before arriving at the bridge over the torrent. From this point one can *return* to Zermatt in 10 minutes. A small châlet, perched on a commanding position on the top of a cliff on the S. side of the Trift Gorge, was opened in 1896. Tea and other refreshments. Good view of the valley can be had here. Time from Zermatt, 45 to 50 min. An extension of this excursion can be made to

§ 7. The **Höhbalm**, about 8600 feet, midway between Zermatt and the Unter Gabelhorn.

This excursion is fit for the afternoon, as this side of the valley gets then into shadow, and the mountains to the east are seen at their best. "Follow the path for the Trift torrent, cross the bridge, and you will discover a rough path leading you up into the woods above the right bank of the stream. Pursue this on to the hillside, and you will find yourself above the precipices and rising obliquely till the path ceases its upward course, and invites you to select your own way among the alternate terraces of grass and rock that rise gently above you. Make a note of the point where you leave the path, and stroll upwards at will, more and more enchanted by views which on a sunny day will not fail to surprise you into admiration. A quiet three hours' walk from the hotel will land you on the summit, an open undulating plateau, about 3500 feet above the village, forming the end of the promontory which descends from the Unter Gabelhorn, where you may roll or ramble at pleasure, and over your lunch drink in to your heart's content beauties of nature remarkable even in Switzerland. The Monte Rosa chain is more interesting in shape than from the Gornergrat, and with the advantage of the Riffelberg as a contrasting middle ground. To compensate for the loss of the upper Gorner Glacier you have the sparkling ice-fall and the deep richness of the valley. . . In returning, if you wish to vary your route, you may either wander on aloft till you look down on the Zmutt Glacier, or descend obliquely in that direction, till you find châlet paths, which will eventually lead you down to Zermatt by a different route."—*Alpine Journal*, vol. viii, p. 284.

§ 8. To the **Täsch Alp and Valley.** See p. 125.

§ 9. To **Heueten (Haueten).** A stroll to the little Chapel (5804 feet, 1769 mètres) and back can be made within an hour. Fine view of Zermatt and the Valley. Wild raspberries round about, and many shady nooks and retired places, good for readers. Go over the Schwebsteg Bridge, and by the path marked R on Plan of Zermatt.

B. Extensions of Excursions 1—9.

§ 10. **To the Gornergrat,** *viâ* **the Riffelalp Hotel and Riffelhaus.** The most popular of all the excursions that are made from Zermatt. The way leads past the front of the Riffelalp Hotel, turns to the left at the angle of the building, and cannot be mistaken. It then makes for the Hotel Riffelberg or Riffelhaus (which is in full view), and for part of the way is steep.[1] After this latter hotel is passed, the gradients are moderate up to the summit.

The **Hotel Riffelberg, or Riffelhaus,** 8429 feet, 2569 mètres; one of the Seiler Hotels; open from June 10 to September 30; 50 beds;

[1] "The Riffelberg, which from the second week in August is about as bare as the South Downs, is in July an almost continuous carpet of flowers, and it would be a good summer's work to botanize this district alone. Half way up the path from Zermatt, in addition to the usual Anemones, there is an abundance of the purple *Anemone Halleri;* and higher up comes the small but elegant *A. baldensis*, and some of the rarer Ranunculuses, such as *R. Pyrenæus* and *R. rutæfolius*."—T. W. Hinchcliff.

Pension 10 to 14 francs per day in July and September (*Pensionnaires* are not taken in August). Post and Telegraph. This Hotel was the earliest established of all the mountain inns round Zermatt, and was formerly called "The Riffel." Originally, it was a very small

THE RIFFELHAUS (THE OLD RIFFEL HOTEL).

affair, started as a speculation by some of the Zermatters. It remains popular, notwithstanding the greater attractions of its big brother down below.

The path leads away from the front of the Hotel, and in half an hour leaves the Riffelhorn on the right. Fine view here of the Breithorn. The prospect around increases in grandeur and extent as one rises, until at last, at the summit, one is encircled by a complete panorama of snowy peaks. For their names and elevations see Map of the Valley of Zermatt. The summit, 10,289 feet, 3136 mètres, is now crowned by an inn, HOTEL-RESTAURANT BELVÉDÈRE (erected by the Commune in 1894-6), which intercepts the view, and does not add to its beauty. The southern portion of the panorama, extending from the Lysjoch to the Breithorn, is perhaps the most striking section (see folding plate at the end of the volume, which is self-explanatory), and can hardly be rivalled in the Alps.

The excursion may be prolonged by going to the Hohthäligrat, and the Stockhorn, or by crossing the Gorner Glacier to the *Cabane* Bétemps, on the rocks called Untere Plattje,—but there is no advantage in doing either. Return home can be varied by descending on to the Gorner Glacier, coming 2 or 3 kils. down the ice, and remounting either upon the upper or the lower side of the Riffelhorn. The times ascending are—

	h.	min.
Zermatt to Riffelalp Hotel	1	30
Riffelalp Hotel to Riffelhaus		40
Riffelhaus to top of Gornergrat	1	15
Total . .	3 hs.	35 min.

Moving briskly, one can come down from the Gornergrat to Zermatt by the regular way (taking advantage, however, of all the short cuts) in 83 min.

CASTOR & POLLUX — THE BREITHORN — PETIT MONT CERVIN

This excursion can be made at any time of the day, but the morning is to be preferred.

§ 11. **Ascent of Gugel,** 8882 feet, 2707 mètres. This can be included in Excursion 10. Gugel is an eminence, well seen from Zermatt, lying to the N.E. of the Riffelhaus, and E. of the Riffelalp Hotel. In descending from the Gornergrat, strike off to the right from the path, when about ¼ h. down, at the drinking-shed kept by Kronig. Though only 453 feet higher than the Riffelhaus, Gugel commands a much finer prospect. It looks right down the Valley of Zermatt, overlooks the Findelen Valley and Glacier, the Trift Valley, and every peak is visible from it that can be seen from the Gornergrat, excepting Monte Rosa. The Riffelhorn groups effectively with the Breithorn, and the view of the Matterhorn is the finest that can be had of it from the North. For obtaining a comprehensive understanding of the surroundings of Zermatt, there is no single *pointe de vue* equal to the summit of Gugel. It can be reached in half an hour from the Riffelhaus. From its summit one can descend direct upon the Riffelalp Hotel, or go down into and return by the Findelen Valley.

§ 12. A visit to **the Hörnli** and the **Matterhorn cabane** on the Hörnli ridge is an extension of Excursion 2.

There is a fair path, starting in front of the Lac Noir Hotel, which leads to the Hörnli; at first over rather rough, stony ground, then past a little lake (of recent formation) by the side of the Furgg Glacier, and then along the moraine on the left bank of the glacier. The path passes underneath and goes *beyond* the Hörnli, and a little clambering is necessary to reach the ridge from the moraine. Then double back to the cairn on **the summit,** 9492 feet, 2893 mètres. The views down the Valley of Zermatt, and (in the reverse direction) of the Matterhorn are striking.

The hut called the Matterhorn *cabane* (see Illustration on p. 80) is situated on the Hörnli ridge, upon the side facing the Furgg Glacier, a few hundred yards from the point where the Matterhorn rises abruptly. The way to it from the Hörnli is mainly along the crest of the ridge. Axes are required for a little cutting here and there in ice or snow. The following remarks upon this *cabane* were printed in *Alpina* (the Official organ of the Swiss Alpine Club), July 1, 1896. "Elle est très fréquentée, mais malheureusement mal construite et toujours humide; il faudrait pour la mettre en état des frais et des travaux considérables. En attendant qu'une décision soit prise à ce sujet, le C. C. a reçu de M. Seiler l'assurance que, pour la saison prochaine, la cabane serait tenue propre et pourvue du mobilier règlementaire. Malheureusement les contrebandiers et les guides eux-mêmes ne se gênent pas pour enlever les couvertures ou les couper en morceaux à leur usage personnel, ce qui n'est pas de nature à encourager à de nouveaux sacrifices."

§ 13. To the **Zmutt Glacier** and **Stockje** is an extension of Excursion 3.

Upon leaving Staffel, continue along the moraine on the right bank of the glacier or close to it; cross it and make for the middle of the ice when tracks die out; steer as directly as possible for the N.E. end of Stockje (a cliffy island surrounded by glacier) and skirt the base of its southern cliffs. Good examples of *glacier-tables* are often to be seen on the Zmutt Glacier. Track is marked on the Map of the Matterhorn and its Glaciers. From the ruined *cabane*, about 9154 feet, 2790 mètres (on the S.W. end of Stockje), there is a magnificent view of the basin of the Tiefenmatten Glacier, with the Matterhorn, Tête du Lion, and the Dent d'Hérens on the farther side. The S.W. ridge of the Matterhorn is seen here nearly in profile, and the Col du Lion, Great Tower, and other points referred to in chap. ii are immediately opposite to the spectator. From this direction the Matterhorn looks its best under afternoon light. A whole day should be devoted to the excursion, starting early, and returning in time for *table d'hôte. Take provisions from Zermatt.*

§ 14. **Ascent of the lower portion of the Gorner Glacier,** to the Riffelhorn, returning by the Riffelhaus or by the Riffelalp.

This is a good excursion for those who wish to see a little of the ice world, and to get instruction in the use of the ice-axe. It is only a *walk* if led by a competent guide. Go *viâ* the Matterhorn Bridge; take to the lower end of the Gorner Glacier (called the Boden Glacier) on the western side, where it is not steep. Use caution not to dislodge the rocks of the moraine which are sometimes poised very insecurely here. Go up the middle of the glacier, inclining, however, towards its W. side, and cross it below the 'ice-fall' when approaching the Riffelhorn. There are ways up the rocks on the N. side of the glacier both on the E. and the W. of the Riffelhorn. The former brings you to the Riffelhaus, and the latter to the Riffelalp Hotel. To make the round comfortably requires 6 or 7 hours.

§ 15. To the **Fluh Alp and the Findelen Glacier** is an extension of Excursion 5.

After passing the Village of Findelen, the path for a time rises to a considerable height above the glacier; but at the Fluh Alp, where there is a little inn which will be reached in 1¾ to 2 hs., they come near together. Notice the lateral moraines. The nearest one is grass-grown; the next is to a large extent composed of ice, having a superficial covering of boulders and moraine matter. The general level of the glacier is now much beneath the moraines, which probably are very ancient. The path is partly carried along them. When it dies out, cross the glacier, and return down the left bank. This excursion can be made longer or shorter, and is another which affords a peep into the ice-world. *Bring provisions from Zermatt.* Guides are necessary for all except experts.

§ 16. To **Triftkummen,** *viâ* the **Trift Gorge** and **Trift Hotel,** is an extension of Excursion 6.

The way up the Trift Gorge leads in about 2 hs. from Zermatt to a little inn. The path in some places is not good, and is not recommended to infirm persons. After the inn is passed, it becomes better, and the valley opens out into a rather considerable basin, bounded by the Unter and Ober Gabelhorns, the Trifthorn, Rothhorn (Moming), and the Mettelhorn. About 40 min. above the Hotel there is a *vallon* (**Triftkummen**) extending northwards (at the head of which there is the Mettelhorn), good hunting-ground for botanists and entomologists. Return can be made by a different path, which will bring you to the Railway Station at Zermatt. The round can be made in an afternoon.

§ 17. From Heueten, *viâ* the **Tufteren Alp** to the **Eggen Alp,** returning by the Findelen Valley, is an extension of Excursion 9.

From the Chapel at Heueten strike upwards towards the E. through the forest. The ground is easy, and paths may be ignored. When well above the trees, bear round to the right (*i.e.* to the S.), along the lower slopes of the Unter Rothhorn, and steer towards the Gornergrat, which will be perceived in the distance. Keep bearing round to the right, and presently you will see the châlets of Eggen. Return home through the Village of Findelen. The excursion may be lengthened by descending upon the Stelli See, instead of upon Eggen. The ground is easy, and one can go anywhere. This excursion is suitable for any hour of the day.

§ 18. The **Ascent of the Riffelhorn,** 9616 feet, 2931 mètres, may be combined with Excursions 1 or 10.

The Riffelhorn is a knob of rock S.S.E. of the Riffelhaus, distant 1½ kils., on the northern side of the Gorner Glacier. It is commonly ascended either from the E. or from the W. It can also be climbed from the S., *viâ* the Gorner Glacier, by more than one way. This side is steep.

Prof. J. D. Forbes, writing in 1855, said no guide of Zermatt had attained the summit of the Riffelhorn. "In 1841, I attempted it by the western side, and arrived within a few fathoms of the top, when I was stopped by a cleft. In 1842, however, some English students of Hofwyl found a circuitous path on the eastern side, by which the top may be gained without much difficulty." But it seems from a letter contributed by Mr. F. C. Grove to the *Alpine Journal* in 1874 that the boys of Hofwyl were not the first to get up the Riffelhorn. "The simple but exciting pastime," says Mr. Grove, "of rolling big stones from the top of the Riffelhorn on to the glacier below was the means last autumn" (1873) "of bringing a curious relic to light. Two American travellers who were enjoying this exhilarating sport last August determined to signalize their visit by sending down a bolt of unusual magnitude. Having fixed upon a stone of such size that it was as much as two men could do to move it, they prized it with great difficulty from its bed, when to their surprise they found in the site thus laid bare a jâvelin or spear-head, which must have been lying under the stone for time indefinite. The weapon thus strangely discovered was of bronze, and may have been some seven or eight inches long; the workmanship was admirable, quite as good as the forging one sees now. The striking end was not pointed, but beaten out into a blade resembling a boldly rounded chisel; the other end must have fitted wedge fashion into a cleft shaft, and had two flanges on each side. . . As it is not impossible that other weapons may be found near the place where this was discovered, it may be worth while for some travellers during the coming season to vary the sport of rolling down stones by a careful examination of the upper rocks."

Mr. Hinchcliff, speaking of the ferns which may be found in this locality, said, "Hidden in the interstices of a group of loose rocks not far from the foot of the Riffelhorn, at a height of about 8600 feet, I know of a few specimens" (of the holly fern) "which, though very interesting in respect of the elevation at which they contrive to exist, are scarcely larger than those for which the Keswick guides endeavour to extort fabulous prices. Close to these, and concealed by the same friendly stones from all but the most inquisitive eyes, may be found a few tufts of *Asplenium viride*, with fronds of about half the usual length, but double the usual number—evidently the very best arrangement that could be devised for their protection at such an unaccustomed altitude. *Cystopteris fragilis*, in the same place, is not only dwarfed, but much beaten about by weather. About 100 yards further, however, in the recesses of a cave facing the Gorner Glacier, and entirely protected from the possibility of a chilling blast, it may be found in thick bunches of delicate green fronds, as perfectly developed as if they were at the bottom of an Italian valley."

There is a legend of a 'wild man of the Riffelhorn,' who was morose and unsociable, and was 'removed' by his neighbours in a way which strongly resembled murder. "A Zermatt, sur le Ryffel, dans le voisinage du Ryffelhorn, est une caverne assez spacieuse avec une étroite entrée. Là demeurait une fois un berger bien étrange. A force de garder seul ses moutons, il était devenu si farouche et misanthrope qu'il en était complétement sauvage et qu'il ne prenait sa nourriture quotidienne que si on la déposait quelque part, sans se laisser voir; car dès qu'il apercevait un être humain, il prenait la fuite et se cachait dans les montagnes. Peu à peu il se déroba aux regards, erra toujours dans la solitude autour des troupeaux, apaisant sa faim avec des moutons qu'il dérobait. Voulant en finir avec ce voleur de moutons, les gens du village cherchèrent à le prendre, mais leurs peines furent inutiles. Dès qu'il s'apercevait qu'on l'épiait, il fuyait toujours sur le Ryffelhorn où l'on arrivait par un sentier unique et dangereux. Il le défendait avec une telle intrépidité et recevait les assaillants avec un telle grêle de pierres, que ceux-ci renonçaient à emporter la forteresse. On ne vit pas d'autre moyen de s'en débarrasser que de tirer sur lui comme sur un chamois, ce que fit un jour un chasseur."—*L'Echo des Alpes*, Geneva, 1873, pp. 27-8.

Easy as the climb is upon the land side, the Riffelhorn has had its victim. On the morning of July 18, 1865, Mr. W. K. Wilson made the ascent with some friends, accompanied by guides, and later in the day attempted to climb the peak alone. He was missed in the evening, and efforts were made from the Riffel to discover him; but, as they were fruitless, Mons. Alex. Seiler called for volunteers at Zermatt. We walked up through the night, and found the body of Mr. Wilson immediately, without search, on the side of the Riffelhorn above the lake. Apparently, he had fallen from a considerable height, and death had been instantaneous. Although so short a time had elapsed, the body was already in a shocking condition. See p. 131.

§ 19. A round *viâ* **Staffel, the Lac Noir,** etc.

A capital excursion (a combination of several of those already mentioned) can be made by going up the Zmutt Valley to Staffel, then turning to the left for the Lac Noir; descending upon and crossing the lower part of the Furgg Glacier, and proceeding by the Théodule route as far as the lower Théodule hut (Gandeck or Gandegg, see section **D**, Passes from Zermatt, and chap. xi); descending thence on to the Unter Théodule Glacier, and going by it *viâ* the Riffelhorn to the Riffelalp Hotel; returning by route § 1, *viâ* Findelen. An entire day should be allowed. Start early. Take lunch No. 1 at the Lac Noir Hotel, No. 2 at the Riffelalp Hotel, and get home in time for *table d'hôte.*

§ 20. By the **Fluh Alp** to the **Findelen Glacier,** and round by the **Stockhorn Pass,** returning down the whole length of the **Gorner Glacier.**

This is the finest excursion of its description that can be made from Zermatt. Every phase in the life of a glacier, from its cradle to its grave, can be seen upon it. There are Crevasses, open and concealed; Seracs and Ice-falls; Glacier-rivers and Moulins; Glacier-tables and Moraines. It is not included in the *Tarif.* Start before daybreak, and take provisions from Zermatt.

The route is by path until beyond the Fluh Alp, and then along the right bank of the Findelen Glacier, partly over moraine (the way so far is the same as for the Adler Pass). Cross the glacier in the direction marked on the Valley of Zermatt Map, and zigzag through some riven ice to the summit, 11,204 feet, 3415 mètres, which lies due E. of the Stockhorn. Grand view of the Lyskamm. Shortly afterwards the route joins that for the Cima di Jazzi and the New Weissthor. Upon arriving at Gadmen, do not take to the lower slopes of the Gornergrat, but continue down the whole length of the Gorner Glacier, and return home by the Matterhorn Bridge. If led by a competent guide, this excursion is a walk.

C. Ascents from Zermatt.

Zermatt itself is not the best starting-point for several of the Ascents which are included in the Zermatt *Tarif.* For some it is better to start from the Riffelalp Hotel (see chapter x), and for others from Randa (pp. 118-121), the Täschalp (pp. 122-5), etc. The following ones are still made from Zermatt, though there are a few of these (Ober Gabelhorn, Zinal Rothhorn, Trifthorn, etc.) for which the Trift Inn is sometimes used.

The **Mettelhorn,** 11,188 feet, 3410 mètres; 7 to 8 hs. up and down. There are two ways from Zermatt, both leading to Triftkummen. See § 16. One can ride up to the head of this *vallon;* thence it is 30 to 40 min. over snow and rock to the top of the Mettelhorn. The view is good from it of the

Weisshorn, Zinal Rothhorn, Gabelhorn and Matterhorn, but it is as a whole much inferior to that from the Gornergrat, which can be seen with less trouble.

The **Unter Gabelhorn**, 11,149 feet, 3398 mètres, 7 to 8 hs. up and down, is reached *viâ* the Trift Inn. As a point of view this is also much inferior to the Gornergrat.

The way for the **Unter Rothhorn**, 10,190 feet, 3106 mètres (6 to 7 hs. up and down), goes by Heueten and the Tufteren Alp (see § 17) round the N.W. slopes of the mountain, and then turns to the S.E. up a *vallon* (Riederkummen) leading to a depression between it and the Ober Rothhorn. From this Col (9800 feet, 2987 mètres) turn to the right, up the peak. Then descend to the Col, and re-ascend by the crest of the ridge to the summit of the **Ober Rothhorn**, 11,214 feet, 3418 mètres. Return again to the Col, and descend into the Findelen Valley, between the Stelli See and Eggen, and return home *viâ* the Village of Findelen. The round can be made in 7½ to 8 hs., and is a good preparatory walk for those who wish to make more difficult excursions.

The **Wellenkuppe**,[1] 12,828 feet, 3910 mètres, and the **Trifthorn**, 12,261 feet, 3737 mètres, are more considerable peaks,—the former on the S. and the latter on the N. of the pass called the Triftjoch, from the summit of which both can be ascended. The view from each is shut out to a large extent by their loftier neighbours the Ober Gabelhorn, and Zinal Rothhorn. These latter are two of the chief mountains one can ascend from Zermatt, and in connection with them there are incidents to relate, which are instructive, without comment. The first illustrates the desirability of making sure, when approaching summits or when climbing *arêtes*, that there are no snow-cornices about; and the second the peril into which a party may be put by the presence of a single inefficient or clumsy person, and the foolishness of placing such an individual last in the line, when *descending*.

The **Ober Gabelhorn** (formerly called simply the Gabelhorn), 13,363 feet, 4073 mètres, was first ascended on July 6, 1865, by Messrs. A. W. Moore and H. Walker, with Jakob Anderegg, who left Zermatt at 12.20 a.m., went over the southern portion of the Trift Glacier (now called the Gabelhorn Glacier) to the wall of rocks at its head; climbed these to the N.E. ridge of the mountain, followed its *arête* to the summit, and returned to Zermatt by 7.15 p.m.

On the following day Lord Francis Douglas, with Peter Taugwalder *père* and Joseph Viennin, ascended the mountain from Zinal, and they saw, by the footsteps, that others had been there before them. "We sat down to dine," he said, in an account found amongst his papers, "when, all of a sudden, I felt myself go, and the whole top fell with a crash thousands of feet below, and I with it as far as the rope allowed (some 12 feet). Here, like a flash of lightning, Taugwald came

[1] The Wellenkuppe is the point marked 3910 mètres on the Valley of Zermatt Map. Its summit appears to have been first reached in July, 1865, by Lord Francis Douglas, upon one of his attempts to ascend the Ober Gabelhorn. The following remarks, which were found after his death among his papers, contain all that is known on the subject. "We had made two previous attempts" (to ascend the Ober Gabelhorn) "in vain. In the first attempt we ascended the Unter Gabelhorn, leaving Zermatt at 11 o'clock at night, but, at 3 o'clock on the following day, found ourselves only at the foot of the Gabelhorn, and had to return. In the second attempt, we reached the summit of another peak of the Gabelhorn, about 13,000 feet in height, which lies immediately to one's left in crossing the Trift pass from Zermatt, but the *arête* connecting this with the Gabelhorn was found impracticable. I cannot conceive why this mountain has no name. It is very often mistaken for the Gabelhorn."

right by me some 12 feet more; but the other guide who had only the minute before walked a few feet from the summit to pick up something, did not go down with the mass, and thus held us both. The weight on the rope must have been about 23 stone, and it is wonderful that, falling straight down without anything to break one's fall, it did not break too. Joseph Viennin then pulled us up, and we began the descent to Zermatt."[1]

Both of these routes are long. On Sept. 3, 1877, Messrs. W. E. Davidson and J. W. Hartley, with Peter Rubi and Johann Jaun, hit off a better one, and it is this which is now usually followed, with a slight variation. They followed the usual path to the Triftjoch until they reached the top of the moraine dividing the Trift from the Gabelhorn Glacier, and crossing the glacier made for a well-defined snow col, at the foot of the final peak, on the S.E. ridge (that running from the Ober to the Unter Gabelhorn, separating the Arben from the Gabelhorn Glacier). From the col, they followed the *arête* of the ridge, sometimes bearing down a little on to the eastern face. From Zermatt and back occupied 11 hours actual walking. The Gabelhorn has also been ascended by several other routes.

In 1895, Mr. W. E. Davidson, with Christian Klucker and Daniel Maquignaz, started from the Trift Inn and ascended the Wellenkuppe; then went straight along the *arête* of the ridge connecting it with the Ober Gabelhorn; crossed the latter mountain and descended to the Arbenjoch; and returned to the Riffelalp Hotel the same evening!

The **Zinal Rothhorn** (or **Moming**),[2] formerly called the Rothhorn only, 13,855 feet, 4223 mètres, was first ascended from the side of Zinal by Mr. F. C. Grove and Mr. Leslie Stephen, with the guides Melchior and Jakob Anderegg, on Aug. 22, 1864. The usual route for the Trift Pass was taken from Zinal as far as the top of the great 'ice-fall' of the Durand Glacier; they then turned to the left, *i.e.* to the north-east, and made for the ridge connecting the Rothhorn with Lo Besso, and went along this ridge until it joined the northern ridge of the Rothhorn, which was then followed to the summit. The difficulties were concentrated in the last part of the ascent. Three principal pinnacles upon the northern ridge had to be turned or surmounted. After the first one had been dealt with, Mr. Stephen says, "A severe piece of chimney-sweep practice then landed us once more upon the razor edge of the *arête*. The second pinnacle demanded different tactics. On the Zermatt side it was impractically steep, whilst on the other it fell away in one of the smooth sheets of rock already mentioned. The rock, however, was here seamed by deep fissures approximately horizontal. It was possible to insert toes or fingers into these, so as to present to telescopic vision (if anyone had been watching our ascent) much the appearance of a fly on a pane of glass. Or, to make another comparison, our method of progression was not unlike that of the caterpillars, who may be observed first doubled up into a loop and then stretched out at full length. When two crevices approximated, we should be in danger of treading on our own fingers, and, the next moment, we should be extended as though on the rack, clutching one crack with the last joints of our fingers, and feeling for another with the extreme points of our toes. . . The third, which now rose within a few yards, was of far more threatening appearance than its predecessors. After a brief inspection we advanced along the ridge to its base. In doing so we had to perform a manœuvre which, though not very difficult, I never remember to have previously tried. One of the plates to Berlepsch's description of the Alps represents a mountain-top, with the national flag of Switzerland waving from

[1] I think this account is exaggerated, and that the rope could not have failed to part if the two fell the distance and in the manner described. The summit of the Ober Gabelhorn and the crests of the ridges near it are frequently garnished with snow-cornices (such as broke away on this occasion), which are distinctly visible from the Lac Noir and Riffelalp Hotels.

[2] There are three other Rothhorns in the Valley of Zermatt. See Appendix E.

the summit and a group of enthusiastic mountaineers swarming round it. One of them approaches, astride of a sharp ridge, with one leg hanging over each precipice. Our position was similar, except that the ridge by which we approached consisted of rock instead of snow. The attitude adopted had the merit of safety, but was deficient in comfort. The rock was so smooth, and its edge so sharp, that as I crept along it, supported entirely on my hands, I was in momentary fear that a slip might send one-half of me to the Durand and the other to the Schallenberg Glacier." Including halts, 16 hs. 50 min. were taken in going from Zinal to the summit and back.

A way up the Rothhorn from Zermatt was found on Sept. 5, 1872, by Messrs. Dent and Passingham, under the leading of that excellent mountaineer and guide the late Franz Andermatten, with two other guides. The route taken on this occasion is substantially that which is followed at the present time. It is marked on the Map of the Valley of Zermatt. The summit is reached from the south. Including halts, 16 hs. were occupied from Zermatt and back. In descending, when not far beneath the top, an incident occurred (happily without serious result) of a closely similar character to another which caused the loss of a life (at almost exactly the same place) in 1894. "Suddenly," says Mr. Dent, "I heard a shout from above; Franz and I both glanced up at once. A large, flat slab of rock that had afforded us good hold on the ascent, but proved to have been only frozen in to a shallow basin of ice, *had been dislodged by the slightest touch*[1] from above, and was coming straight at us. . . Just above me it turned its course slightly. Franz, who was close beneath me more in its direct line of descent, attempted to stop it, but it ground his hands cruelly against the rock, and passed on swiftly, straight to Imseng. A yell from us hardly awoke him to the danger; the slab slid on faster and faster; but, just as we expected to see our guide swept away, it gave a bound for the first time, and, as with a startled expression he flung himself against the rock face, it leapt up, and flying by within a few inches of his head thundered disappointed down below."

On Sept. 20, 1894, Dr. P. Horrocks was descending the Rothhorn, with the guides Peter Perrn[2] and Joseph Marie Biner, both of Zermatt; and, when at almost precisely the spot mentioned above, very nearly came to his death, through the dislodgment of a boulder. "Perrn, who was last, was standing behind and holding on to a fair-sized rock, round which he was paying out the rope; while Dr. Horrocks crossed the slab, and Biner gradually pulled in the slack. Suddenly the rock in which Perrn placed such confidence came out, and bounded down the mountain side. Perrn slid rapidly down the steep rocks; Dr. Horrocks, who had no foothold and very little handhold, was jerked from his position, turning a somersault, and becoming momentarily stunned from his head striking against the rock. The strain on the rope was too great for Biner to withstand, and he was dragged down too. The whole party half tumbled, half slid, down the very steep smooth rocks for 30 or 40 feet, when the rope between Dr. Horrocks and Perrn caught behind a projecting rock, and brought them both to a standstill. Perrn found himself landed in a small patch of soft snow some 15 feet below the rock which had so fortunately engaged the rope, while Dr. Horrocks, some 7 feet higher up, though at first suspended with his back to the steep rocks, was very soon able to get more or less foothold. Poor Biner had the extra length of his own rope still to fall, and, when the strain came, the rope broke, according to one account, half-way between him and Dr. Horrocks; according to another, rather nearer to the latter. Biner fell down on to the Durand Glacier some 2000 feet below." Dr. Horrocks was rescued from his perilous position by some guides who were closely following.

The Rothhorn was climbed from the W. in 1878. Time from the Mountet *cabane* to Zermatt 10½ hs. On Aug. 9, 1873, "Mr. F. Morshead, with Melchior

[1] In the original, these words are not in italic. Although the name of the guide who dislodged this rock is not stated, it is easy to tell who he was. He is a man notorious for accidents.

[2] Not the Peter Perrn who is mentioned in earlier pages of this volume.

Anderegg and Christian Lauener, started from the Zinal hut" (Mountet) "and crossed over the top of the Rothhorn to Zermatt in the astonishingly short space of nine hours (halts included)."—*Alpine Journal*, vol. vi, p. 365.

Certain of the ascents which are included in the Zermatt *Tarif* may be dismissed from consideration (**Plattenhörner** or **Blattenhörner**, S. of and less elevated than the Mettelhorn; **Ebihorn**; **Mominghorn**; **Mont Durand** or **Arbenhorn**; **Pointe de Zinal**; **Schallhorn** or **Schallihorn**). Others are best made from the Riffelalp Hotel (**Monte Rosa**; **Lyskamm**; **Castor** and **Pollux**). The **Breithorn** and **Petit Mont Cervin** are usually ascended *vià* the Théodule Pass, and are referred to in section **D. Passes from Zermatt.** The **Dent d'Hérens** is ordinarily ascended from Prerayen (Valpelline), or from Breuil (Val Tournanche). The ascent of the **Tête Blanche**, when made, is generally combined with the passage of the Col de Valpelline.

The **Dent Blanche**, 14,318 feet, 4364 mètres, is the most important of the residual mountains included in the *Tarif*, but its ascent is better made from the head of the Val d'Hérens (Valley of Evolena) than from Zermatt, and upon such occasions as it is attempted from Zermatt it is usual to pass a night on Stockje. It is not easy to say what length of time is likely to be occupied upon any of the several ways up the Dent Blanche, for it is known by experience that the time will largely depend upon the state of the weather and the condition of the mountain, and this is very variable.

The first ascent of the Dent Blanche was made on July 18, 1862, by Mr. T. S. Kennedy and Mr. Wigram, with the guides Jean-Baptiste Croz[1] (brother of Michel-Auguste Croz) and — Kronig of Zermatt, under unfavourable conditions. They started from the châlets of Abricolla (Alpe Bricolla), on the eastern side of the Glacier de Ferpècle, about 3 hs. above Evolena, and ascended partly by the S.W. face, and partly by the ridge running southwards from the summit. This track is marked on the Map of the Valley of Zermatt.

The Dent Blanche has also been ascended by the S. ridge; from the Schönbuhl Glacier; from Zinal by the E. ridge; and from Ferpècle by the westerly ridge. The following times have been occupied on various occasions.

1862. First Ascent. From Abricolla and back, 16 hs.

1864. Second Ascent, by Mr. Finlaison. From Abricolla and back, about 13 hs.

1874. Mr. Whitwell took 16 hs. 20 min. from a camping-place on the Schönbuhl Glacier, 6 hs. from Zermatt, to the top and back to Zermatt.

1876. Mr. F. Gardiner took 16¼ hs. from the Stockje *cabane* (now in ruins) to the top, and down to Ferpècle.

1882. Messrs. Anderson and Baker from the Mountet *cabane* to Stockje occupied about 19½ hs.

1886. Messrs. Lorria and Lammer took the whole of a long day in going from Stockje to the top, and did not get back to their starting-point at nightfall.

1889. Mr. Eckenstein, from Zermatt and back to Zermatt, took 27½ hs. *vià* the Schönbuhl Glacier. Their route "is believed to be the worst yet taken."—*Alpine Journal*, vol. xiv, p. 499.

1890. Three Members of the Alpine Club took 38 hours from Stockje to the top, and back to Stockje.

[1] Some of his early friends will be glad to hear that this excellent guide (whose name is associated with several of the first ascents in the Zermatt district) is still living; and that he is, though retired from his profession, in good preservation.

In April, 1893, the Dent Blanche was ascended from Abricolla and back in about 21½ hours.

On August 11, 1882, Mr. W. E. Gabbett (a Durham Tutor) passed the night at Stockje, with Joseph-Marie Lochmatter and his eldest son, intending to make the ascent of the Dent Blanche on the next day, and to return to Zermatt. As they did not re-appear, search was made for them on the 14th, and the bodies of the three were found, 200 feet apart, about 2500 feet below the summit, all frightfully disfigured and scarcely recognisable. Most of their clothing was gone, and neither watches nor ice-axes could be discovered. Mr. Gabbett was buried at Zermatt (see p. 131), and the Lochmatters at St. Nicholas (p. 110). The cause of the accident is unknown. The mountain is said to have been at the time in the best possible condition.[1]

D. Passes from Zermatt.

The **Theodule Pass**[2] **(Matterjoch or Colle S. Teodulo)**, 10,899 feet, 3322 mètres, is the most frequented of the snow-passes leading out of the Valley of Zermatt, and perhaps was the first that was discovered. See chap. i. It is easy to traverse, and is useful as a route between the upper Valley of the Rhone and the Valley of Aosta. De Saussure took mules across in 1789, and Ruden said (in 1870) that according to some of the old inhabitants the traffic between Zermatt and Aosta was very considerable. One might see, "though very seldom, a string of 25 to 30 beasts of burden" crossing it at one time. Cows and mules are still taken over occasionally. Of late years the glaciers which have to be traversed have shrunk considerably, especially that upon the Italian side. Although the crevasses on the route are seldom large, rope should always be employed. I have seen, upon various occasions, Italian peasants crossing alone, provided with no implement except an umbrella. Skeletons of persons unknown are found upon this pass from time to time.

The way to the Theodule from Zermatt leads over the Matterhorn Bridge, and at the beginning is the same as the route for the Lac Noir. See p. 139. It then goes away to the left from the latter path, and mounts along the right bank of the Gorner Glacier, at some height above the ice; crosses the stream (Furggbach) coming from the Furgg Glacier, and ascends (sometimes in zigzags) towards the edge of the Ober Theodule Glacier (for track see Map of Matterhorn and its Glaciers), which it skirts, over rocky ground (part of this is called Leichenbretter),[3] until arriving at Z'Wangen, the southern extremity of the rocks, where there is a small inn, at about 9900 feet, **Gandeck** or **Gandegg**, known as **the lower Theodule cabane**. Not recommended. [When H.M. the Queen of Italy came this way in 1894, she stopped a night at Gandeck. Next morning when the bill was presented there was found an

[1] Joseph-Marie Lochmatter was a large and powerful man, and was one of the best guides in the Valley. See p. 68.

[2] Sometimes written Théodulepass, Theodul Pass, St. Theodule Pass. The height given above is the elevation assigned to it on the Siegfried Map. The *Carta d'Italia* makes it 2 mètres more. In ordinary conversation the pass is simply called "the Theodule."

[3] The word Leichenbretter may be translated 'floored' or 'paved' with corpses. Mons. Alfred Cérésole says that the quietude of the Theodule has often been disturbed by murderous combats. "Il y en eut un si formidable jadis entre Piémontais et Valaisans qu'on ne sut où enterrer la masse des cadavres. Ils furent laissés sur le sol en si grand nombre que pendant bien longtemps le glacier rejeta leurs squelettes et leurs armures jusque sur les rochers inférieurs qui se trouvent du côté du nord; ceux-ci portent encore aujourd'hui le nom significatif de *Leichenbretter*."

item of 100 francs for firewood! Her Majesty demurred at this royal charge, and took advice upon the subject.] From Zermatt to Gandeck will occupy 3½ to 4 hs. The inn is situated close to the edge of the Ober Theodule Glacier. The *path* ends there, and mules go no farther. In fine weather, the way can hardly be mistaken up to this point, but the higher part of it is readily obscured even by a slight fall of snow. For routes to Gandeck from the Riffelalp Hotel and from the Lac Noir Hotel, see chaps. x, xi.

The distance from Gandeck to the summit of the Theodule, as the crow flies, is less than 3 kils.,—all over snow-covered glacier. Put on the rope before embarking on the ice. Steer S.W. for about 10 min., until well on the glacier, and then make direct for the small cliffs of the Theodulhorn which will be seen in front, towards the south. Skirt them on the east, and at their southern end turn sharply to the right, where you will find the **Inn (Pavillon du Col St. Théodule)** on the summit of the pass. Beds. Civil proprietor. Prices reasonable. When the place is not overcrowded, one may pass a night comfortably here. From Gandeck to the summit of the pass takes about 1 h. 30 min.

The **View from the Summit** is interesting all round. The Matterhorn looks gigantic, and finer than from the Breithorn. One sees 'the shoulder,' and the notch between it and the final peak which stopped Tyndall; 'the Great Tower,' the Tête and Col du Lion, and various other points referred to in chap ii. See outline on p. 44. The Theodulhorn comes in front of the Matterhorn, and it can be readily ascended from the Pass. On the Italian side the Grand Paradis, Grivola and Ruitor are amongst the most prominent features in the distance, and the Bec de Luseney and Dent d'Hérens are the chief ones upon the right hand (western side) of the Val Tournanche. In the *séracs* close at hand, on the south, the stratification of the snow is generally well seen.

[**The Petit Mont Cervin and the Breithorn.**—In 1792, after measuring the height of the Matterhorn, De Saussure and his son, guided by Marie Coutet (Couttet) of Chamonix, went up the Petit Mont Cervin, and said that at that time it had never been ascended by mortal man. [*Voyages*, § 2247.] He called it 'la Cime-Brune du Breit-Horn,' but this appellation has not been adopted. The De Saussures declined the ascent of the Breithorn, partly on account of "the fatigue and dangers which the steepness of the slopes would have caused them," and also because examination of its rocks could not be made, from their being entirely covered with snow. "As it," he said, "presents a large and rounded summit to those who approach it on the side of Zermatt, the name *Breit-horn* or *Cime-Large* appears to suit it very well."

The Breithorn is said to have been first ascended by Mons. Henri Maynard in 1813.[1] Sir John Herschell went up it in 1821 (or 1822), and is said to have been "led to believe that he had attained the most elevated point of this great cluster, and to maintain that Saussure had greatly overrated its height" [*i.e.* the height of Monte Rosa] "in his trigonometrical measurement on the side of Macugnaga."[2] Lord Minto went up the Breithorn in 1830, with his son William (a boy of sixteen), who "excited much compassion" [at Zermatt] "as they thought it hard that so young a boy should be led up to perish so cruelly."

The Ascent of the Breithorn, 13,685 feet, 4171 mètres, has become extremely popular. It is best to start at an early hour from the inn on the Theodule (rather than from Zermatt or the Riffelalp), and to arrive on the summit *soon after daybreak.* The panorama that may be enjoyed from the top is one of the finest (some say *the* finest)

[1] I take this from Conway's *Climber's Guide to the Eastern Pennine Alps*, p. 6, but I have not been able to verify the statement.

[2] Quoted from Lord Minto's diary in *Alpine Journal*, vol. xvi, p. 232. Lord Minto says that it was the wish to determine this doubtful point that first induced him to project his expedition.

In *Peaks, Passes and Glaciers*, 2nd series, vol. ii, p. 260, Mr. Tuckett says that he believed *no Zermatt guide had made the ascent of the Breithorn before* 1859!

ON THE TOP OF THE COL THEODULE.

that can be seen in the Zermatt district; and, although less extensive, is more picturesque than the views from the summits of the still loftier peaks. Rope should be used. Time from the inn on the Theodule to the top about 2 hs. 40 min. The track is marked on the Valley of Zermatt Map. Time descending to the inn 1 h. 15 min.

On leaving the inn, the way to the Breithorn at first slightly descends. It then mounts (for a time rather steeply) to a large snowy plateau, which is invisible from below, and, after that is crossed, turns N. towards the mountain, and leads up a steep bank of snow to the western end of the summit ridge, which is followed to the top. When descending, the **Petit Mont Cervin** (Klein Matterhorn), 12,750 feet, 3886 mètres, can be taken *en route* at the cost of a little more than an hour.]

The descent from the summit of the Theodule into the Val Tournanche commences at first in a N.W. direction, and the way skirts the base of the cliffs of the Furgg Grat, shewn in the illustration on p. 29. In less than half an hour the snow is quitted for *terra firma*, and the path descends in a (generally) W.S.W. direction to Breuil. The slopes are gentle, and one can go anywhere, but it is best to adhere to the path.

Breuil (Breil); HOTEL DU MONT CERVIN (ALBERGO DEL MONTE CERVINO), 6880 feet, 2097 mètres; HOTEL DES JUMEAUX, 6575 feet, 2004 mètres. The former is the larger. The Hotel des Jumeaux (opened in 1895) is kept by Mons. Gab. Maquignaz, one of the very earliest explorers of the S. side of the Matterhorn. See p. 21.

The principal excursions from Breuil are—1. The Ascent of the Matterhorn. 2. Ascent of the Tête du Lion. 3. Ascent of the Dent d'Hérens. 4. Ascent of the Cimes Blanches. The view from the Cimes Blanches is not much inferior to that from the Breithorn, and the ascent can be made at any hour of the day, though early morning is to be preferred.

It often happens that there is a lack of guides at Breuil. In the middle of the season, the Val Tournanche men are more likely to be found at Zermatt than in their own valley. Those at present upon the Register are—

THE HOTEL DES JUMEAUX, BREUIL.

ANSERMIN Agostino di Antonio.
AYMONOD G. Battista di Franc.
BARMASSE Giuseppe di G. Pietro.
BICH Luigi Alberto di Antonio.
BICH Pietro Daniele di Antonio.
CARREL Cesare di G. Giacomo.
CARREL G. Batt. di G. Antonio.
CARREL Luigi di Antonio.
GORRET Carlo di Antonio.
GORRET Massimiliano di G. Pietro.
MAQUIGNAZ Antonio di Pietro.
MAQUIGNAZ Daniele di G. Pietro.
MAQUIGNAZ Giov. Battista.
MEYNET Alberto di Salomone.
MEYNET Salomone di Battista.
PELLISSIER Gius. Andrea di Ant.
PELLISSIER G. Batt. di G. Agost.
PERRON Pietro Luigi di Agostino.
PERRUQUET G. Batt. di Anselmo.
PESSION Alessandro di Pietro.
PESSION Bernardo di Pietro.
PESSION Elia di Antonio.
PESSION Franc. di M. Antonio.
PESSION Pietro Gius. di Nicola.
PESSION Silvano di Pietro.
RAVAZ Salomone di Battista.

About 20 min. below Breuil, a few hundred feet to the E. of the path to Val Tournanche, there is a small lake **(Lac de Layet)** with water of exquisite purity. The lake has no streams flowing into it, yet maintains an almost constant level, although two small streams flow out of it. One of these falls into the Val Tournanche torrent, and the other into a lakelet or pool slightly below the larger one. This lakelet has no visible outlet, yet the level of the water remains almost always the same. The vicinity is well-wooded, and extremely picturesque, and at midday, in good sunlight, the colouring is brilliant.

Upon leaving Breuil **the path to Val Tournanche** follows the left bank of the valley, and for 35 min. keeps close to the torrent and descends gently. At about 50 min. from Breuil it comes to an abrupt descent, alongside the commencement of the **Gouffres de Busserailles,** where the valley narrows, and the torrent disappears in a profound gorge. A little plain succeeds, and then there is another, smaller, descent. In 1 hour from Breuil the path crosses to the right bank. Châlet against the bridge (with wine, beer, etc. at moderate prices), at the entrance to the **Gouffres,** which should be inspected. Admittance 1 franc. The torrent at this part of the valley passes through a fissure, which it has hollowed and polished in a remarkable manner. In Nov. 1865, Jean-Antoine Carrel induced two of the Maquignaz's to lower him by a rope into the chasm. One of the Maquignaz's subsequently descended in the same manner, and they were so struck by what they saw that they forthwith set to work with hammer and chisel to make a way into this romantic gulf, and constructed a rough but convenient plank gallery along its walls. In some places the torrent has wormed the rock and left natural bridges. The most extraordinary features of the Gouffres are the caverns which the water has hollowed out of the heart of the rock. The plank path leads into one of the largest, about 28 feet in diameter, with the torrent 50 feet or so below. The cavern is lighted by candles, and talking in it can only be managed by signs. See *Scrambles amongst the Alps,* chap. vi.

The valley now opens out, and in about 20 min. you arrive at the Village of

Val Tournanche, pop. 1200 (in the Commune); 4813 feet, 1467 mètres; HOTEL DU MONT ROSE, small and plain. Very civil proprietor, who has kept the house for 40 years. *Order Trout.* They are sometimes taken here up to 6 lbs. in weight. The Church of Val Tournanche is ornate internally, and has tablets outside to the memory of Canon Carrel (see p. 75), Jean-Antoine Carrel (p. 86, etc.), and J.-J. Maquignaz (p. 78). The principal **Excursions** are the ascent of

VILLAGE OF VAL TOURNANCHE.

the **Grand Tournalin,** 11,086 feet, 3379 mètres, situated due E. of the village, from the summit of which there is a magnificent panoramic view (see *Scrambles amongst the Alps,* chap. vi); and the passage of the **Va Cornère** (Gra Cornère, Col Courgnier, or Col du Mont Cornière), 10,325 feet? 3147 mètres? to the W.N.W. of the village,—a convenient way of getting across country to Prerayen in the Valpelline. The mule-path ends and a carriage-road begins at Val Tournanche. A post-cart goes in the afternoon, in 2 hs., to Châtillon, and comes up in the morning in 4 hours. *Before starting, have a clear understanding as to what the charge will be.* Voitures from Val Tournanche to Châtillon cost 8 to 12 francs, according to the bargaining power of the traveller.

Upon leaving Val Tournanche the road descends rapidly, and soon crosses to the right bank of the valley, on which side it continues nearly all the way to Châtillon. It becomes increasingly picturesque, and for the most part of the distance passes through and under luxuriant foliage. Near **Antey,** notice the arches of an aqueduct on the western side of the valley, high above the road. They are *not* Roman, as some guide-books say; and appear to be the remains of an *unfinished* work. In 4 hs. from Val Tournanche you arrive at **Châtillon,** in the Valley of Aosta. HOTEL DE LONDRES (against the bridge); HOTEL-PENSION SUISSE. Trains go up the valley to Aosta in ¾ h., and down the valley to Ivrea and Chivasso for Turin, etc. etc.

NEAR ANTEY.

The following are average times on the Theodule Pass.

Zermatt to Châtillon.

	h.	min.
Zermatt to Gandeck (Gandegg)	3	45
Gandeck to Summit of Theodule Pass	1	30
Summit of Theodule Pass to Breuil	2	10
Breuil to Val Tournanche	1	20
Val Tournanche to Châtillon (on foot)	3	5
Total .	11	50

Châtillon to Zermatt.

	h.	min.
Châtillon to Val Tournanche.	4	
Val Tournanche to Breuil	2	10
Breuil to Summit of Theodule Pass	3	20
Summit of Theodule Pass to Gandeck		45
Gandeck to Zermatt	2	10
Total .	12	25

The **Breuiljoch** and **Furggjoch,** two passes to the W. of the Theodule, at the foot of the Matterhorn, are referred to in chap. xi. The next pass to the west, the **Col de Tournanche,** 11,378 feet, 3468 mètres, crosses from the head of the Tiefenmatten Glacier, a little W. of the Tête du Lion, to the head of the Val Tournanche. On the first passage, made on Aug. 25, 1864, 13 hs. 40 min. were occupied between Zermatt—Breuil. It is seldom traversed, and as a pass is useless. The **Tiefenmattenjoch,** 11,788 feet, 3593 mètres, between the Dent d'Hérens and the Tête de Valpelline, from the head of the western branch of the Tiefenmatten Glacier to the head of the Valpelline, like the last-mentioned, is useless as a pass, and is rarely crossed. Not recommended. Mr. A. W. Moore, who was its discoverer, said of it that it was evidently only passable under the Dent d'Hérens. "It unfortunately happens that this is the exact direction which every prudent man would desire to give as wide a berth as possible. . . The north face of the Dent d'Hérens immediately above is for the most part precipitous rock, but at about half its height runs a broad band of broken *séracs.* How the ice clings to the cliffs at all is a marvel, but that portions of it are liable to, and actually do, come down with a run at varying intervals of time, is a fact which the merest novice would see at a glance. The danger was palpable, and theoretically we ought not to have incurred it."—*Alpine Journal*, vol. v, p. 322.

The **Col de Valpelline,** 11,687 feet, 3562 mètres, the next pass on the west, leading from Zermatt to the Valpelline, is of a more practical character than the last-mentioned passes. For route see the Map of the Valley of Zermatt. It leads up the Zmutt Glacier, Stockhi, and Stock Glacier; passes between the Tête Blanche, 12,303 feet, 3750 mètres, and the Tête de Valpelline, 12,510 feet, 3813

THE VILLAGE OF BIONA.

mètres (either of which may be ascended in 1½ hs. from the summit of the pass); and descends upon Prerayen at the head of the Valpelline, *viâ* the Za-de-Zan Glaciers. From Zermatt to Prerayen or *vice versâ* reckon 10 hours. At Prerayen there is a small inn (poor place); thence to Biona (path sometimes rough) 4 hours. No inn. Wine can be had at the Curé's,—a chamois hunter, gunny and genial. Biona to Valpelline, path good, 1 h. 50 min.; small inn. Valpelline to Aosta in char-a-banc, 1¾ to 2 hs., or on foot a little more. At **Aosta,** HOTEL VICTORIA, against the Railway Station. Excellent hotel, kept by Sig. Bertolini of the Hotel Royal at Courmayeur.

The Valpelline cannot compare in picturesqueness with the Val Tournanche. The most striking view to be seen on the pass is of the Matterhorn, just after crossing the summit from the Italian side. The following deviations from the ordinary route may be made by those who do not mind a little additional labour.

[From the head of the Haut Glacier de Za-de-Zan one can reach Prerayen by crossing the Col du Mont Brulé and the Col de Collon. Upon getting to the highest rocks on the Italian side of the Col de Valpelline, bear round to the right, to the right bank of the glacier, to the **Col du Mont Brulé** (a

THE MATTERHORN, FROM THE TOP OF THE COL DE VALPELLINE.

little to the north of Mont Brulé). Thence descend steep rocks mixed with snow to the head of the **Glacier d'Arolla**; and, upon touching the highest part of the moraine on its right bank, cross the glacier, steering almost due West, to the foot of the cliffs of the peak called l'Evêque. Skirt the base of these cliffs, and presently sweep round to the South, and so arrive at the **Col de Collon** (3130 mètres, 10,269 feet), which is one of the easiest of the high snow-passes in this district. Time, top of Col de Valpelline to highest rocks, 1 h.; rocks to Col du Mont Brulé, 2 hs. 10 min.; Col to moraine, 1 h.; moraine to summit of Col de Collon, 90 min.; Col de Collon to Prerayen, 3 hours.

Prof. Forbes crossed the Col de Collon in 1842, and said, "the only *traveller* I am aware of as having passed here is M. Godefroy," but the pass was well known to the people of the country at that time, and was frequently used by smugglers. In descending towards the Arolla Glacier, Forbes' party came across the body of a man who had perished at the foot of Mont Collon, and lower down discovered remnants of two others. "A dark object was descried on the snow to our left, just under the precipices of Mont Collon. . . This proved to be the body of a man fully clothed, fallen with his head in the direction in which we were going. From the appearance of the body as it lay, it might have been presumed to be recent; but when it was raised, the head and face were found to be in a state of frightful decay, and covered with blood, evidently arising from an incipient thaw, after having remained perhaps for a twelvemonth perfectly congealed. The clothes were quite entire and uninjured, and, being hard frozen, still protected the corpse beneath. It was evident that an unhappy peasant had been overtaken in a storm, probably of the previous year, and had lain there covered with snow during the whole winter and spring, and that we were now, in the month of August, the first travellers who had passed this way. The hands were gloved and in the pockets, in the attitude of a person maintaining the last glow of heat, and the body being extended on the snow, which was pretty steep, it appeared that he had been hurrying towards the valley when his strength was exhausted, and he lay simply as he fell. . . A very little farther on we found traces of another victim, probably of an earlier date;—some shreds of clothes, and fragments of a knapsack; but the body had disappeared. Still lower, the remains of the bones and skin of two chamois, and near them the complete bones of a man. The latter were arranged in a very singular manner, nearly the whole skeleton being there in detached bones, laid in order along the ice,—the skull lowest, next the arms and ribs, and finally the bones of the pelvis, legs, and feet, disposed along the glacier, so that the distance between the head and feet might be five yards." It was subsequently found that the body first discovered was that of a man who had started with eleven others to cross into Italy. Being overtaken by storm, they resolved to return; but three of the number, worn out by fatigue, dropped behind and perished.]

The Col d'Hérens (formerly called **Col d'Erin**), 11,418 feet, 3480 mètres, leading from Zermatt to the Val d'Hérens, is an old pass, which is traversed rather frequently during the season. Track is marked on the Valley of Zermatt Map. Prof. Forbes, who crossed it in 1842, said he proposed to call it the **Col d'Erin**, *as it had not yet received a name;* and remarked that Venetz wrote in 1833 that this pass was so dangerous that he had never known but one man who had accomplished it. "I first heard of it," said Forbes, "from a guide at Zermatt, Peter Damatter, who told me, in 1841, that he had passed it."

As a whole it is easy. When going from Zermatt, the route is the same as for the Col de Valpelline so far as the middle of the Stock Glacier. It then turns N.N.W., and crosses the ridge leading from the Tête Blanche to the Wandfluh. There is a small, rather steep, wall of rock and snow to ascend, at the base of which there is usually a small bergschrund. On the northern side of the pass the slopes are gentle. From Zermatt to Alpe Bricolla (Abricolla) reckon 10-11 hours.

The **Col de la Dent Blanche** (originally called **Zinaljoch**), 11,483 feet, 3500 mètres, leading from Zermatt to Zinal and the Val d'Anniviers, which passes between the Dent Blanche and the Pointe de Zinal, was first crossed on Sept. 6, 1872, by Mr. T. S. Phillpotts, with Peter Knubel and Elie Petter. They took 7¾ hs. from Mountet to Zermatt. "Three hours to summit from Mountet. Nearly 2 hs. were taken descending on the right of the Schönbuhl Glacier to Stockje. Ascent and descent easy. The first part of south side much exposed to stones from Dent Blanche, and therefore had better be taken early . . . 2¾ hs. Stockje to Zermatt."—*Alpine Journal*, vol. vi, p. 437. The track is marked on the Valley of Zermatt Map. Confusion has been caused by changing the original name of this pass.

The **Col Durand**, 11,398 feet, 3474 mètres, between the Pointe de Zinal and Mont Durand (Arbenhorn),[1] leading to the Val d'Anniviers, is one of the easier of the high snow-passes in this district. According to Conway's *Climber's Guide to the Central Pennine Alps*, the summit has been reached in 2 hs. from Mountet, and descent from the summit to Zermatt has been effected in 3 hours. When going from Zermatt over the Col Durand, pass through the village of Zmutt, and keep on the left bank of the Zmutt Valley.

The **Arbenjoch**, 11,975 feet, 3650 mètres, between Mont Durand (Arbenhorn) and the Ober Gabelhorn, leading from Zermatt to the Val d'Anniviers, is one of the loftiest passes to the W. of Zermatt, and one of the finest, from the Alpinist's point of view. Its passage was first effected on July 8, 1875, by Mr. W. E. Davidson, with Laurent Lanier (Courmayeur) and a porter from Vissoie. They left Zinal at 2.45 a.m., proposing to cross the Col Durand, but at the Roc noir changed their intention, and "turned to the left, bore diagonally across a snow plain, and passing beneath a range of enormous ice-cliffs, which rendered a direct approach to the Col impossible, arrived without difficulty at the foot of the N.W. face of the Gabelhorn, . . . passing upwards between two gigantic tiers of ice-cliffs, which were in a most unstable condition. The passage of the *séracs* was a work of much difficulty. . . It was not until 2 p.m. that we reached the plateau above the ice-fall, and we were then compelled, by the size and number of the crevasses, to bear to the left a long way out of our course until, at a point about 300 feet below the western arête of the Gabelhorn, we crossed the bergschrund which guards its N.W. face. The final slope was hard ice, and it cost us 1½ hs. of constant step-cutting to gain the ridge. . . The descent was by steep but easy rocks to the Arben Glacier, whence the route to Zermatt, which was reached at 8.45 p.m., presents no difficulty whatever. . . All the difficulties are on the Zinal side. . . Time from Zinal to the Col, 13 hs. actual walking; Col to Zermatt, 3 hs. 20 min. actual walking."—*Alpine Journal*, vol. vii, p. 321. The Ober Gabelhorn can be ascended from the Arbenjoch. See p. 150.

The **Triftjoch**, 11,614 feet, 3540 mètres, between the Trifthorn and Wellenkuppe, leading from Zermatt to the Val d'Anniviers, is reputed to be an old pass, and it is the most direct one that can be taken. Frequently used during the season. Route is marked on the Valley of Zermatt Map.

The way from Zermatt leads up the Trift Gorge, passes the Trift inn and Triftkummen (see p. 146), and ascends for a considerable distance by a path on the crest of a moraine on the left bank of the Trift Glacier. Then there is a little piece of glacier to be traversed, which is separated by a small bergschrund from the final bit leading to the pass. This is a mixture of snow and rock.

The descent is at first by steep rocks, much broken up and not difficult. At the base of this cliff there is another small bergschrund; and, when this is left behind, a nearly straight course can be steered to the Mountet *cabane*, 9475 feet, 2888 mètres, at the southern foot of Besso. At this hut there is a guardian, from whom food can be purchased.

	h.	min.
Zermatt to summit of Triftjoch	4	45
Summit of Triftjoch to Mountet	2	
Mountet to Zinal	3	10
Total .	9	55
Zinal to Mountet	4	15
Mountet to summit of Triftjoch	3	
Summit of Triftjoch to Zermatt (moving briskly) .	2	45
Total . .	10	

[1] This name is not given on the Valley of Zermatt Map. The peak is marked 3744.

In re falling stones.—Mr. T. W. Hinchcliff went over this pass in 1857, and said that, so far as he had been able to discover, it "had only been twice crossed in modern times." He dwelt in his account upon the risk from falling stones on the Zinal side, and since that time it has been well-known that they come down in such numbers and with such frequency as to be dangerous,—more particularly after the sun strikes the upper cliffs of the Trifthorn. He had halted for lunch, some distance from the base of the cliffs, "when," he said, "a booming sound, like the discharge of a gun far over our heads, made us all at once glance upwards to the top of the Trifthorn. Close to its craggy summit hung a cloud of dust, like dirty smoke, and in a few seconds another and a larger one burst forth several hundred feet lower. A glance through the telescope showed that a fall of rocks had commenced, and the fragments were leaping down from ledge to ledge in a series of cascades. Each block dashed off others at every point of contact, and the uproar became tremendous; thousands of fragments, making every variety of noise according to their size, and producing the effect of a fire of musketry and artillery combined, thundered downwards from so great a height that we waited anxiously for some considerable time to see them reach the snow-field below. As nearly as we could estimate the distance, we were 500 yards from the base of the rocks, so we thought that, come what might, we were in a tolerably secure position. At last we saw many of the blocks plunge into the snow after taking their last fearful leap; presently much larger fragments followed, taking proportionably larger bounds; the noise grew fiercer and fiercer, and huge blocks began to fall so near to us that we jumped to our feet, preparing to dodge them to the best of our ability. 'Look out!' cried some one, and we opened out right and left at the approach of a monster, evidently weighing many hundredweight, which was coming right at us like a huge shell fired from a mortar. It fell with a heavy thud not more than twenty feet from us, scattering lumps of snow into the circle where we had just been dining; but scarcely had we begun to recover from our astonishment when a still larger rock flew exactly over our heads to a distance of 200 yards beyond us. . . Even Cachat" [Zacharie Cachat, of Chamonix] "looked somewhat bewildered, and . . exclaimed 'Ah! si ma femme pouvait savoir où je suis à présent!'"—*Peaks, Passes and Glaciers*, 1st series.

A Tragedy on the Trift.—Two English ladies, Miss Sampson and Miss Growse, left the Riffelalp Hotel at 2 a.m. on Aug. 30, 1895, with Louis Carrel (Val Tournanche) and Anton Biener (Zermatt), intending to cross the Triftjoch on the same day! They went down to Zermatt, walked up to the Trift Hotel, and stopped to get provisions there. The people of the inn had not risen, delay occurred, and, in consequence, they arrived on the top of the Pass somewhere about 10 a.m.—later than was advisable. However, they descended the cliff on the Mountet side all right, and were about to cross the small bergschrund at its base,—Carrel leading, followed by Miss Growse, then Miss Sampson, with Biener behind her. Carrel was just at the bergschrund, cutting steps. "All at once," said he, "I heard a great noise, and saw stones coming down. Said I to myself, 'We are all lost.' I shouted 'cachez-vous!'" a thing which it was impossible for them to do. Louis crouched down against the upper lip of the bergschrund, and was only struck by some small fragments. Miss Growse was rather severely bruised by the blows she received, but was not seriously hurt. Miss Sampson was hit in the back, and so was Biener. A flask he carried was crushed. "How large was the stone which struck Miss Sampson, Louis?" "I am not sure," he said, "one couldn't see clearly, but I think about as large as this,"—indicating a cube of about 16 inches. "What did you do then?" "She could not walk, and I took her on my back; but more steps had to be cut, and we got along slowly." "You cut with one hand, and held her on with the other?" "Yes. "Had she any strength?" "Yes, she hung on to me, with her hands over my shoulders." "Could she talk?" "Yes, but I couldn't understand what she said, for she spoke in English." "Go on with the story." "I carried her until we were out of reach of falling stones, and then laid her on the snow, on my coat and other things. She was then alive." "How long was this after the accident?" "About an hour. Just then, the guardian of the Mountet hut came up, with two of his men. He had seen that there was something wrong, and hurried across the glacier to meet us. 'She is dying,' he said to me. It was so. She turned pale, her eyes closed, and it was all over."

Miss Sampson was buried at Zermatt on Sept. 2 (see p. 132). An unusual degree of sympathy was manifested by the Zermatters upon this occasion.

The **Moming Pass**, 12,444 feet, 3793 mètres, which goes between the Zinal Rothhorn and the Schallhorn (Schallihorn), is another way which may be taken from Zermatt to Zinal and the Val d'Anniviers. Circuitous. Not recommended. See *Scrambles amongst the Alps*, chap. xii.

Zinal, 5505 feet, 1678 mètres; **Hotels**—HOTEL DURAND (the oldest); HOTEL DIABLONS; HOTEL DU BESSO; is growing in public estimation, and many persons wish to go there from Zermatt. The easiest, quickest, and most economical way is to take train from Zermatt to Sierre; telegraph beforehand to have a char waiting at the Railway Station; ride to **Vissoye**, 3980 feet, 1213 mètres, HOTEL-PENSION D'ANNIVIERS; and walk from Vissoye to Zinal. It can be done in 9 hs., at a cost of 28 frs.

Leave Zermatt	6.40 a.m.
Arr. Sierre	10.13 ,,
do. Vissoye (in char)	1.10 p.m.
do. Zinal (on foot)	3.40 ,,
Total .	9 hours.

The cost is 11 frs. 50 cts. for the train from Zermatt to Sierre (3rd class), and 16 frs. 50 cts. for a char from Sierre to Vissoye, including *bonnemain* to driver.

This brings us to the end of the Passes to the South and West of Zermatt. For others, situated to its East and South-east, it is more convenient to start from the Riffelalp Hotel. See Chap. x.

MONUMENT TO T. W. HINCHCLIFF.

CHAPTER X.

EXCURSIONS FROM THE RIFFELALP AND RIFFELBERG HOTELS.

EARLY ATTEMPTS TO ASCEND MONTE ROSA—THE FIRST ASCENT OF MONTE ROSA—THE HÖCHSTE SPITZE (DUFOURSPITZE)—*CABANE BÉTEMPS*—WINTER ASCENT OF MONTE ROSA—THE NORD END—THE LYSKAMM (SILBERBAST)—DEATH OF MR. CHESTER—LOSS OF MESSRS. LEWIS AND PATERSON—ANOTHER SNOW-CORNICE ACCIDENT—CASTOR AND POLLUX (ZWILLINGE, OR THE TWINS)—THE BREITHORN FROM THE NORTH—A TOUR ROUND THE BREITHORN—CIMA DI JAZZI—THE STRAHLHORN—PASSES—THE ADLERPASS—SCHWARZBERG WEISSTHOR—NEW WEISSTHOR—OLD WEISSTHOR—SESIAJOCH—LYSJOCH—FELIKJOCH—ZWILLINGSPASS—SCHWARZTHOR.

IN a certain sense, excursions from the Riffelalp Hotel (or from the Riffelhaus) are also excursions from Zermatt; but most persons will find it to their comfort to use the Riffelalp Hotel as a starting-point for those which are mentioned in this chapter. There are, besides, a number of little excursions that can be made in the vicinity of the Hotel, which has the advantages of being free from external noises and nuisances, and of being surrounded by ground (partly open and partly tree-covered) over which the tourist can roam at pleasure. A path to the Findelen Valley starts at the back of the Hotel (by the side of which there is a monument erected to the late Mr. T. W. Hinchcliff), and various other erratic paths, leading nowhere in particular, will be found in the same direction. It goes without saying that excursions to the Gornergrat or the Findelen Valley, and ascents of Gugel and the Riffelhorn are made from the Riffelalp Hotel (or from the Riffelhaus) with even greater facility than from Zermatt itself.

The Ascent of Monte Rosa, 15,217 feet, 4638 métres, has become extremely popular. As no records are preserved, it is impossible to say how many ascents are made. They are probably much more numerous than those of Mont Blanc. The first ascent of the highest point was effected by the Messrs. Smyth in 1855. See pages 15, 17.

THE RIFFELALP HOTEL.

Prior to their success several efforts had been made to get to the top *vià* the Silbersattel, the *depression* between the Nord End and Monte Rosa proper (or Dufourspitze, as it is now termed by the Swiss). The height of this Col is 14,731 feet, and the difference of level between it and the very highest point is only 486 feet, but this small distance proved too much for the early explorers.

It is stated that Prof. Ulrich got to the Silbersattel in 1848; and again, with G. Studer, in 1849. In 1851, Hermann and Adolph Schlagintweit (who afterwards became known as Himalayan travellers) appear to have mounted to some height *above* the Silbersattel, and in

1854, an Englishman, Mr. S. D. Bird,[1] is said to have climbed within a hundred feet of the top,—which is, perhaps, doubtful. Shortly afterwards, Messrs. Smyth made the first ascent of the Strahlhorn, and the majestic appearance of Monte Rosa when seen from that direction induced them to make the attempts which followed. Their first effort was in Aug. 1854, and the next upon the succeeding Sept. 1. By the courtesy of Canon Smyth I am able to give the following extracts from an account which was written shortly afterwards.

ASCENT OF MONTE ROSA. Friday, Sept. 1, 1854.

"The following Ascent was made by three brothers—Captain Edmund Smyth, 13th Bengal N.I.; James Grenville Smyth, Vicar of N. & S. Elkington, Lincolnshire; Christopher Smyth, Rector of Woodford, Northampton.

After an unsuccessful attempt to ascend this beautiful mountain, owing to cloudy weather,[2] we determined to make another trial, and accordingly, after an early breakfast, started at 2 a.m. from the Hotel de Riffel, ourselves three in number, with four guides, one of whom carried a ladder, and a porter to carry part of the baggage for the first 3 or 4 hours. One of these guides was Ulrich Lauener of Lauterbrunnen,[3] a man whose value we had learnt by experience, having crossed with him some of the highest and most difficult passes in the Alps,—the rest were Zermatt guides. . . .

Our path for the first 40 minutes lay along the West side of the Riffel, leaving the Riffelhorn on the right,—from this point is obtained the first view of the upper part of the Gorner Glacier. Here our path turned to the left, passing along the side of a steep slope, inclined at an angle occasionally of 60°. Above us was the path leading to the Gornergrat, about 700 feet below us was the glacier. The path continued in the same direction, keeping along the side of, and gradually descending towards the glacier, which we reached in about 2¾ hours from the Hotel. . . We were longer about this part of our journey than we should otherwise have been, for it was still too dark to see clearly, and we had nothing but one tallow candle to help us. Fortunately, on arriving at the glacier, the twilight was sufficiently advanced for us. Here, as may be supposed, all traces of a path ceased. Our way now lay directly across the glacier towards the rocks at the foot of Monte Rosa, leaving what is called in the maps the Gorner See on the left. This See or Lake no longer exists. It has been drained since last year by new crevasses in the Glacier. The site of the Lake is marked by a large hollow in the ice of some acres in extent. . . It takes an hour to cross this enormous glacier, which stretches from the Old Weiss Thor Pass to within about 2 miles of Zermatt.

We arrived at the opposite side in about 3 hours from the Hotel, during which time we had advanced very little in actual height. Now, however, the ascent began in earnest, at first over the rocks, which was comparatively easy work. Soon we had again to walk upon the glacier by the side of the rocks. Here it was more crevassed, and in consequence greater care was required. The danger in walking over glaciers consists not so much in what you can see as in what you cannot see. . . It is seldom the guides are deceived. A good guide will go on steadily until he comes to the treacherous places, which are

[1] I have been unable to learn anything about Mr. Bird, and shall be glad of information.

[2] "The Riffelberg Hotel, a poor shanty then, had just been opened. Having previously surveyed our ground, we started in the afternoon, and slept under the slight shelter of some rocks a few hundred feet above the Gorner Glacier, on the side of Monte Rosa, with sheep-skins to keep us warm. Beware of sheep-skins!! I remember that night well enough, when we had hardly room to scratch ourselves, fitting into each other like spoons! The next morning we made for the Sattel between the highest point and the Nord End, but finally a change in the weather, with a south wind drove us back to the friendly Riffel to wait for better times."—*Letter from the Rev. Christopher Smyth.*

[3] Two others were Johann and Matthias zum Taugwald.—*E. W.*

generally known by the increased whiteness of the snow. Here he digs in his bâton, finds out the breadth of the crevasse, and if practicable leaps across; or, if not, walks along the side until he comes to a practicable place. Sometimes he divides his weight by crawling on his hands and knees, while the rest cautiously follow in his footsteps. This was our manner of proceeding for 5 hours, occasionally stopping to rest, or eat, or to admire the increasing beauty of the scenery, as we gradually rose to the level of all the surrounding mountains.

On approaching the summit the crevasses became larger and more picturesque, the huge masses of ice stood out in bold relief far above us, on one side. . . One of these crevasses stretched completely across our way, with no means of passing except by a narrow bridge of snow. Fortunately, this natural bridge was strong enough to bear our weight; we all crossed in safety, and in due time arrived at the ridge between the Northern and the Highest peaks. This spot I believe to be about 14,800 feet above the sea. Here we sat down on our waterproofs for about 20 minutes to rest ourselves, and to enjoy the view, before proceeding to the most difficult part of our expedition.

The Highest Peak of Monte Rosa consists of a long ridge of rock partially covered with snow and ice. Very narrow at the top, and so steep as to be almost inaccessible,—indeed I should imagine it was wholly inaccessible to any but first-rate guides. We were fortunate enough in having as good a guide with us as any in Switzerland. We had brought up the ladder from below with a view of climbing this rock, but it was useless. Even our bâtons were of no use to us here. From this point to the top it was a scramble up steep rock covered with ice.

On making a start we were each of us attached by a short rope to a guide, a most necessary precaution, as a single slip might (and probably would) have been fatal. The first part of this ascent being less steep was the easiest, and by treading in each other's footsteps we managed to get along pretty easily, but this did not last long. We soon came to the steeper rocks, and then every muscle in the body was brought into action. . . Here our guides left us for half an hour while they cut steps in the ice.

This was the most disagreeable part of all. As long as we were in the sunshine or in exercise we felt pretty well, but now sitting, or rather half-reclining, in the shade, with nothing but a rock covered with ice to rest upon, to which I suppose may be added the rarefaction of the air, all these things combined brought on excessive faintness. The feeling was one of entire helplessness, as if the proper place for one were a comfortable bed, where one could lie down and go to sleep. . . Fortunately, this feeling did not last long. A little cognac soon restored us, and when the guides were ready for us, we were ready to continue our scramble. The remainder of the journey to the top was so steep and so slippery that we had to be helped up the whole distance, notwithstanding the steps cut in the ice.

I might mention here that the guides are generally more careful of travellers than travellers are of themselves, their fault (if fault it can be called) is *over-caution*, they *will* help you when you feel you don't want help. . . On the present occasion there was good reason for the greatest caution; for, although we were all three of us accustomed to climbing, yet the scrambling up a precipice over blocks of stone covered with ice was quite a new thing. The three ropes by which we had been before attached to three of our guides were now fastened together, and one by one we were helped up the rocks by a guide who sat above us, in this way we proceeded the rest of the distance to the summit.

I said the highest peak of Monte Rosa consisted of a long narrow ridge. Upon this ridge there are three small peaks of nearly equal height,—the middle one of the three being a few feet higher than the others. The point at which we were now arrived was the most Eastern, had time and weather allowed us, we should have liked to have proceeded to the other two points, but as it was now 12 o'clock, and the clouds were beginning to gather all round us, we thought it inadvisable to venture, especially as the road appeared to be

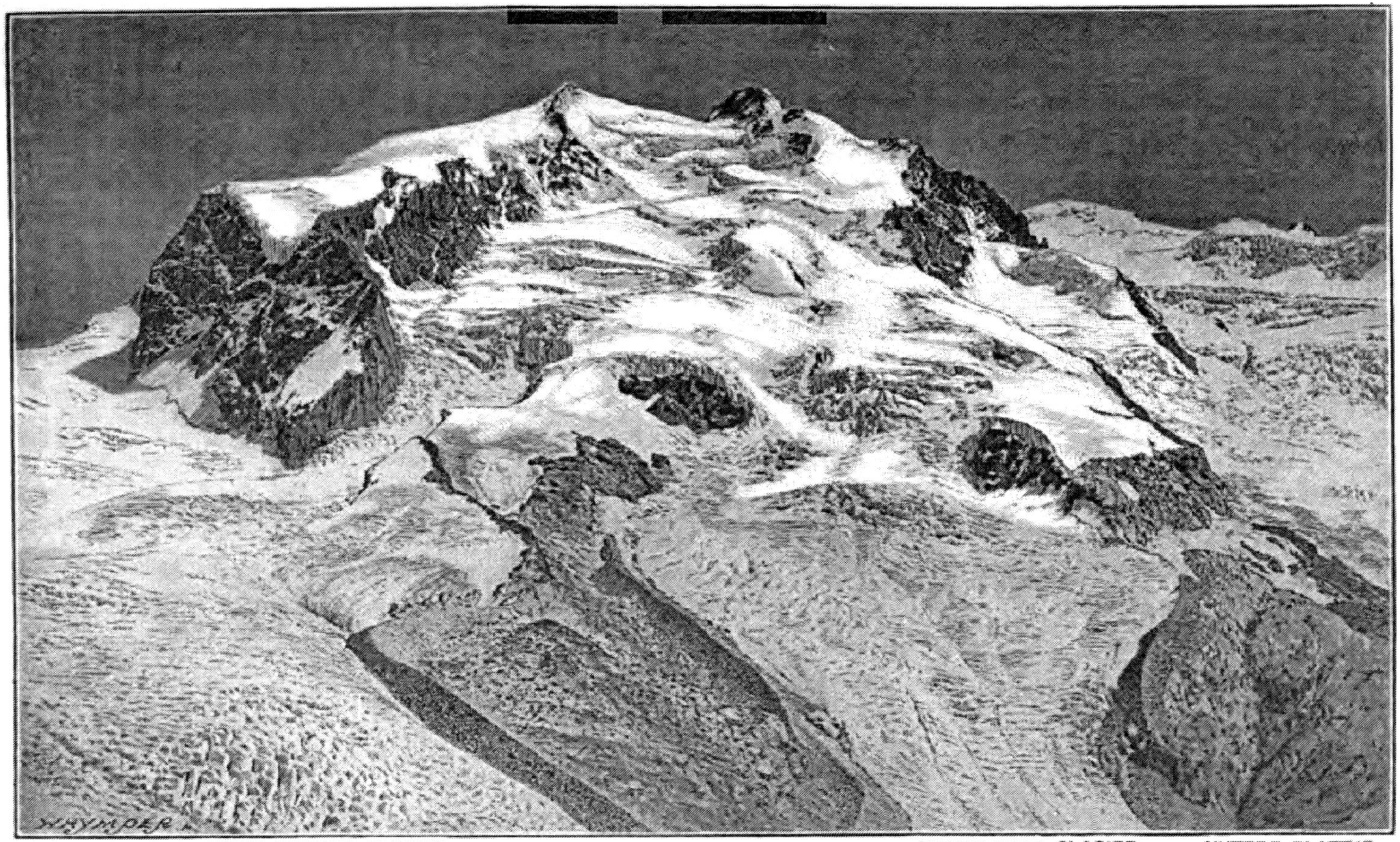

MONTE ROSA, FROM THE GORNERGRAT.

more dangerous than anything we had yet encountered, owing to the narrowness of the ridge and the quantity of black ice upon the rocks. We stayed at the summit about half an hour during which time our guides amused themselves by building a cairn and planting our flag.[1]

. . . .

We now began to think of returning. Again the ropes were brought into requisition, and we were one by one let down a short distance at a time, until we were beyond the most dangerous parts. We then clambered down as best we could, until we arrived at the foot of the peak in safety. It took us an hour and a half to reach the summit from this point, and nearly the same time to return, although the distance was really so small.

The descent from here was comparatively easy. We went over the snow very rapidly, performing in two hours what had taken five in ascending. The same care, however, was required in crossing the crevasses,—but with this exception the descent was easy. In two hours we reached the rocks at the foot of the mountain. We now crossed the Gorner Glacier, and in an hour reached the path we had used in the morning. We arrived at the Hotel de Riffel at ½ past 7, having been 17 hours on the expedition."

It is obvious from this relation that Messrs. Smyth were aware that they had not reached the very highest point, as it is mentioned explicitly that there were three peaks of nearly equal height, the middle one being a few feet higher than the others, and that they went upon *the most Eastern one.*

In July, 1855, Messrs. Christopher and Grenville Smyth were again at Zermatt, and amongst other things ascended the Breithorn and Petit Mont Cervin, with some friends.

"Two days after this, as some of the party wished to ascend Monte Rosa, and as Chris. and I only looked upon the expedition as rather a long day's walk, we determined to join them. Accordingly we were called at 11 p.m.!! On Tuesday, July 31, breakfasted about ¼ to 12, and started (5 of us with 4 guides) at ½ past 12. The moon was about full and the night most beautiful. We went over nearly the same ground as last year, until we arrived about two hours from the top. Here the glacier by which we formerly ascended was so broken that we were obliged to turn to the right and began to ascend the highest peak from the West instead of from the East. The snow was very steep and in many places had become ice, so that more than a hundred steps had to be cut. . . Whilst steps were being made, after about an hour's halt, we started again,—the wind was still very cold, though not violent, and the sun had some little power. There were now two steep ridges of snow to mount, almost every step of which had to be cut, after which there was about half an hour's climbing up and down steep rocks, and then we stood the first human beings upon the very highest point of the highest peak of this glorious mountain. . . We descended in safety, and much more quickly than we went up, sliding and running down the snow which had taken so long a time in ascending, and arrived at the Hotel not very late in the afternoon."[2]

From this account it appears that the adoption of the new way was partly accidental rather than intentional, and this arose from

[1] "Having no flag, my brother, Col. Smyth, sacrificed his alpenstock and one of two shirts he was wearing. Apropos of this banner. An Englishman ascending shortly afterwards by the same route cut from the shirt the portion on which my brother's name was marked, and one day at a dinner-table was relating the story of his climb, and of the trophy he had brought down with him, and had then in his possession. My brother overheard the conversation, and asked him to produce it, which he did at once."—*Letter from the Rev. Christopher Smyth.*

[2] Extract from a letter from Canon Smyth, dated Aug. 9, 1855. Ulrich Lauener was again the leading guide.

the glacier by which they had formerly ascended being so broken that they "were *obliged* to turn to the right" and so began to ascend the highest peak from the West. The Rev. Christopher Smyth, however, informs me that they were determined to try the new way from doubting the practicability of the old one, and that when they made off for the ridge the guides lagged behind and moved on slowly towards the Sattel. "Nor did they rejoin us till they saw us begin the ascent of the dome-shaped slope of ice and snow which leads to the final rocks. Perceiving that we were prepared to go on without them, and that our success without them might be prejudicial to their prestige as guides, they once more took the lead; but were not very useful, nor do I think much credit was due to them.[1] We did not rope, nor was the helping hand needed. I think Ulrich Lauener cut a few steps. He was head of the party, and reached the top first."

The route taken by Messrs. Birkbeck, Hudson, Stevenson and Smyth on Aug. 1, 1855,[2] is the route which is followed still, so far as the *upper* part of the mountain is concerned. It goes along the ridge which leads due W. from the highest point. See Map of the Valley of Zermatt. But at the commencement it differs from the way they took. It now leads over the rocks called Untere Plattje. See Illustration on p. 169, and the View from the Gornergrat at the end of the volume. The *cabane* Bétemps, built upon the western side of these rocks, is now commonly used as a starting-point. This little place (completed in 1894) cost nearly £600 to erect, towards which the Swiss Alpine Club contributed 11,792 francs! It has a guardian, from whom food can be obtained. The authorized *tarif* for provisions, etc., should be posted up in the *cabane* and in the Hotels of Zermatt.

THE CABANE BÉTEMPS.

The highest point of Monte Rosa (or Monte Rosa proper) has also been ascended from the South (*Alpine Journal*, vol. vii, p. 107); and by its S.E. ridge (*A. J.* vol. viii, p. 339). "Our route is recommended to future climbers, who do not mind rotten rocks, plenty of falling stones, and but little good handhold or footing during three and a half hours." It has been ascended,

[1] The Rev. E. W. Stevenson writes much to the same effect. "On arrival at the summit," he says, "the guide who had been cutting the steps" (Lauener) "was with us; one came up some time afterwards, and one never came up at all."

[2] Not July 31, as is frequently stated.

too, from Macugnaga, by the E. face. Although this latter is a very fine excursion, those who undertake it should not conceal from themselves that it is a hazardous one (*A. J.* vol. vi, pp. 91, 232-44).

The highest point and the Nord End in one day.—On Aug. 10, 1877, Messrs. W. Penhall and G. Scriven, with Ferdinand Imseng and P. J. Truffer, combined the ascent of the Nord End and the highest point. They followed the usual Monte Rosa route to a little above Auf'm Felsen, and bearing away to the left took to the rocks of the Nord End. Descending to the Silbersattel, they remounted to the highest point.

A Winter ascent of Monte Rosa.—Signor Vittorio Sella camped under canvas on the moraine of the Grenz Glacier on Jan. 25, 1884, with Joseph and Daniel Maquignaz (Val Tournanche). Starting next morning at 4 a.m., they gained the summit at 1.30 p.m. Up to the height of 3700 mètres (12,139 feet), the snow was soft and powdery. Higher up it was harder. The camp was regained at 5.30 p.m. On the third day they reached Zermatt *viâ* the Gornergrat and Riffel. Temperature on the summit was - 16° C., and the minimum observed during the expedition was - 17° C.

Accidents.—A fatal accident of a vulgar type occurred upon Monte Rosa on July 27, 1865. Two Englishmen, with three guides and two porters, started to make the ascent soon after the fall of a large amount of snow; and when near the Saddle (close to the top) started an avalanche, and were all more or less buried in it, except two of the guides. One porter was smothered. On Aug. 8, 1881, Sig. Marinelli, with Ferdinand Imseng and B. Pedranzini, attempted to ascend Monte Rosa by its E. face, and, getting in the track of an avalanche, were all killed. Avalanches of sorts fall frequently on that side.

The **Nord End,** 15,132 feet, 4612 mètres, the second highest peak of Monte Rosa, was ascended in 1861 (date not recorded) by Mr. Edward North Buxton, Sir T. Fowell Buxton (now Governor of South Australia) and Mr. J. J. Cowell, with Michel Payot and other guides. See *Peaks, Passes and Glaciers,* 2nd series, vol. ii, pp. 412-22.

The positions and elevations of the lower peaks of Monte Rosa (Jägerhorn, Balmenhorn, Ludwigshöhe, Parrotspitze, Signalkuppe, and Zumsteinspitze) are given in Appendix E.

The **Lyskamm (Silberbast),**[1] 14,889 feet, 4538 mètres, is exceeded in elevation by mountains in the Zermatt district only by Monte Rosa and the Dom. It forms the most prominent object seen from the Gornergrat, and looks its best from 9.30 to 11 a.m. The first ascent was made on Aug. 19, 1861, by the party whose names are given on p. 18, led by Peter Perren (Perrn).[2] The course was for the greater part of the way the same as that which leads to the Lysjoch (up the Grenz Glacier, formerly called the Monte Rosa Glacier), but, before reaching the Col, turned off to the right, up 'a rather stiffish snow-slope,' to the ridge leading E.S.E. from the summit. When the crest of this was reached, they doubled back (*i.e.* turned to the right), and followed the crest or *arête* of the ridge to the top. Perren went up "in magnificent style, kicking and cutting steps with a skill and rapidity which I have seldom seen

1 "The old name 'Silberbast' for the Lyskamm has almost been forgotten. . . Yet the word 'Bast' must be familiar to many visitors to Zermatt, for it is applied in the local dialect to the wooden saddles of the pack-mules. It does not require a great deal of imagination to suppose that the name 'Silberbast' was given to the Lyskamm because, seen from the Gornergrat, it has the appearance of a huge snowy pack-saddle, and the name is therefore very appropriate."—*Herr A. Lorria.*

2 Not the Peter Perrn mentioned on p. 151.

equalled, stopping only now and then to shout down to us a hoarse query as to the state of the snow above him, lest he should unwarily tread upon an overhanging cornice."—*Peaks, Passes and Glaciers*, 2nd series, vol. i, pp. 389-90. 17 hs. 20 min. were occupied from the Riffel to the top and back. The Lyskamm has been ascended from several other directions, but the route generally taken from the Riffel-alp Hotel is substantially that which was first adopted. Though the ordinary way up the Lyskamm cannot be accounted difficult, it affords various possibilities, some of which will be illustrated presently.

Winter Ascents.—Signor Vittorio Sella, the accomplished photographer, reached the top from the Italian side on Mar. 22, 1885, and this was again done by two other Italians on Mar. 4, 1889.

Co-operation.—In 1866, Messrs. F. Morshead and H. Walker, with Melchior and Jakob Anderegg, and Mr. J. H. Kitson with Christian Almer, left the Riffel together for the Lyskamm. Separating on the Gorner Glacier, the former gentlemen ascended by the Zwillinge Glacier and the Western *arête*, arriving at the summit at 10.15; and Mr. Kitson ascended by the Eastern *arête*, arriving at 9.35. Thus the two parties were together on the top, and descending each by the *arête* by which the other had ascended, they met on the Gorner Glacier again.—*Alpine Journal*, vol. ii, p. 414.

A Tour of the Lyskamm and its Ascent combined.—In July, 1867, Messrs. C. E. Mathews and F. Morshead, with Christian Almer, left the Riffel at midnight; ascended to the top of the Felikjoch by a few minutes past 5; bore round to the left on to the western part of the Lys Glacier, and made for the rocks running South from the Lyskamm. These were ascended. At 10.15 a.m. they were on the summit; then descended to the Lysjoch, and got back to the Riffel at 6 p.m.

Death of Mr. Henry Chester (1869).—At 4 a.m. on Sept. 15, 1869, Mr. Chester (a London solicitor) left the Riffel with two guides, to ascend the Lyskamm. A little before 10 on the evening of the same day the guides returned with the news that he was dead. They stated that they had reached the summit at 2.45 p.m., and had almost immediately commenced the descent. "Mr. Chester, being very tired, had stumbled several times, but he had got to the end of the narrow part of the *arête* without an actual fall. At this point he insisted upon going" to look for traces of a dog which he had taken with him, and which had disappeared during the ascent. In going, he fell forwards on his face; the guides were not alert at the moment, and were dragged off their feet by his fall. "The whole three had immediately bounded over an ice-cliff, and at last, after slipping down a slope estimated by the guides as being some eight hundred to a thousand feet in height, had lodged on the Grenz Glacier beneath." This was the account given by the two guides.

At 3 a.m. on the following morning four Englishmen, Mr. W. E. Hall (barrister), Mr. (now the Right Hon. Lord Justice) Rigby, Mr. Porter (now Master of St. Peter's Coll., Cambridge), and Mr. Fowler, started with ten men for the scene of the accident, and found Mr. Chester dead, with his neck broken. The tracks on the snow, and other circumstances, led to the belief that the story of the guides was, at least in part, an invention. An official investigation of the usual character was subsequently held at Zermatt. As the result of this was not made known, Mr. Hall communicated a paper to the Alpine Club upon the subject, in which he said, "M. Clemenz" (who held the investigation) "promised to me—and when Mr. Chester's brother arrived at Zermatt to him also—that his decision and the grounds of it should be fully communicated to us. For a long time expectation that M. Clemenz would fulfil his promise naturally and necessarily closed our mouths. But when more than six months have gone by, and when a date, fixed after several letters as that in which the decision should arrive in England has been passed by nearly eight weeks, it becomes necessary, if any good effect is to be produced during the coming summer by the publication of the truth, that the dilatory courtesy of M. Clemenz should no longer be waited for. . . I am content that my action should be sufficiently justified by the fact that like promises were made after the accident on the Matterhorn, and that they were never fulfilled."[1] Mr. Hall concluded by saying that, whatever might be the motive for M. Clemenz's silence, the effect of it was unfortunate on the Guides of Zermatt, and, in that opinion, I entirely concur.

The death of Mr. Chester remains a mystery. There *was* a dog with the party, but it is by no means certain that Mr. Chester went to look after it, or that it had anything to do with his death.

Three Guides and two Tourists perish by breaking through a snow-cornice (1877).—"On Sept. 6, 1877, Messrs. William Arnold Lewis and Noel H. Paterson, with Niklaus, Johann and Peter Joseph Knubel" (of St. Nicholas) "left the Riffelhaus at 2 a.m., to make the ascent of the Lyskamm. As they did not return that night, Mr. J. A. Carfrae, accompanied by Peter Knubel, Joseph Imboden and J. J. Truffer" (of St. Nicholas) "started the following morning at 6.30 in search. They followed the tracks of Mr. Lewis's party to the foot of the *arête* leading down from the summit of the mountain towards the Lysjoch, and there found two knapsacks which had been left by them at this spot on the preceding day, before they began the final climb. This circumstance caused them at once to fear that an accident had occurred, and after skirting the lower slopes on the Italian side for nearly an hour, they reached a point from which they saw the whole of the party lying upon the snow at some distance beneath them. Being unable to reach the bodies from this point, they retraced their steps, and after making a slight detour arrived at the spot. The cause of the accident was at once apparent: a snow-cornice on the *arête* about 500 feet below the summit of the mountain had given way under the weight of the party, and they had fallen some 1200 feet on to the glacier beneath. The whole of the party had received such injuries that death must have been instantaneous in every case. Portions of the broken cornice were lying round the bodies, and the line of their fall could be traced by two axes belonging to members of the party, one of which was found upon the ice slope some 300 feet above, and the other upon rocks still higher up. . . Messrs. Lewis and Paterson were buried in the English Churchyard at Zermatt, on the afternoon of the 10th." (See p. 132.)

"The cornice had broken away in two places, leaving some 10 feet in the middle still adhering to the mountain. The length of the parts which broke away was, perhaps, 40 feet on each side of the remaining portion. The distance of the fall was estimated at from 1200 to 1500 feet. The bodies, from the nature of the injuries they had received, had evidently fallen upon their heads on the rocks, and then, in one great bound, had reached almost the spot where they were found."—*Alpine Journal*, vol. viii, pp. 346-7.

The Editor of the *Alpine Journal* remarked that "at Zermatt it may be believed no warning" (in respect to snow-cornices) "will be wanted for many years." History, however, repeats itself.

Two Guides and a Tourist perish by breaking through a snow-cornice (1896).—On Sept. 6, 1896, Dr. Max Günther left the Bétemps *cabane* at 4 a.m., with Roman Imboden (St. Nicholas) and Peter Joseph Ruppen (Balen, Saas Thal), for an ascent of the Lyskamm. They were accompanied as far as the Lysjoch by another German with his guide. The two latter went towards the Ludwigshöhe to watch the ascent of the others, who left the Lysjoch soon after 9 a.m. At 10.30 the roar of an avalanche was heard, and a cloud of snow was seen blowing from the ridge of the Lyskamm. Upon proceeding to a point where the Italian side of the mountain could be inspected, the bodies of Dr. Günther and his guide could be seen lying on the snow at the base of a pre-

[1] See note to p. 70.

cipice about 1500 feet in height. They had broken through a snow-cornice, and the hole made in it was clearly visible from below.—*Alpine Journal*, vol. xviii, p. 269.

Castor and Pollux (Zwillinge or the Twins) are overshadowed by the Lyskamm and Breithorn. They can both be bagged in one day from the Zwillingspass. **Castor**, 13,878 feet, 4230 mètres, was ascended by Messrs. W. Mathews and F. W. Jacomb with Michel-Auguste Croz and J. B. Croz, on Aug. 23, 1861, in 1 h. from the Zwillingspass; and **Pollux**, 13,422 feet, 4094 mètres, is said to have been first ascended by Mons. Jules Jacot in 1864, from the Schwarzthor.

The Breithorn from the North.—On the 15th Sept. 1869, Mr. R. Fowler, with Peter Knubel and G. Ruppen, went up the Breithorn from the North,—going *viâ* the slopes called Triftje, and then ascending partly by the Breithorn Glacier and a small glacier above which feeds it, finally struck the summit-ridge to the E. of the summit. Descent was effected by the ordinary route. From the Riffelhaus to the top and back occupied 12½ hours.

The Breithorn is sometimes ascended from the Riffelhaus or Riffelalp Hotel by crossing the Gorner Glacier, and taking up the ordinary route at Gandeck; but it is best (for the reason already given) to sleep at and to start from the inn on the top of the Theodule.

A Tour round the Breithorn.—On July 21, 1866, Mr. S. Winkworth with J. B. Croz and Peter Perren made a tour round the Breithorn from the Riffelhaus to Zermatt. After crossing the Gorner Glacier, they ascended the Schwärze Glacier, and went over the Schwarzthor; then turned to the right, still ascending, to cross a snow-ridge running southwards from the Breithorn. They then passed along the southern face of the mountain nearly on a level, though ascending somewhat to a second ridge, which was the highest point reached,—perhaps 400 feet higher than the Schwarzthor. Descending from this, they joined the ordinary route for the Breithorn *viâ* the Theodule, and returned by the Theodule to Zermatt. Twelve hours were occupied, excluding halts.

The walk to the **Cima di Jazzi**, 12,526 feet, 3818 mètres, is one of the most popular excursions made from the Riffelhaus or the Riffelalp Hotel. For most of the way it is the same as the route for the New Weissthor. Several variations on the route may be made.

1. By the (rough) path from the Riffelalp Hotel which passes to the W. of the Riffelhorn, and descends on the Gorner Glacier. This gives a good deal of glacier. 2. By the (rough) path which descends directly upon the Gorner Glacier on the E. of the Riffelhorn. 3. By the path which passes between the Riffelhorn and Gornergrat and skirts the base of the latter. This is the most usual way, and it is marked on the Map of the Valley of Zermatt. 4. By a path descending to the Gorner Glacier from the top of the Gornergrat.

Between Stockknubel and the Cima there are many concealed crevasses, and rope should always be employed. Early in the season there are concealed crevasses *lower* down the glacier than Stockknubel. The slopes of the Cima are gentle upon the western side, but on the Italian side they descend precipitously. "Travellers are strongly cautioned against approaching too close to the verge, as the cap of frozen snow that covers the summit usually forms a cornice projecting several feet from the rock, and is liable, every now and then, to break away and fall some thousands of feet down towards the Macugnaga Glacier."—*Mr. John Ball.* The view on the Italian side is very extensive. To have the best chance of seeing it, and for general comfort, *start early.*

The **Strahlhorn**, 13,750 feet, 4191 mètres, was ascended in August, 1854 (date not recorded), by Capt. E. Smyth, the Rev. J. G. Smyth, and the Rev. C. Smyth, with 'the landlord of the Hotel at Saas' (presumably Franz Andermatten), from the Adlerpass. The ascent ordinarily presents no difficulties on the Saas side, and on that of Zermatt the only point which requires labour is the rather steep bank of snow just before arriving at the summit of the pass.

There are nine **Passes** leading to the E., S.E. and S. out of the basin of the Gorner Glacier, for which the Riffelalp Hotel is a natural starting-point. Though interesting as glacier-excursions, they are, however, of little utility as *passes.* For *tarif* see Appendix D.

The **Adlerpass**, 12,461 feet, 3798 mètres, leading between the Strahlhorn and Rymfischhorn to the Valley of Saas, is reputed to be an old pass. Track is marked on the Map of the Valley of Zermatt. The **Schwarzberg Weissthor**, 11,811 feet, 3600 mètres, leading between the Strahlhorn and the Cima di Roffel (Rofel) is perhaps the easiest way of getting into the Valley of Saas out of the basin of the Gorner Glacier. There are two ways to it (both marked on the Map), one by the Findelen Glacier, and the other round the southern side of the Gornergrat, for most of the way identical with the routes to the Cima di Jazzi and the New Weissthor. This latter way is the easier of the two.

The **New Weissthor**, 11,811 feet, 3600 mètres, between the Cima di Roffel (Rofel) and the Cima di Jazzi, leading to the Val Anzasca, is one of the most practical of the passes going out of the basin of the Gorner Glacier, and is frequently crossed during the season. The route is the same as for the Cima di Jazzi so far as the foot of the Cima. It then bears away to the left, and arrives at the summit of the pass by going over what appears to be an innocent snow-field. There are concealed crevasses close up to the edge of the cliff overlooking the Italian side, and the rope should on no account be cast off before the rocks are reached. For track see Map of the Valley of Zermatt. The precipice above the Val Anzasca is startlingly abrupt. The rocks are good, but very steep. At the foot of the steepest part there is the **cabane Eugenio Sella.** Below it, for a good part of the way, the route leads down ordinary slopes. Grand view of the Macugnaga Glacier and of Monte Rosa towering above, on arriving at the head of the Val Anzasca. After this, it is still 5 kils. to Macugnaga. Hotels.—HOTEL MONTE MORO; HOTEL MONTE ROSA. In crossing from the side of Zermatt, reckon 6 to 6½ hs. from the Riffelhaus (halts included) to the top of the pass; 1 h. 35 min. from the top to the *cabane* Eugenio Sella; and 2¼ to 2½ hs. thence to Macugnaga.

In a recently-published work, the author mentions the Weissthor as one of the passes over which he had 'strolled.' It may be said roundly that no one has ever strolled across the New Weissthor. If the writer crossed the pass *alone* (as he leads one to believe) he did a foolish thing. Untrue statements relating to the Weissthor do no harm to those who are acquainted with the pass; but they are likely to be mischievous with those who are *not*, and especially with persons who, for the sake of economy, desire to dispense with the services of Guides. The best of the Val Anzasca guides prefer descending to Stalden and going over the Monte Moro Pass to crossing the New Weissthor *alone.*

On July 28, 1894, a German (G. A. Meyer), "despite all remonstrances, persisted in going quite alone" (from the E. Sella hut towards Zermatt). "He followed a guided party for some distance, and when they were on the pass was seen by them on a ridge below. . . He was missed and searched for. His body was found four days later on the glacier, at the foot of a rock precipice."—*A. J.*, vol. xvii, p. 268. This occurred on the Italian side, where a decent mountaineer *may* go alone, without imprudence.

The **Old Weissthor**, 11,733 feet, 3576 mètres, between the Cima di Jazzi and the Fillarhorn, also leads into the Val Anzasca. There are several variations. Not recommended.

The **Sesiajoch**, 14,472 feet, 4411 mètres, between the Parrotspitze and Signalkuppe, was traversed by Messrs H. B. George and A. W. Moore with Christian Almer and Matthias zum Taugwald on July 11, 1862, from chālets 2½ hs. above Alagna to the Riffel, in 18 hours. This pass is seldom used. Perhaps, with the facilities afforded by the Bétemps *cabane*, it may become more fashionable. See Map of the Valley of Zermatt.

The route for the **Lysjoch**, about 14,000 feet, leading to the valley of Gressoney, between Ludwigshöhe and the Lyskamm is for the greater part of the way on the Northern side the same as for the Lyskamm or the Sesiajoch. See View from the Gornergrat at the end of the volume, and Map of the Valley of Zermatt. The *cabane* Bétemps can be used as a starting-point. "The first expeditions to the Lysjoch on record date back so long ago as 1778-80."—*A. J.*, vol. v, p. 136.

In 1894, a dramatic incident occurred on the Zermatt side of the Lysjoch, Her Majesty the Queen of Italy was crossing the pass on Aug. 25, with a caravan of 30 persons, led by Alessandro Welf of Gressoney, under the general direction of Baron Louis Peccoz. The summit was crossed, and for the first hour and a half Her Majesty and two ladies were dragged down in sledges. When this manner of progression could no longer be continued, Welf took the lead, followed by the Baron and the Queen. Presently they approached some crevasses, and the Baron called out loudly "Crevasses! Take care of the Queen!" A few seconds afterwards, Welf felt a pull on the rope, and, turning, saw the Baron falling on the snow. The others gathered around, but they could do nothing. Baron Peccoz gave one or two gasps, and expired. The spot where this occurred is marked with a cross on the View from the Gornergrat. The body was brought down to Zermatt on the evening of the 28th; the next day was conveyed by special train to Visp, and thence back to Italy over the Simplon. It is stated that physicians had recommended the Baron not to undertake long expeditions on account of his heart.

The **Felikjoch**, 13,347 feet, 4068 mètres, between the Lyskamm and Castor leads either to Fiery (Val d'Ayas) or to Gressoney (V. of Gressoney). It was first crossed on Aug. 23, 1861, by Messrs. W. Mathews and F. W. Jacomb, with Michel-Auguste Croz and J. B. Croz, who took 14 hs. 40 min. from a chālet 2½ hs. above Gressoney to the Riffel (including the ascent of Castor *en route*). They called this pass the Col des Jumeaux, but this name is now superseded. The *cabane* Bétemps can be used as a starting-point for the Felikjoch. See View from the Gornergrat, and Map of the Valley of Zermatt.

The **Zwillingspass**, 12,668 feet, 3861 mètres, between Castor and Pollux, leads to the Val d'Ayas. Mr. Winkworth, who made the first passage on July 31, 1863, took 6¼ hs. from the Riffel to the Col, and proposed the name Col de Verra for the pass, as it led on the Italian side to the Combe di Verra. The name has not been adopted.

The **Schwarzthor**, 12,274 feet, 3741 mètres, between Pollux and the Breithorn, leading to the Val d'Ayas, was first crossed by Mr. John Ball in 1845. From the Riffelhaus to the summit reckon 6 hs. The Breithorn was ascended from the Schwarzthor on Aug. 16, 1884, by Mr. J. S. Anderson with Ulrich Almer and Aloys Pollinger, who arrived on the top at 6.45 p.m.! having taken 16¼ hs. from the Riffelhaus!

THE LAC NOIR HOTEL.

CHAPTER XI.

EXCURSIONS FROM THE LAC NOIR HOTEL.

THE LAC NOIR—THE FURGG GLACIER—THE THEODULE PASS—THE BREUILJOCH—THE FURGG GRAT—THE FURGG JOCH—ROUTES UP THE MATTERHORN—THE NORTHERN OR ZERMATT ROUTE—THE SOUTHERN OR BREUIL ROUTE—THE ZMUTT ROUTE—DEATHS OF BAUMANN, IMSENG, MUMMERY, PENHALL, PETRUS, ETC.

THE Lac Noir Hotel takes its name from a small piece of water which is drying up. The only sport to be had in it is fishing for water-beetles. The "Matterhorn Hotel" would not be an inappropriate title for this establishment, since it is to all intents and purposes *the* Hotel for the Matterhorn. It is the nearest one to the summit, and it is the natural base for supplies. Even those who make the Ascent of the Matterhorn by the southern route often start from the Lac Noir Hotel, and get to the Col de Lion by crossing the Breuiljoch.

Simultaneously with the partial drying up of the Lac Noir a new lakelet has been formed on the southern side of the Hörnli, which may, in course of time, grow to large dimensions; and it seems probable that the Lac Noir, formerly, was at least partly maintained by drainage from the Furgg Glacier, which drainage has latterly been diverted in consequence of the shrinkage of the glacier. The new lake is against the lateral moraine on the left bank of the Furgg Glacier. A short distance away to the south, the shrinkage of the glacier has caused the exposure of a cliff in the middle of the ice, which formerly was completely covered up by it. The surface of the glacier at this part was always much riven (indicating that it was passing over a rugged bed), but it is now seen that it actually passed over a perpendicular cliff, and yet maintained its continuity. These two features,—the formation of an entirely new lake, and the demonstration that glaciers can maintain their continuity when passing over perpendicular cliffs—have particular interest for those who are concerned in the study of glaciers.

By sleeping at the Lac Noir Hotel, the time occupied on the passage of the **Theodule Pass** can be abbreviated. Gandeck (see pp. 153, 158) may be reached in 2½ hs. by crossing the lower part of the Furgg Glacier. This route meets the ordinary one from Zermatt when about half the distance to Gandeck has been accomplished, and thenceforward the two ways are identical. See Map of Matterhorn and its Glaciers. Returning from Gandeck to the Lac Noir Hotel takes 75 to 80 minutes.

Breuil can be reached from the Lac Noir Hotel more quickly by the **Breuiljoch** (about 10,900 feet) than by the Theodule. To get to the Breuiljoch, follow the regular path to the Hörnli (pp. 139, 145); go along the lateral moraine on the left bank of the Furgg Glacier so long as there is a path, and then take to the ice, and make for the left hand (or eastern) side of the first small peak on the Furgg Grat that is to the E. of the Matterhorn. This little peak has no name. It is marked 3357 mètres on the Siegfried Map. The last bit before arriving at the Col is a slope, half-rock and half-snow. On the Italian side there is first a small bank of snow to descend, followed by a little bit of glacier and a good deal of moraine. This is succeeded by ordinary grass-slopes, over which one can go anywhere. By bearing a little round to the left, the Theodule path can be struck about 35 min. above Breuil; or an independent track may be made. See Map of Matterhorn and its Glaciers.

The **Furgg Grat** is the name given to the ridge connecting the eastern base of the Matterhorn with the Theodule. A short day can be pleasantly occupied by going from the Lac Noir Hotel to the Theodule, then following the *arête* of this ridge to the Breuiljoch, and returning *viâ* the Furgg Glacier. This excursion was first brought into notice by Mr. J. C. Leman, who took between 3 and 4 hours in passing from one end of the ridge to the other. It is best to go from E. to W., thus having the Matterhorn in view during the whole time.

The **Furgg Joch** is upon the W. side of the little peak 3357, at the extreme western end of the Furgg Grat. It was first crossed on July 10, 1863, by Mr. F. Morshead with P. Perrn (Perren) and Moritz Andenmatten, from Zermatt to Breuil, and the name Matterjoch was proposed for it; but, as this was one of the names already applied to the Theodule, another title had to be found, and it was christened Furgg Joch on the Siegfried Map. The name Breuiljoch was also given officially. The Furgg Joch is sometimes impassable. In 1865 I wanted to cross it from S. to N., and found that it was not possible to descend the northern side. During the two years which had elapsed since the first passage, the Furgg Glacier had shrunk so much that it was completely severed from the summit of the pass.

There is at the present time a curious confusion among the guides of the Zermatt district as to these two passes (Breuiljoch and Furgg Joch). The Furgg Joch alone is on the *Tarif*, and guides when engaged for the Furgg Joch conduct the tourist over the Breuiljoch! In Conway's *Zermatt Pocket Book* (p. 68), published in 1881, it is stated (correctly) that the Furgg Joch is on the W. and the Breuiljoch is on the E. of the peak 3357. In Conway's *Central Pennine Alps* (p. 151), published in 1890, it is stated (incorrectly) that the pass on the W. of the peak 3357 "used to be called the Breuiljoch!"

These and other excursions can be made from the Lac Noir Hotel, but its great excursion is the Ascent of the Matterhorn. The northern or Zermatt route is the popular one, and nearly all of those who go by it either start from, or must pass, the Lac Noir Hotel. In the last edition of *Scrambles amongst the Alps* the ascents which had been made of the Matterhorn were tabulated down to the end of 1879, and it appeared that those made from Zermatt and back to Zermatt were as compared with those made from Breuil and back to Breuil about six to one. The disproportion has become, perhaps, greater.

The route now followed for the Ascent of the Matterhorn from Zermatt is the same as that which was taken upon the first ascent, with the exceptions which will be pointed out. There are now *two* paths to the Lac Noir Hotel. Upon the first ascent the old, or more northern, path was followed. The other path and the Hotel were not then in existence. From the Hotel to the Hörnli ridge the present way is the same as that which was taken on the first ascent, but in 1865 there was mostly a track (not a *path*) and in some places not even a track. On the Hörnli ridge there was no track in 1865, but now there is a *path*.[1] The *cabane* on the Hörnli ridge (see p. 80) is a little short of the place where the real Matterhorn begins to rise. A large part of those who make the ascent from Zermatt use this *cabane* as a starting-point, in which they perhaps make a mistake, as the small amount that is gained in time does not compensate for the weariness of getting through a night in such a place, under the usual conditions.[2]

In passing from the end of the Hörnli ridge on to the actual peak, the exact ledges are traversed over which I myself led on the first ascent, and the track presently passes close to the spot where my tent was placed on July 13-14, 1865. In 1874, 1876, and 1892, I visited the tent-platform which was made here. In the two former years the wall of stones which was built around it was still standing, and my initials were to be seen on the rock behind; but in 1892 I found it difficult to recognise the spot. By natural decay, the platform was nearly obliterated, and the inscribed rock had fallen down.

So long back as 1874 there was a strongly marked track up the East Face as far as the *cabane* which was first erected (see p. 79), and little piles of stones, placed in prominent situations, pointed out the way, even to the dullest person. The route taken now-a-days

1 Which might be made into a good mule-path, or even into a carriage-road, up to the base of the mountain.

2 See p. 145 for remarks in *Alpina* upon this *cabane*.

at this part goes rather closer to the *arête* of the North-East ridge than we went, in 1865. We bore more away on to the East Face, and proceeded more directly towards the 'shoulder' at the foot of the final peak. At the top of the 'shoulder' we went to the right, on to the northern side (see pp. 59-60), to turn the nearly perpendicular cliff which rose in front. Now, the usual way is to climb directly upwards by aid of fixed ropes and chains. **The time occupied** upon ascents is very variable. Those who start from the *cabane* on the Hörnli ridge are usually able to get back to Zermatt the same evening, if they wish. Some, however, are not so fortunate. For *tarif*, see Appendix D.

Most ascents are made in the latter part of July, August and September.[1] Signor Vittorio Sella was the first to succeed in **an Ascent in Winter.**

"Accompanied by J.-A. and Louis Carrel he left Breuil at 11 p.m. on March 16, 1882, the night being very fine. The Glacier du Lion was gained just before 3 a.m., the snow near it being in a very powdery condition, and the Col du Lion reached at 6 a.m., the party up to this point having walked by lantern-light. The rocks were then attacked, and, says Signor Sella, 'no extraordinary difficulty' was encountered, so that at 10 a.m. the party reached the Pic Tyndall and halted for breakfast. The passage of the ridge" (*i.e.* the southern shoulder) "was somewhat awkward, but the rocks of the final peak were free from snow, and the summit was gained at 2 p.m. The air was perfectly still and the view cloudless. . . After a short halt the descent of the Zermatt face was commenced, hardly any snow being found on the *arête.* This side of the mountain was already in shade, but the way was fairly easy until after the" (northern) "shoulder was passed. From that point numerous serious difficulties had to be overcome. . . The Swiss hut was reached at 7.30 p.m., and after a very uncomfortable night Zermatt gained the next day. . . Signor Sella states that he suffered scarcely at all from the cold, save near the Glacier du Lion."—*Alpine Journal,* vol. x, p. 494.

This remarkable Winter Ascent was actually effected in less time than is frequently occupied on summer ones.

The Southern or Breuil route, though it has been largely 'facilitated,' still remains a more difficult route than the Zermatt or Northern one. Up to the top of the southern 'shoulder' there is only one way that can be regarded as the established route on the southern side,[2] but there are three ways up the final 500 feet.

1. The route originally taken by Jean-Antoine Carrel upon the first ascent on the Italian side (see pp. 73-4). So far as I am aware this has only been used on two subsequent occasions. Mr. F. C. Grove went by it in 1867 (see pp. 76-7) and in 1895 Carrel's ascent was repeated by Mr. W. E. Davidson, with Christian Klucker and Daniel Maquignaz. All of the party considered the passage of the Zmutt face excessively difficult, and are of opinion that this route is beyond all comparison harder than any of the others up the mountain, with all of which (except the lower part of Penhall's route) both Mr. Davidson and his guides are personally acquainted. 2. The route which was discovered by J.-J. and J.-P. Maquignaz (see pp. 77-8). This leads very directly towards the summit, and is largely provided with rope. 3. Another

[1] The first ascent in 1897 was made on July 7.

[2] Some variations have been made below the Col du Lion, but the regular way to the Col is up the 'little' and the 'great staircase,' and by skirting the base of the cliffs of the Tête du Lion. See pp. 23, etc.

way which was discovered in July, 1887, by J.-B. Maquignaz, J.-B. Perruquet, and J. Aymonod, which goes diagonally up the precipice facing Breuil, to the E. of route 2.

The main peak of the Matterhorn on the Italian side is now festooned with rope from the top down to the Col du Lion, and several hundred feet are even fixed along the base of the cliffs of the Tête du Lion! Altogether there cannot I think be less than 1200 feet of fixed rope at one part or another. Notwithstanding the assistance this affords, comparatively few ascents are made on the Italian side.

There is, finally, what is called the Zmutt route, that was first used by Messrs. Mummery, Penhall, and Baumann (see pp. 84, 85), leading from the upper end of the Zmutt Glacier up the long snow-slope which is a prominent feature of the north-west side of the Matterhorn. The top of this slope is shewn on the right of the diagram on p. 69, and on the left of the Illustration on p. 160. This snow-slope affords an easy way up to a very considerable elevation. The top of it is nearly on a level with the 'Great Tower' on the south-east ridge.[1] At its upper end there are some prominent pinnacles which are not easy to pass; but, after that, the ascent of the rocks above does not present unusual difficulties. The face of the Matterhorn between the Penhall couloir and the Col du Lion is almost incessantly raked by falling stones, and the couloir affords a natural path for the descent of a great many of them.[2] Though the snow-ridge is free from this objection, there are loose rocks on the arête above, which require care in handling. No ascent was made again, I believe, by this way until 1894. Since then the route has been used occasionally, but it is not likely that it will be traversed frequently, as it is circuitous, and tourists, like trade, drift into the easiest channels.[3]

[1] See the accompanying outline, in which A marks the Summit; B, the southern 'shoulder'; C, the 'Great Tower'; D, the Col du Lion; E, Penhall's couloir; F, F, the Zmutt snow-ridge; G, G, the Tiefenmatten Glacier; H, a feeder of the Tiefenmatten Glacier; K, K, Penhall's routes; L, L, Mummery's route.

[2] This corner was the scene of the mad prank which is mentioned in the note at the foot of p. 85.

[3] Of the three amateurs and six guides who were concerned in the first ascents of the Zmutt side of the Matterhorn six have perished. 1. Ferdinand Imseng was killed by an avalanche on Monte Rosa, Aug. 8, 1881. See p. 172. 2. Johann Petrus was killed on the Aig. Blanche de Peuteret, July, 1882. Cause of accident is unknown. See *Guide to Chamonix*, pp. 58-9. 3. Mr. W. Penhall was killed by an avalanche on Aug. 4, 1882, near Grindelwald. 4. Mr. J. Baumann disappeared in South Africa at the end of 1890 or beginning of 1891. 5. Mr. A. F. Mummery disappeared on Nanga Parbat in Aug. 1895. 6. Emile Rey slipped while descending the Aig. du Géant, on Aug. 24, 1895, and was killed on the spot. See *Guide to Chamonix*, pp. 63-4.

Three others who were concerned with the southern side of the Matterhorn have also come to premature ends, namely Dr. Tyndall and his guide Bennen, and J.-J. Maquignaz. The sad death of Dr. Tyndall will be remembered by all. Bennen was smothered by an avalanche on the Haut de Cry, Feb. 28, 1864. See *Scrambles amongst the Alps*, Appendix A; and J.-J. Maquignaz disappeared on Mont Blanc in Aug. 1890. See *Guide to Chamonix*, pp. 60-1.

A
B
C
D
L
F
L
E
F
K
K
K
E
K
H
H
G
G
G

CHAPTER XII.

ON THE VALLEY OF SAAS (SAAS THAL).

EXPLANATIONS — A YEAR OF AVALANCHES — STALDEN — EISTEN — HUTEGGEN—BALEN—SAAS (IM GRUND)—EXCURSIONS FROM SAAS —ALMAGELL—PASSES TO ANTRONA AND THE SIMPLON ROAD— MATTMARKSEE AND MATTMARK HOTEL—THE BLAUENSTEIN— MONTE MORO PASS—MACUGNAGA—THE MONDELLI PASS—SAAS-FÉE—EXCURSIONS FROM SAAS-FÉE—THE WEISSMIES HOTEL— EXCURSIONS FROM IT—HOW TO GET HOME.

FORMERLY when one spoke of **Saas** the village was meant which now is called sometimes Saas im Grund and sometimes im Grund. The hamlet of **Fée** (774 feet above Saas), which formerly was invariably called Fée, is now almost universally called Saas-Fée.[1] At present, if one asks for Saas, the natives will perhaps answer enquiringly 'im Grund?' being in doubt whether the real, original Saas or the upstart Saas-Fée is meant. Im Grund may be translated 'at the bottom,' or 'at the lowest part.' Saas-Fée means 'Fairy Saas.'

The **Saas Thal** extends from Stalden to the Monte Moro Pass. [For Stalden, see chap. vii.] The lower part of the valley, from Stalden to Saas (im Grund), is extremely picturesque, and is fairly populated;[2] but the upper portion of the valley, from Almagell to the Monte Moro, is sterile and naked, and in all probability has never had a permanent population. The few châlets which are found there are not tenanted in winter. The valley in general is rather especially liable to snow-avalanches. Ruppen says that, 'according to the chronicle writers,' 1741 was 'a year of avalanches,' and refers [p. 69] to the case of a woman who was swept away by one, and lay for 100 hours buried under the snow. *She* could hear people digging, and even listen to them speaking, but *they* could not detect her

[1] De Saussure speaks [§ 2222] of the Valley of Sass. Prof. J. D. Forbes in his *Travels* [pp. 350-54] mentions Saas and Fée. Both places are referred to under these names in the 1854 ed. of Murray's *Handbook*, and in Ball's *Guide to the Western Alps*, in 1863. But in Sheet xxiii of the Carte Dufour, published in 1862, Saas is called im Grund, though Fée remains Fée; and in the Siegfried Map the nomenclature continues the same.

[2] It is stated in *Die Chronik des Thales Saas*, by Peter Joseph Ruppen, Sion, 1851, that the population of the four Communes Almagel, Balen, Fée and Grund amounted to 801 persons in 1850. At the census of 1888 it had increased to 1000. According to Ruppen, Burgener was the most common family name in the Valley.

smothered cries. At last, she and her spinning-wheel were found and saved. The way up the valley is liable to be interrupted even in summer or autumn when newly-fallen snow is melting quickly. This happened on Oct. 1, 1896, when the path was cut in several places by boulders that were brought down by the rapid liquefaction of a heavy fall which had occurred on the previous day. The women of the Saas Thal are famed for their strength. In 1894 I saw some of them carrying full-sized doors on their backs, up the valley, for some of the new hotels at Saas-Fée; and I was told that the large mirrors which can be seen in those establishments had been transported from Stalden in a similar fashion.

The path from Stalden to Saas is a mule-path all the way. Rough carts are used by the natives at some places, but the route is nowhere fit for carriages. Walking time from Stalden to Saas is about 3 hs. 5 min.; returning 2½ hs.

Ascending.	min.	Descending.	min.
Stalden to Eisten	60	Saas (im Grund) to Balen . .	35
Eisten to Huteggen	30	Balen to Huteggen	40
Huteggen to Balen (Aballa) .	55	Huteggen to Eisten	25
Balen to Saas (im Grund) . .	40	Eisten to Stalden	50
Total .	3 hs. 5 min.	Total .	2 hs. 30 min.

The path from Stalden to Saas crosses the Railway *at the Station;* and descends in 3 min. to a bold bridge thrown across the Mattervisp. Good views from this bridge both up and down the valley. Very shortly after passing it, the path divides. Take the one to the left, with telegraph posts. [The other path leads to the Hannig Alp. See chap. vii.] It at once commences to rise steeply, on the left bank of the valley, and soon attains a great elevation above the Saaservisp. The village seen on the other side of the valley, nearly in front, is **Staldenried**, 3468 feet, 1057 mètres; pop. 241. Look back occasionally at the mountains on the N. side of the Rhone Valley. The prominent, pyramidal peak is the **Bietschhorn**, 12,969 feet, 3953 mètres. At about 35 min. from Stalden the path is carried for a short distance along the face of a cliff, on a shelf cut in the rock; and in 25 min. more arrives at the village of

Eisten, 3557 feet, 1084 mètres; pop. 222. Post. This village was formerly united with Stalden, but it now forms a separate Commune. It is the abode of a number of Guides, who are seldom at home during the season. For their names see Appendix G. The church, which occupies a prominent position, was erected recently. The path up the valley still continues on the left bank, and in 30 min. reaches

Huteggen, 4088 feet, 1246 mètres, where there is a small Hotel-Restaurant by the wayside, which is the *only* inn between Stalden and Saas. A path leading across country to St. Nicholas *viâ* the Hannig Alp starts on the N. side of Huteggen; and about 200 yards south of the hamlet another one goes away through forest to the châlets of Schweiben, 5581 feet, 1701 mètres, whence one can cross the Ferrichlücke or the Gabelhorn Pass to St. Nicholas. [See chap. vii.] Six or seven min. south of Huteggen the path up the Saas Thal crosses to the right bank of the valley, by a fine, stone bridge, constructed in 1896. Notice the manner in which the rocks here have been hollowed by the torrent. The way continues on the right bank

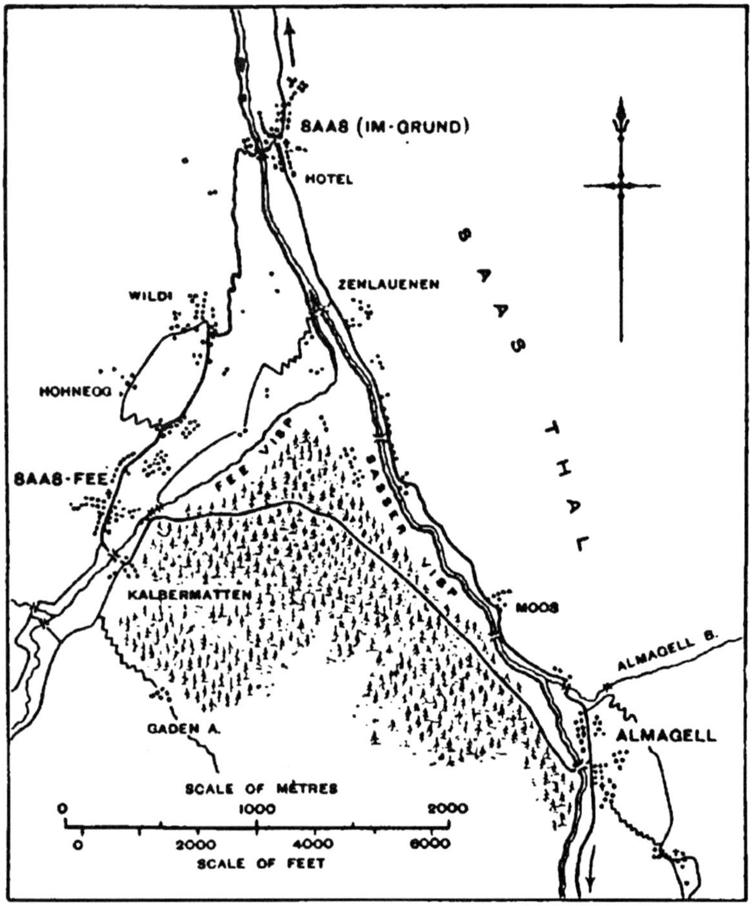

ENVIRONS OF SAAS.

for about 23 min., and then recrosses to the left bank. In about 20 min. more it passes the church of

Balen (Aballa), 4984 feet, 1519 mètres; pop. 172; a Commune composed of several hamlets, situated upon nearly level ground; and in 3 min. more again goes over to the right bank, and continues upon that side until Saas. Upon approaching that place, the bottom of the valley opens out, and affords the largest expanse of flat grazing-ground in the district.

Saas, or Saas im Grund, or im Grund, 5125 feet, 1562 mètres; pop. 386. Post and Telegraph. **Hotel.**—HOTEL-PENSION MONTE MORO, quite at the southern end of the village. Saas is pleasantly situated, and is increasing in public favour, though the great peaks cannot be seen from the village. It was formerly a starting-point for a large number of excursions, but the Weissmies Hotel has become the natural base for some of those towards the East, and Saas-Fée for most of those on the West. Almagell also, as it now possesses an inn, is available for the Antrona and Zwischbergen passes, and for various ascents. Saas, however, remains the starting-point for the easiest way from the Saas Thal to the Simplon Road, which is by the

Simeli Pass, 9934 feet, 3028 mètres, which leads *viâ* the Mattwald Alp (east of Huteggen) past the S.E. side of the Mattwaldhorn, 10,673 feet, 3253 mètres (seldom ascended), from the Valley of Saas into the Gamser Thal [This valley is also called Nanzer Thal or Nanz Thal. The village of Gamsen, in the Rhone Valley, 3½ kils. to the W. of Brieg, is at its mouth. Dynamite factory there.] Mr. Ball said in his *Guide to the Western Alps*, 1863, "This valley has not yet attracted the attention of Alpine travellers," and that remains the case. Those who cross the Simeli Pass only descend to the *head* of the Nanz Thal, and then remount to the

Sirwolten Pass, 8740 feet, 2664 mètres, and descend upon the Simplon Road (which is scarcely 3 kils. away to the E.), near Refuge vii, about half-way between the summit of the Simplon and Simpeln, 4852 feet, 1479 mètres. Time from Saas to the top of the Simeli Pass 4½ to 5 hs., and from the top to the Simplon Hospice or the village of Simpeln about 3 hs. The total time occupied is about the same if the passes are taken in the reverse direction.

The principal of the little excursions from it are, (1) to the Hotel Weissmies, (2) to Saas-Fée, and (3) up the Valley to the Monte Moro Pass. Guides are unnecessary in fine weather. For other excursions see pp. 190-92, and for **Tarif of Excursions from Saas** see Appendix C.

(1) There are two ways to the **Hotel Weissmies,** a small mountain inn situated to the N.E. of, and about 3000 feet above Saas, on a lower slope of the Laquinhorn. These two paths unite a little above the châlets on the Trift Alp, and by either of them the Hotel Weissmies can be gained in 3 hours.

(2) There are two paths from Saas (im Grund) to **Saas-Fée,** one commencing nearly opposite to the Hotel Monte Moro, and the other about half a mile to its south, at Zenlauenen (see Plan of Environs of Saas). By either route it takes 35 to 40 min. to get to Saas-Fée. The great attraction of this spot is the magnificent *cirque* of the Mischabel, which is one of the finest things of its kind in the Zermatt district. For Hotels and Excursions from Saas-Fée, see later.

(3) To Mattmark See and the Monte Moro Pass. We will take this first.

The path up the bottom of the valley continues on the right bank, and leads in about 35 min. to the village

Almagell, Almagel or Almengell, 5509 feet, 1679 mètres; pop. 207. Post. A small inn called RESTAURANT PORTIENGRAT was opened here in 1896. Fine waterfall. See Appendix G for names of Guides. Almagell is near the entrance to the Furggthal, at the head of which is the Antrona Pass.[1]

[1] This pass has been known for a very long time. Dr. Schiner says in his *Descrip. du Dép. du Simplon*, p. 166, "on passait autrefois fréquemment par Antrona . . . avec les chevaux et autres bétails. On appelait ces passages déjà en 1440 *fort vieux passages.*"

The **Antrona Pass** affords the easiest and quickest way of getting from the Saas Thal to the Italian Lakes. Almagell to the summit (9331 feet, 2844 mètres) takes about 4 hours. Nowhere steep. Mules were formerly taken over this pass (see note, p. 187), but at the present time they cannot cross it, although they can go within an hour of the top. The summit lies between the Latelhorn (10,561 feet, 3219 mètres, easily ascended from this direction) and the Jazzihorn, and on it there is an old, roofless cabane which was formerly used as a stable. The path on the Italian side at first descends steeply, and in about 45 min. passes near the southern side of the little Lago di Cingino, 7191 feet, 2192 mètres, and presently arrives at the first châlets (Alpe Cingino), 6663 feet, 2031 mètres, in the Val Antrona. The path thence to the village of Antronapiana, 2959 feet, 902 mètres, small hotel, is good. Time from summit about 4 hs. A carriage-road leads from Antronapiana to Villa d'Ossola Railway Stn., whence one goes (southwards) to the Lake of Orta.

Antronapiana can also be reached from the Saas Thal by the **Ofenthal-pass**, 9311 feet, 2838 mètres, which leads through the Ofenthal (see p. 189), and crosses the chain S. of the Jazzihorn, joining the route of the Antrona Pass a little below the Alpe Cingino. Time Almagell to Antronapiana about 9 hours.

The **Zwischbergen Pass**, 10,656 feet, 3248 mètres, at the head of a small valley running towards the E. from Almagell, goes between the Weissmies and the Portjengrat, and leads by a rather roundabout way to the Simplon Road. Not often used. Almagell to summit 3¾ to 4 hs. Sometimes upon this side of the pass there is little or no snow. On the eastern side, the route leads at first over snow, and then across the small Gemein Alp Glacier to the Val Varia. There are tracks on each side of the stream at the head of this valley, but lower down it there is a path on the left bank *only*. From the summit to Gondo on the Simplon Road, 6 hours.

The path up the valley for the Monte Moro Pass continues on the right bank, and in 5½ kils. from Almagell passes the end of the **Allalin Glacier**, and arrives at the **Mattmarksee.** Notice the two great, lateral moraines. "The moraine supplies," says J. D. Forbes (*Travels*, p. 352), "the well-known blocks of gabbro, containing Smaragdite, which are recognised so extensively over the plains of Switzerland, and which have no native locality in the Alps but here. They are brought down by the glacier from the inaccessible heights of the Saasgrat, . . so that the rock may probably never be found *in situ.*" This glacier extends to the bottom of and almost across the valley, leaving only just room for the stream flowing out of the lake. This was reputed to be deep. It is evidently shallow, and is now almost annihilated. The **Mattmark Hotel** (This is the *only* inn between Amagell—Macugnaga. *Persons crossing the Monte Moro Pass, in either direction, do well to bring food along with them*), 6965 feet, 2123 mètres, is 1 kil. south of the southern end of the lake, or about 7½ kils. from Almagell and in time about 1 h. 40 min. A few hundred yards south of the hotel, and against the path, there is the great erratic block called the **Blauenstein,** which is one of the largest boulders in the Alps.

According to Charpentier (*Essai sur les Glaciers*), who quotes Venetz and does not seem to have seen the boulder himself, it measures 68 feet (French ?) long, 57 broad, and 63 high, and contains 244,000 cubic feet. I think these dimensions are in excess of the truth. The calculation of its volume is erroneous, as allowance is not made for the rounding of the angles. Charpentier says that it was deposited at this place by the Schwarzenbergg Glacier in 1818, and that in 1821 there were old men living at Saas who had heard their fathers say that they had seen it upon the back of the glacier.

The end of the Schwarzenbergg Glacier is now a kilomètre from the boulder, and is the next object of interest on the way. A mile south of the Mattmark Hotel, one passes some châlets at the **Distel Alp,** 7120 feet, 2170 mètres, which are the last on this side of the pass [The Ofenthal, at the head of which is the Ofenthalpass to Antronapiana, leads away hence to the E.]. The path now steepens, and in 2 kils. arrives at **Thälliboden,** 8189 feet, 2496 mètres, at the

THE BLAUENSTEIN, VALLEY OF SAAS, AND MATTMARK HOTEL.

end of the glacier of that name. Mules stop here, and the rest of the way to the summit of the pass (which as the crow flies is distant 1⅓ kil.) is generally over snow lying between the Thälliboden Glac. on the E., and the Seewineng Glac. on the W. The scenery here is desolate, but on arriving at **the Col (Monte Moro, or Passo del Moro),** 9390 feet, 2862 mètres, one is rewarded with a superb view of the Italian side of Monte Rosa. The immediate summit of the pass is shelterless. Protection can be obtained during bad weather by descending a short distance on the southern side. From Mattmark Hotel to the summit reckon 2¾ to 3 hs. From the summit to Mattmark can be accomplished in 1 h. 30 min.

Upon commencing the descent into Italy, the route leads at first over snow-beds and then by rocky ground, towards the S.S.W., as far as the châlets of Galkerne, 6894 feet, 2101 mètres. It then goes S.S.E., and descends rather more rapidly (principally through forest) into the Val Anzasca, which it joins at Pratti, one of the hamlets of **Macugnaga,** 3937 feet, 1200 mètres. **Hotels.**—HOTEL MONTE MORO (moderate prices), HOTEL MONTE ROSA. The descent from the summit to Macugnaga occupies about 2¾ hs.; from Macugnaga to summit is a little less than 4 hs. For the head of the Val Anzasca, and route from Zermatt by the New Weissthor, see chap. x.

[There is another way from the Saas Thal to the Val Anzasca by the **Mondelli Pass,** 9321 feet, 2841 mètres. This diverges from the Monte Moro route at Thälliboden, crosses the chain about mid-way between the Joderhorn and Pizo d'Antigine, and descends S.E. to Mondelli and a little farther on to Prequartera, in the Val Anzasca, about 7 kils. below Macugnaga.][1]

I return now across the Monte Moro Pass to speak of the excursions from Saas-Fée and the Weissmies Hotel. **Saas-Fée,** 5899 feet, 1798 mètres; pop. 235. **Hotels.**—GRAND HOTEL SAAS-FÉE; GRAND HOTEL BELLEVUE; GRAND HOTEL DU DOM; HOTEL-PENSION SAAS-FÉE. Tailor, Shoemaker, Restaurant, and several knick-knack shops in the village. A large church has been erected recently.

Saas-Fée cannot be seen from im Grund or from the bottom of the Saas Thal. It is situated in a lateral valley (at some height above the main one), which leads towards the West to the foot of the Mischabelhörner. The Fée basin is surrounded by the Allalinhorn, Alphubel, Täschhorn, and Dom, and these great mountains form a sort of *cirque*, at the end of the valley. The distance of the village from the summit of the Dom is about 4½ miles, and the difference of level is about 9000 feet. Precipitous cliffs and fine glaciers bound the head of the basin, while down below, "embosomed in this imposing scene of desolation and solitude is the sweetest pastoral valley that ever God created or man enjoyed. The pasture grounds are rich and well-watered, the grass is of the freshest green."—*Mr. Justice Wills.*

This (the eastern) side of the Mischabelhörner is much more striking than the western one, facing the Nicolai Thal, and is better seen; but to thoroughly appreciate the proportions of these noble mountains one must get higher than the bottom of the valley of Saas-Fée. In the immediate neighbourhood, the **Egginerhorn,** 11,080 feet, 3377 mètres (about 4¾ hs. ascending, 2¾ descending), and the **Mittaghorn,** 10,328 feet, 3148 mètres (about 3 hs. ascending), are favourite points of view. The **Egginergrat** from the Mittaghorn to the Egginerhorn, keeping on the crest of the ridge the whole way, is a good climb. On the opposite side of the Saas Thal (to the E., N.E., and S.E. of im Grund) the positions are even better, and are numerous.

[1] De Saussure refers (vol. iv, p. 387) to the strength of the women in the valleys around Monte Rosa. "I will give a notion of their strength," he says. "I had made up at Macugnaga an extremely heavy box of minerals, and asked my host if he could find a man who would carry it to Vanzon" [Vanzone], "whence it might be sent to Geneva. He answered quite seriously that there wasn't a man in the district who could carry such a burden such a distance; but that if it was all the same to me to have a woman, he could easily find one who would carry it willingly, and it is the fact that two were sufficient to carry a mule-load."

The principal **ascents made from Saas-Fée** are those of the Balfrinhorn, Ulrichshorn, Süd-Lenzspitze, Dom, Täschhorn, Alphubel and Allalinhorn. Those of the Dom and Täschhorn are effected more easily from other directions, and this side of those peaks has been very generally condemned, from the frequency of falling stones. See p. 120. The principal **passes from Saas-Fée** are the Ried Pass (to St. Nicholas), the Nadeljoch and Domjoch (to Randa), and the Mischabeljoch, Alphubeljoch and the Féejoch (to the Täsch valley and Zermatt). It is better to take the three latter in the reverse direction. One of the nicest **little walks** from Saas-Fée is through forest to Almagell, by the track marked on the Plan on page 186. In shade the whole way; fine examples of *roches moutonnées* near Saas-Fée. On arriving opposite to Almagell, cross the bridge, and return down the right bank of the Saas Thal to Zenlauenen or im Grund, and back home by one of the usual paths. The same walk may be extended to Mattmark and the Blauenstein (which will take, going, about 2 hs. 20 min.); or it may be continued to the top of the Monte Moro Pass, without undue fatigue.

THE WEISSMIES HOTEL.

The **Tarif** of excursions from Saas embraces some which are made from Saas and others which belong properly to Saas-Fée. No distinction is made. See Appendix C. For **Guides** see Appendix G. The **Season** at Saas-Fée closes earlier than at Zermatt. By the end of September the place, sometimes, is almost or quite deserted.

The **Weissmies Hotel** (about 8125 feet) is a little inn (opened in 1894 by the proprietor of the Hotel Monte Moro at Saas) placed in an excellent position as a point of view, intended to facilitate the ascents of the Fletschhorn, Laquinhorn and Weissmies, and the passage of the Rossboden Pass, Fletschjoch and Laquinjoch. The view from it is very extensive, and embraces the whole of the Italian side of Monte Rosa as far as the Col de la Loccie, the whole of the range of the Mischabel, and (near at hand) the Fletschhorn, Laquinhorn and

Weissmies. The very highest point of the Fletschhorn is not visible, and not much of the Oberland can be seen.

The **Fletschhorn**, 13,127 feet, 4001 mètres, is the most northern of three considerable peaks on the eastern side of the Valley of Saas. They are all comparatively easy of access, and all have been ascended from several directions. Whether the Fletschhorn is mounted from the W. or S. the time occupied will be nearly the same. Ascending, about 5 hs.; descending, 3 hs. The **Laquinhorn**, 13,140 feet, 4005 mètres, is only 1⅓ kil. S. of the Fletschhorn. Ascending, 4½ to 5 hs. I am informed that a descent has been effected from the summit to Saas in 3 hs. The **Weissmies**, 13,225 feet, 4031 mètres, is 3⅓ kils. S. of the Laquinhorn. From the Hotel to the top occupies about 5 hs. The descent may be made in 2½ to 3 hours.

The **Rossboden Pass**, about 10,800 feet, is the easiest of the three ways of getting from the Weissmies Hotel to the Simplon Road. From the Hotel to the top takes 4 hs. and from the top to Eggen (2 kils. above Simpeln) about 3½ hs. This pass appears to have been known for a long time. In 1833, a description of a passage of it was published at Geneva, entitled *Passage du Roth-horn*, par Marc Viridet. The author set out from Saas at 6 a.m., on Aug. 1, 1833, with a couple of young friends and the Innkeeper, Moritz Zurbrucken. Two of the party had bâtons, M. Viridet carried an umbrella, and the fourth had no support. They were without rope or ice-axe, and experienced some of the vicissitudes which are usual, when traversing glaciers, under such circumstances. M. Viridet advises his readers not to cross the Roth-horn (Rossboden Pass), and concludes by saying, "but if you *will* try this journey, *munis-toi de guides, de cordes, et de bâtons ferrés.*" Good advice.

The **Fletschjoch**, (the next pass in order, proceeding from N. to S.), 12,051 feet, 3673 mètres, leads between the Fletschhorn and Laquinhorn to the Simplon Road. Its passage seems to have been first effected by Messrs. Jacomb and Chater with Christian Michel and Peter Baumann in 1863. Not recommended. The **Laquinjoch**, 11,473 feet, 3497 mètres, between the Laquinhorn and Weissmies (also leading to the Simplon Road) is more practical. It takes about 2½ hs. from the Hotel to the top of the pass, and 4 to 5 hs. from the top to Simpeln.

And now, How are you going to get back? Perhaps time is up, or money running short? Then return the way you came, for it is the quickest and cheapest route. But if anything is left return by Bern,[1]—saunter on the Cathedral Platform, and then feed the Bears. Dine leisurely at the Buffet in the Station (reasonable prices); take your seat *in good time* in a through carriage to Calais (by the Delle route),[2] and go to sleep,—knowing that the Douaniers at Belfort will be sure to wake you up and turn you out about midnight. After that, you can go to sleep again, and dream of Home, sweet Home!

[1] Bern can be reached most *quickly* from Zermatt by taking train to Visp, thence travelling *viâ* Lausanne and Fribourg; but a person who is so happy as to be free from baggage can get to Bern from Zermatt more *economically* by walking from Louèche (Suste or Souste) to Leukerbad, and over the Gemmi Pass. See p. 99, and Plan on p. 97.

[2] One of the advantages of this route is that luggage registered to London is not examined *in France*, or until it arrives at the Station to which it was registered from Bern.

APPENDIX.

A.—'TARIF' of Excursions from ST. NICHOLAS.

	Guides. Francs.	Porters. Francs.
Ascent of the **Balfrinhorn**	25	20
do. **Brunneggh orn**	40	25
do. **Grabenhorn**	25	15
do. **Nadelhorn**	35	20
do. do. descending to **Saas**	45	25
do. do. descending to **Randa**	40	20
do. **Rothhorn (Jungthal)**	15	10
do. **Schwarzhorn**	15	10
do. **Sparrenhorn**	15	10
do. **Ulrichshorn**	30	20
Over the **Balfrin Glacier** to **Saas**	20	15
By the **Hannig Pass** to **Saas-Fée**	15	10
do. **Jung Pass** to **Gruben**	15	10
do. **Ried Pass** to **Saas-Fée**	30	20

B.—'TARIF' of Excursions from RANDA.

	Guides. Francs.	Porters. Francs.
Ascent of the **Bieshorn**	50	30
do. **Dom**	60	40
do. **Durrenhorn**	30	20
do. **Hohberghorn**	30	20
do. **Südlenspitz**	80	40
do. **Täschhorn**	60	40
do. **Weisshorn**	80	45
To the **Weisshorn Cabane**	20	15
By the **Biesjoch** to **Gruben**	40	25
do. do. **Zinal**	45	25
do. **Nadeljoch** to **Saas-Fée**	45	30
do. **Schallijoch (Schallenjoch)** to **Zinal**	50	30

C.—'TARIF' of Excursions from SAAS.

	Guides. Francs.	Porters. Francs.
Over the **Dom** to **Randa**	100	70
Ascent of the **Allalinhorn**	25	15
do. **Almagellhorn**	20	10

N.B.—This tarif should be posted in all mountain hotels in the Canton Valais, and in the Cabanes.

Before engaging Guides or Porters, it is desirable to have a clear understanding whether the agreed price includes return.

	Guides. Francs.	Porters. Francs.
Ascent of the **Alphubel**, by the **Alphubeljoch**	35	25
do. do. by the **Mischabeljoch**	40	30
do. **Balfrinhorn**	30	20
do. **Egginerhorn**	20	10
do. **Fletschhorn**	40	30
do. **Joderhorn**	12	10
do. **Latelhorn**	10	8
do. **Laquinhorn**	40	30
do. **Mittaghorn**	10	8
do. **Nadelhorn**	40	30
do. **Portjengrat**	40	30
do. **Rimpfischhorn**	40	30
do. **Sewinenhorn**	10	8
do. **Simelihorn**	12	10
do. **Sonnighorn**	25	15
do. **Stellihorn**	20	10
do. **Strahlhorn**	30	20
do. **Täschhorn**	80	50
do. **Ulrichshorn**	30	20
do. **Weissmies**	40	25
By the **Adler Pass** to **Zermatt**	30	20
do. **Allalin Pass** to **Zermatt**	30	20
do. **Alphubeljoch** to **Zermatt**	30	20
do. **Antrona Pass** to **Antrona**	15	10
do. **Domjoch** to **Randa**	50	35
do. **Feejoch** to **Zermatt**	30	20
do. **Fletschhorn Pass** to **Simpeln**	30	20
do. **Furggen Pass** to **Antrona**	20	15
do. **Laquinjoch** to **Simpeln**	20	15
do. **Mischabeljoch** to **Zermatt**	80	50
do. **Mondelli Pass to Anzasca**	15	10
do. **Monte Moro Pass** to **Macugnaga**	20	15
do. **Nadeljoch** to **Randa**	45	30
do. **Ofenthal Pass** to **Antrona**	15	10
do. **Portjen Pass** to **Antrona**	20	15
do. **Rossboden Pass** to **Simpeln**	20	15
do. **Sewinen Pass** to **Macugnaga**	30	20
do. **Sirwolten Pass** to **Simpeln**	20	15
do. **Sonnighorn Pass** to **Antrona**	20	15
do. **Zwischbergen Pass** to **Gondo**	20	15
To the **Aleusser Thurm**	10	8
do. **Almagell Alp**	6	4
do. **Furgg Alp**	6	4
do. **Innerer Thurm**	12	10
do **Mattmark Hotel**	6	6

	Guides. Francs.	Porters. Francs.
To the **Ofenthal**	8	6
do. **Thälliboden**	8	6
do. **Trift Alp**	6	6
do. **Triftgrat**	10	8

D.—'TARIF' OF EXCURSIONS FROM ZERMATT.

Ascent of the **Allalinhorn**	35	20
do. do. descending to **Saas**	40	25
do. **Alphubel** by the **Alphubeljoch**	35	20
do. do. descending to **Saas**	50	30
do. do. by the **Mischabeljoch**	40	25
do. **Blattenhörner** (**Plattenhörner**)	10	8
do. **Breithorn** from the **North**	50	30
do. do. from the **South,** in one day . .	25	15
do. do. from the **South,** sleeping on the **Theodulpass**	30	20
Ascent of the **Breithorn** from the **South,** sleeping on the **Theodulpass,** descending to **Breuil**	40	25
Ascent of **Castor,** and back to the **Riffel**	35	20
do. **Castor and Pollux,** in one day	55	30
do. do. descending to **Gressoney** .	50	35
do. the **Cima di Jazzi** from the **Riffel**	15	10
do. do. *viâ* the **Findelen Glacier** .	20	15
do. **Dent Blanche**	80	45
do. do. descending to **Ferpècle** . .	90	50
do. **Dent d'Hérens**	80	60
do. do. descending to **Prerayen** .	90	70
do. **Ebihorn**	30	20
do. **Gabelhorn, Ober**	70	40
do. **Gabelhorn, Unter**	20	15
do. **Gornergrat**	8	8
do. **Hohthäligrat**	10	10
do. **Hörnli**	8	...
do. **Jägerhorn,** from the **Riffel**	30	20
Ascent of **Klein Matterhorn** (**Petit Mont Cervin**) . .	15	10
do. do. sleeping on the **Theodulpass**	25	15
do. **Lyskamm**	100	60
do. **Mominghorn**	40	25
do. **Matterhorn**	100	70
do. do. as far as the northern shoulder . .	60	40
do. do. descending to **Breuil**	150	100

	Guides. Francs.	Porters. Francs.
Ascent of **Mettelhorn**	10	8
do. do. as far as the saddle	8	6
do. **Mont Durand** (**Arbenhorn**)	30	20
do. do. descending to **Zinal**	40	30
do. **Monte Rosa, highest point**	50	35
do. do. **Ludwigshöhe**	40	25
do. do. **Nordend**	50	35
do. do. **Parrotspitze**	50	35
do. do. **Signalkuppe**	50	35
do. do. **Vincent Pyramide**	40	25
do. do. do. descending to **Alagna**	60	40
do. do. **Zumsteinspitze**	50	35
do. **Plattenhörner** (**Blattenhörner**)	10	8
do. **Pointe de Zinal**	30	20
do. **Pollux,** and back to the **Riffel**	30	20
do. **Rimpfischhorn,** from the **Allalin Pass**	50	35
do. do. from the **Adler Pass**	40	20
do. do. from the **Fluh Alp**	35	20
do. **Rothhorn, Ober**	10	10
do. **Rothhorn, Unter**	8	8
do. **Rothhorn, Zinal**	80	45
do. do. descending to **Zinal**	100	60
do. **Schallhorn**	40	25
do. **Stockhorn**	15	12
do. **Strahlhorn**	30	20
do. do. descending to **Saas**	40	25
do. **Täschhorn,** from the **Täsch Alp**	80	50
do. **Tête Blanche**	25	15
do. do. descending to **Prerayen**	30	25
do. do. do. **Arolla** or **Ferpècle**	35	30
do. **Tête du Lion**	60	50
do. **Trifthorn**	30	15
do. **Wellenkuppe**	40	20
To the **Bétemps Cabane** from the **Riffelberg** (**Riffelhaus**)	8	6
do. do. from **Zermatt**	15	10
do. **Findelen Glacier**	6	6
do. **Gorner Glacier**	3	...
do. **Gorner Glacier,** and through the *séracs* to the **Riffel** or **Riffel Alp**	12	...
do. **Höhbalm**	5	...
do. **Matterhorn Cabane** (**Hörnli ridge**)	15	10
do. **Plattje,** from the **Riffel**	8	6
do. do. from **Zermatt**	15	10
do. **Riffel Alp Hotel**	4	4
do. **Riffelberg** (**Riffelhaus**)	5	5

	Guides. Francs.	Porters. Francs.
To the **Riffelhorn,** from the **Riffel Alp**	8	...
do. do. from the **Riffelhaus**	6	...
do. do. by the *séracs* of the **Gorner Glacier**	20	...
do. do. from **Zermatt**	10	...
do. **Schwarzsee (Lac Noir)**	6	6
do. **Stockje** (ruins of Cabane)	15	10
do. **Théodule,** hut on **top of Pass**	10	...
do. do. lower hotel (**Gandegg**)	8	...
do. **Trift Hotel**	8	...
do. **Zmutt Glacier**	5	...
By the **Allalin Pass** to **Saas**	30	20
do. **Alphubeljoch** to **Saas**	30	20
do. **Arbenjoch** to **Zinal**	40	30
do. **Bertol, Col de,** to **Arolla**	30	25
do. **Bouquetins, Col de,** to **Arolla**	30	25
do. **Cimes Blanches** to **Fiery**	25	15
do. **Durand, Col,** to **Zinal**	35	25
do. **Feejoch** to **Saas**	30	20
do. **Felikjoch** to **Gressoney**	40	25
do. **Furggjoch** to **Breuil**	25	15
do. **Hérens Col d',** to **Ferpècle**	30	25
do. **Jägerjoch** to **Macugnaga**	40	30
do. **Lysjoch** to **Alagna**	50	40
do. do. to **Gressoney**	45	30
do. **Mischabeljoch** to **Saas-Grund**	35	25
do. **Moming, Col de,** to **Zinal**	50	35
do. **Rothhornjoch** to **Zinal**	40	30
do. **Schwarzthor** to **Fiery**	40	25
do. **Sesiajoch** to **Alagna**	60	45
do. **Theodul Pass (Matterjoch)** to **Breuil**	20	15
do. **Tiefenmattenjoch** to **Prerayen**	40	25
do. **Tournanche, Col de,** to **Breuil**	40	25
do. **Trift Pass (Triftjoch)** to **Zinal**	35	25
do. **Valpelline, Col de,** to **Prerayen**	35	20
do. do. the **Col du Mont Brulé,** and the **Col de l'Evêque** to **Mauvoisin**	60	40
do. **Valpelline, Col de,** and the **Col du Mont Brulé** to **Arolla**	30	25
do. **Weissthor, New,** to **Macugnaga**	35	25
do. do. **Old,** to **Macugnaga**	40	30
do. do. **Schwarzberg,** to **Mattmark**	30	20
do. **Zinal, Col de (Zinaljoch, Col de la Dent Blanche),** to **Zinal**	35	25
do. **Zwillings Pass** to **Fiery**	40	25

'TARIF' FOR HORSES AND MULES AT ZERMATT.

		Francs.
To the	**Village of Findelen**	8
do.	**Glacier of Findelen**	10
do.	**Gorges of the Gorner**	5
do.	**Gorner Glacier**	8
do.	**Gornergrat**	15
do.	do. returning by the **Findelen Valley**, or *vice-versa*	18
do.	**Mettelhorn**[1]	18
do.	**Lac Noir (Schwarzsee)**	10
do.	do. returning by the **Staffelalp**, or *vice-versa*	15
do.	**Plattje Cabane**	20
do.	**Riffelalp**	8
do.	do. returning by the **Findelen Valley**, or *vice-versa*	10
do.	**Riffelberg**	10
do.	do. returning by the **Findelen Valley**, or *vice-versa*	12
do.	**Täschalp**	15
do.	**Col Theodule**, as far as the moraine	15
do.	do. as far as **Hotel Gandegg**	17
do.	**Trift Hotel**	15
do.	**Village of Zmutt**	8
do.	**Zmutt Glacier**	10

'TARIF' AT ZERMATT FOR 'PORTEURS À CHAISE' (PER MAN).

To the	**Village of Findelen**	4
do.	**Glacier of Findelen**	6
do.	**Gorges of the Gorner**	3
do.	**Gorner Glacier**	4
do.	**Gornergrat**	8
do.	do. returning by the **Findelen Valley**	10
do.	**Mettelhorn**[1]	10
do.	**Lac Noir (Schwarzsee)**	6
do.	do. returning by **Staffelalp**	8
do.	**Plattje Cabane**	12
do.	**Riffelalp**	4
do.	do. returning by the **Findelen Valley**	6
do.	**Riffelberg**	6
do.	do. returning by the **Findelen Valley**	8
do.	**Col Theodule**, as far as the **Hotel Gandegg**	10
do.	do. to the **summit of the Pass**	12
do.	do. and across to **Breuil**	15

[1] Enquiry should be made whether horses or *chaises à porteur* can go to the top.

E.—Mountains in and around the Basin of the Valley of ZERMATT.

Name of Peak.	Height in Mètres.	Height in Feet.	Situation.
Allalinhorn . . .	4034	13,235	E.S.E. ½ E. of Täsch; E.N.E. of Zermatt; N.E. of Allalinpass.
Alphubel . . .	4207	13,803	E. ½ S. of Täsch; S. of Mischabeljoch; N.W. of Alphubeljoch.
Arbenhorn (Mt. Durand)	3744	12,284	W. by N. of Zermatt; E. of Col Durand; W. of Arbenjoch.
Augstbordhorn . .	2974	9757	West of Stalden.
Balfrin (Balenfirn) .	3802	12,473	S. of Stalden; E. of Herbrigen.
Balmenhorn (Monte Rosa)	4324	14,187	E. by S. of Lysjoch.
Barrhorn . . .	3621	11,880	W.S.W. of St. Niklaus.
Bieshorn . . .	4161	13,652	W.N.W. of Randa; W. of Biesjoch.
Bigerhorn . . .	3180	10,433	S.E. of St. Niklaus.
Breithorn . . .	4171	13,685	South of Zermatt.
Brunnegghorn . .	3846	12,619	N.W. of Randa; S.E. of Brunnegg-joch.
Castor	4230	13,878	S.S.E. of Zermatt; S.E. of Zwillings-pass.
Cima di Jazzi . .	3818	12,526	E.S.E. of Zermatt; S. of the New Weissthor.
Cima di Roffel . .	3645	11,959	N.E. of Cima di Jazzi.
Dent Blanche . .	4364	14,318	W. by N. of Zermatt.
Dent d'Hérens (d'Erin)	4180	13,714	W.S.W. of Zermatt; E. of Tiefenmattenjoch.
Dom	4554	14,941	E. by S. of Randa; N.E. of Zermatt; S. of Nadeljoch.
Dreizehnenhorn . .	3056	10,026	W. by S. of Stalden.
Durchlochhorn . .	2704	8872	East of St. Niklaus.
Dürrenhorn . . .	4035	13,238	N.E. by E. ½ E. of Randa; N. of Hohberg Pass.
Ebihorn . . .	3343	10,968	W. of Zermatt.
Egginerhorn . .	3377	11,080	Between the Feegletscher and the Saas Thal.
Ferrichhorn . . .	3292	10,801	S.E. by E. of St. Niklaus; S. of Ferrichlücke.
Festihorn . . .	3249	10,660	W. of St. Niklaus.
Fillarhorn . . .	3679	12,070	S.E. by E. of Zermatt; S. of the Old Weissthor.
Fluchthorn . . .	3802	12,473	N.E. of the Strahlhorn.
Fluhhorn . . .	3318	10,886	E. of Zermatt; W. of Langenfluh-pass.
Furggen, Gr. . .	2820	9252	E.S.E. of Grächen.

Name of Peak.	Height in Mètres.	Height in Feet.	Situation.
Furggen, Kl. . .	2650	8694	E. ½ S. of Grächen.
Furgg-grat . . .	3498	11,477	Between the summit of the Theodul-pass and the Matterhorn.
Furggwanghorn . .	3163	10,377	W.N.W. of St. Niklaus; N. of Jungpass.
Getschunghorn . .	2860	9383	W. of Täsch.
Gabelhorn . . .	3135	10,276	E. ½ S. of St. Niklaus.
Gabelhorn, Ober . .	4073	13,363	W.N.W. of Zermatt.
Gabelhorn, Unter .	3398	11,149	W. by N. of Zermatt.
Galenhorn . . .	3360	11,024	E. of Herbrigen; N. of Galenpass.
Gemshorn . . .	?	?	N.W. of Saas-Fée; E.N.E. of the Ulrichshorn.
Gornergrat . . .	3136	10,289	North side of the Gorner Glacier.
Grabenhorn . . .	3375	11,072	E.S.E. of Randa.
Gugel	2707	8882	E.N.E. of the Riffelhaus.
Hohberghorn . .	4226	13,865	E.N.E. of Randa; S. of Hohberg-pass.
Hohthäligrat . .	3289	10,791	S.E. by E. of Zermatt.
Hohwänghorn . .	3482	11,424	W. of Zermatt; N. side of Zmutt Glacier.
Hörnli	2893	9492	S.W. ½ W. of Zermatt.
Jägerhorn . . .	3975	13,042	S.E. by E. of Zermatt; N. of Jäger-joch.
Leiterspitz . . .	3218	10,558	E. by N. of Täsch.
Ludwigshöhe . .	4344	14,252	Head of the Grenz Glacier.
Lyskamm . . .	4538	14,889	S.E. by S. of Zermatt; E. of Felik-joch; W. of Lysjoch.
Matterhorn or **Mont Cervin**	4482	14,705	S.W. by W. of Zermatt.
Mettelhorn . . .	3410	11,188	S.W. by W. of Täsch; N. of Zermatt.
Mittaghorn . . .	3148	10,328	Between the Feegletscher and the Saas Thal.
Monte Rosa . . .	4638	15,217	S.E. of Zermatt.
Nadelhorn . . .	4334	14,218	E. by N. of Randa.
Nordend (Monte Rosa)	4612	15,132	N.N.E. of the Höchste Spitze.
Petit Mont Cervin .	3886	12,750	S. by W. of Zermatt; E. of Theodul-pass.
Parrotspitze (Mte. Rosa)	4463	14,643	Head of the Grenz Glacier.
Plattenhörner . .	3136	10,261	N. of Zermatt.
Platthorn . . .	3249	10 660	E. by S. of St. Niklaus; N. of Ferrichlücke.
Pollux	4094	13,432	S.S.E. of Zermatt; N.W. of Zwillingspass.
Riffelhorn . . .	2931	9616	S. by E. of Zermatt.

Name of Peak.	Height in Mètres.	Height in Feet.	Situation.
Rimpfischhorn . .	4203	13,790	E. of Zermatt; N. of Adler Pass.
Rothhorn . . .	3262	10,702	W. by N. of St. Niklaus; S. of Jungpass.
Rothhorn or **Moming** .	4223	13,855	S.W. by W. of Randa; W. of Täsch; S. of Momingpass.
Rothhorn, Ober . .	3418	11,214	E. by N. of Zermatt.
Rothhorn, Unter . .	3106	10,190	E. of Zermatt.
Schallihorn . . .	3978	13,051	W.S.W. of Randa; S. of Schallijoch; N. of Momingpass.
Schwarzhorn . .	2805	9203	W. of Saas-Fée.
Schwarzhorn . .	3204	10,512	W. of Kalpetran; N. of Augstbordpass.
Seethalhorn . . .	3038	9967	E. of St. Niklaus.
Signalkuppe (Mte. Rosa)	4561	14,964	Head of the Grenz Glacier.
Sparrhorn . . .	2990	9810	W. by N. of St. Niklaus.
Steinthalhorn . .	3113	10,213	N.W. of St. Niklaus; S. of Augstbordpass.
Stellihorn . . .	3415	11,204	W. by S. of St. Niklaus.
Stockhorn . . .	3534	11,595	E.S.E. of Zermatt; W. of Stockhornpass.
Stockje . . .	3097	10,161	W. by S. of Zermatt.
Strahlhorn . . .	4191	13,750	E. by S. of Zermatt; S.E. of Adlerpass.
Sud-Lenzspitze . .	4300	14,108	E. of Randa; N. of Nadeljoch.
Täschhorn . . .	4498	14,757	E.S.E. of Randa; E. by N. of Täsch; S. of Domjoch.
Tête Blanche . .	3750	12,303	W. by S. of Zermatt; N. of Col de Valpelline.
Tête du Lion . .	3723	12,215	Between the Matterhorn and the Dent d'Hérens.
Tête de Valpelline .	3813	12,510	W.S.W. of Zermatt; S. of Col de Valpelline.
Theodulhorn . .	3472	11,391	S.S.W. of Zermatt; N. of Theodulpass.
Trifthorn . . .	3737	12,261	N.W. by W. of Zermatt; N. of Triftjoch.
Ulrichshorn . . .	3929	12,891	E.N.E. of Randa; S. of Riedpass.
Wasenhorn . . .	3340	10,958	W. ½ S. of St. Niklaus.
Weisse Egg . . .	3168	10,394	N.W. by W. of St. Niklaus.
Weisshorn . . .	4512	14,803	W. of Randa.
Wellenkuppe . .	3910	12,828	N.W. by W. of Zermatt.
Zinal, Pointe de . .	3806	12,487	W. ½ N. of Zermatt; W. of Col Durand.
Zumsteinspitze (Monte Rosa)	4573	15,004	Head of the Grenz Glacier.

F.—Passes in the Basin of the Valley of ZERMATT and its Environs.

Name of Pass.	Height in Mètres.	Height in Feet.	Position of Summit.
Adlerpass . . .	3798	12,461	Between the Strahlhorn and Rimpfischhorn.
Allalinpass . . .	3570	11,713	Between the Allalinhorn and Rimpfischhorn.
Alphubeljoch . .	3802	12,474	Between the Alphubel and Allalinhorn.
Antronapass . .	2844	9331	E. by S. of Mattmark See.
Arbenjoch . . .	3650	11,975	Between Ober Gabelhorn and Mont Durand (Arbenhorn).
Augstbordpass . .	2893	9492	Between the Schwarzhorn and Steinthalhorn.
Biesjoch . . .	3549	11,644	Between the Bieshorn and Brunnegghorn.
Breuiljoch . . .	about	10,900	At the head of the Furgg Glacier; S.E. of the Matterhorn.
Brunneggjoch . .	3383	11,099	N.W. of the Brunnegghorn.
Domjoch . . .	4286	14,062	Between the Dom and Täschhorn.
Durand, Col . . .	3474	11,398	Between the Dent Blanche and Mont Durand (Arbenhorn).
Feejoch	3812	12,507	W.N.W. of the Allalinhorn.
Felikjoch . . .	4068	13,347	Between Castor and the Lyskamm.
Ferrichlücke . .	2889	9479	Between the Platthorn and Ferrichhorn.
Fillarjoch . . .	?	?	Between the Fillarhorn and Jägerhorn.
Furggjoch . . .	about	10,900	At the head of the Furgg Glacier; S.E. of the Matterhorn.
Gabelhornpass . .	about	10,170	Between the Gabelhorn and Platthorn.
Galenpass . . .	3240	10,630	Between the Galenhorn and Dürrenhorn.
Ginanzthalpass . .	2912	9554	E. of Dreizehnenhorn.
Hérens, Col d' . .	3480	11,418	N.E. of the Tête Blanche.
Hohbergpass . .	?	?	Between the Dürrenhorn and Hohberghorn.
Jägerjoch . . .	?	?	Between the Nord End (Monte Rosa) and Jägerhorn.
Jungpass . . .	2994	9823	Between the Furggwanghorn and Rothhorn.
Langenfluhpass . .	3200	10,499	Between the Fluhhorn and Rimpfischhorn.

Name of Pass.	Height in Mètres.	Height in Feet.	Position of Summit.
Laquinjoch . . .	3497	11,473	S. of Laquinhorn ; N. of Weissmies.
Lion, Col du . . .	3577	11,736	Between the Tête du Lion and Matterhorn. The height is according to the Italian Map scale $\frac{1}{50000}$.
Lysjoch . . .	about	14,000	Between the Lyskamm and Ludwigshöhe (Monte Rosa).
Mischabeljoch . .	3856	12,651	Between the Täschhorn and Alphubel.
Momingpass . .	3793	12,444	Between the Schallihorn and Rothhorn (Moming).
Mondellipass . .	2841	9321	Head of Saasthal, a little E. of Monte Moro.
Moro, Monte (Passo del Moro).	2862	9390	Between Saas Thal and Macugnaga.
Nadeljoch . . .	4167	13,672	Between the Nadelhorn and Dom.
Ofenthalpass . .	2838	9311	N.E. of Monte Moro.
Piodejoch . . .	?	?	Between the Parrotspitze and Ludwigshöhe.
Riedpass . . .	about	11,900	Between the Balfrin (Balenfirn) and Ulrichshorn.
Rossbodenpass . .	?	?	N. by W. of the Fletschhorn.
Schallijoch . . .	3751	12,307	Between the Schallihorn and Weisshorn.
Schallijoch, Ober .	3745	12,287	Between the Schallihorn and Momingpass.
Schwarzberg Weissthor	3600	11,811	Between the Strahlhorn and Cima di Roffel.
Schwarzthor . .	3741	12,274	Between the Breithorn and Pollux.
Sesiajoch . . .	4411	14,472	Between the Parrotspitze and Signalkuppe.
Silbersattel . . .	4490	14,731	Between the Nord End and Höchste Spitze (Monte Rosa).
Simelipass . . .	3028	9934	E. of Eisten (Saasthal).
Sirwoltenpass . .	2664	8740	Head of Gamserthal, east side.
Stockhornpass . .	3415	11,204	E. of the Stockhorn, between the Findelen and Gorner Glaciers.
Theodulpass or **Matterjoch**	3322	10,899	Between the Theodulhorn and Klein Matterhorn (Petit Mont Cervin).
Tiefenmattenjoch .	3593	11,788	Between the Tête de Valpelline and Dent d'Hérens (Mont Tabor).
Tournanche, Col de .	3468	11,378	Between the Dent d'Hérens and the Tête du Lion.
Triftjoch . . .	3540	11,614	Between the Trifthorn and Wellenkuppe.

Name of Pass.	Height in Mètres.	Height in Feet.	Position of Summit.
Valpelline, Col de .	3562	11,687	Between the Tête Blanche and the Tête de Valpelline.
Weisshorn Pass . .	?	?	Between the Weisshorn and the Bieshorn.
Weissthor, New . .	3600	11,811	Between Cima di Jazzi and Cima di Roffel.
Weissthor, Old . .	3576	11,733	Between Cima di Jazzi and the Fillarhorn.
Zinaljoch . . .	3500	11,483	Between the Dent Blanche and the Pointe de Zinal.
Zwillingspass . .	3861	12,668	Between Pollux and Castor.
Zwischbergenpass .	3248	10,656	Between the Weissmies and Portjengrat.

AN OLD PUBLIC SERVANT.

G.—List of Guides of ZERMATT, TÄSCH, RANDA, ST. NICHOLAS, STALDEN, VISP, SAAS, etc.

ANDENMATTEN Adolph (*Almagell*).
ANDENMATTEN Baptist (*Almagell*).
ANDENMATTEN Basil (*Eisten*).
ANDENMATTEN David (*Eisten*).
ANDENMATTEN Moritz (*Stalden*).
ANDENMATTEN Polycarp (*Stalden*).
ANDENMATTEN Xavier (*Almagell*).
ANTHAMATTEN Aloys (*Balen*).
ANTHAMATTEN Franz (*Saas*).
ANTHAMATTEN Joh.-Jos. (*Saas*).
ANTHAMATTEN Johann-Peter (*Saas*).
ANTHAMATTEN Roman (*Saas*).
AUFDENBLATTEN Emmanuel (*Zermatt*)
AUFDENBLATTEN Johann (*Zermatt*).
AUFDENBLATTEN P.-Jos. (*Zermatt*).
AUFDENBLATTEN Séverin (*Täsch*).
BIENER Alois (*Zermatt*).
BIENER Franz (*Zermatt*).
BIENER Franz (*Zermatt*).
BIENER Ignaz (*Zermatt*).
BIENER Joseph (*Zermatt*).
BIENER Joseph-Marie (*Zermatt*).
BIENER Joseph-Lorenz (*Zermatt*).
BIENER Joseph-Marie (*St. Nicholas*).
BIENER Marius (*Zermatt*).
BIENER Peter-Anton (*Zermatt*).
BIENER Raphael (*Zermatt*).
BIENER Theodul (*Zermatt*).
BIFFIGER Jos.-Marie (*St. Nicholas*).
BLUMENTHAL Joseph-Marie (*Eisten*).
BRANTSCHEN Adolph (*Randa*).
BRANTSCHEN Joseph (*St. Nicholas*).
BÜMANN Gottfried (*Randa*).
BURGENER Alois (*Eisten*).
BURGENER Alexander (*Eisten*).
BURGENER Franz (*Eisten*).
BURGENER Fridolin (*St. Nicholas*).
BURGENER Elias (*Balen*).
BURGENER Emmanuel (*Balen*).
BURGENER Joseph-Marie (*Saas-Fée*).
BURGENER Peter-Joseph (*Almagell*).
CHANTON Peter-Ludwig (*St. Nicholas*).
FURRER Alphons (*Zermatt*).
FURRER Elias (*Stalden*).
FURRER Ferdinand (*Eisten*).
FURRER Franz (*Eisten*).
FUX Joseph-Mario (*St. Nicholas*).
GENTINETTA August (*Zermatt*).
GENTINETTA Emmanuel (*Glis*).
GENTINETTA Joseph (*Glis*).
GRAVEN Emil (*Zermatt*).
GRUBER Alphons (*St. Nicholas*).
GRUBER Peter (*St. Nicholas*).
GUNTERN Alexander (*Zermatt*).
IMBODEN Alois (*St. Nicholas*).
IMBODEN Ambrose (*St. Nicholas*).
IMBODEN Felix (*Täsch*).
IMBODEN Ferdinand (*Täsch*).
IMBODEN Friedrich (*Täsch*).
IMBODEN Joseph (*St. Nicholas*).
IMBODEN Joseph-Marie (*Täsch*).
IMBODEN Nicholas (*St. Nicholas*).
IMBODEN Theodul (*St. Nicholas*).
IMBODEN Theophil (*St. Nicholas*).
IMSENG Abraham (*Saas-Fée*).
IMSENG Aloys (*Saas-Fée*).
IMSENG Emil (*Saas-Fée*).
IMSENG Moritz (*Saas-Fée*).
IMSENG Xavier (*Saas-Fée*).
JULEN Edouard (*Zermatt*).
JULEN Elias (*Zermatt*).
JULEN Emmanuel (*Zermatt*).
JULEN Felix (*Zermatt*).
JULEN Gabriel (*Zermatt*).
JULEN Hieronymus (*Zermatt*).
JULEN Julius (*Zermatt*).
KALBERMATTEN Joseph (*Almagell*).
KALBERMATTEN A. (*Balen*).

KALBERMATTEN Emmanuel (*Saas*).
KARLEN Polycarp (*Törbel*).
KNUBEL Cæsar (*St. Nicholas*).
KNUBEL Peter (*St. Nicholas*).
KNUBEL Salomon (*St. Nicholas*).
KRONIG Aloys (*Zermatt*).
KRONIG Fridolin (*Zermatt*).
KRONIG Johann (*Zermatt*).
KRONIG Leopold (*Täsch*).
KRONIG Mathias (*Zermatt*).
LAGGER Alfred (*St. Nicholas*).
LAGGER Jos.-Marie (*St. Nicholas*).
LAUBER Elias (*Zermatt*).
LERJEN Aloys (*Täsch*).
LERJEN Johann (*Täsch*).
LOCHMATTER Jos.-Marie (*St. Nicholas*)
LOCHMATTER Joseph (*St. Nicholas*).
LOCHMATTER Julius (*St. Nicholas*).
MOSER Anton (*Täsch*).
MOSER Fridolin (*Täsch*).
MOSER Joseph (*Täsch*).
MOSER Joseph (*Zermatt*).
MOSER Léo (*Täsch*).
MOSER Robert (*Täsch*).
PERREN Emil (*Zermatt*).
PERREN Clemens (*Randa*).
PERREN Franz (*Zermatt*).
PERREN Fridolin (*Randa*).
PERREN Hermann (*Zermatt*).
PERREN Moritz (*Zermatt*).
PERREN Peter, 1882 (*Zermatt*).
PERREN Peter, 1886 (*Zermatt*).
PERREN Peter-Anton (*Zermatt*).
POLLINGER Alois (*St. Nicholas*).
POLLINGER Joseph (*St. Nicholas*).
RUPPEN Ad. (*Saas-Fée*).
RUPPEN Aloys (*Saas*).
RUPPEN Peter (*Visp*).
SARBACH Peter (*St. Nicholas*).
SCHALLER Adolph (*Randa*).
SCHALLER Anton (*Emd*).
SCHALLER Joseph (*Randa*).
SCHALLER Victus (*Emd*).
SCHANTON Jos.-Marie (*St. Nicholas*).
SCHWARZEN Heinrich (*Randa*).
SCHWARZEN Quirinus (*Randa*).
SCHWARZEN Viliam (*Randa*).
SIGRIST Joseph (*Zermatt*).
SUMMERMATTER Alph. (*Randa*).
SUMMERMATTER Clemens (*Randa*).
SUMMERMATTER Friedrich (*Randa*).
SUMMERMATTER Johann (*Randa*).
SUPERSAXO Albert (*Balen*).
SUPERSAXO Aloys (*Saas-Fée*).
SUPERSAXO Alphons (*Saas-Fée*).
SUPERSAXO Ambros (*Saas-Fée*).
SUPERSAXO Ambros (*Saas-Fée*).
SUPERSAXO Anton (*Saas-Fée*).
SUPERSAXO Benedikt (*Saas-Fée*).
SUPERSAXO Ignaz (*Saas-Fée*).
SUPERSAXO Johann-Peter (*Saas-Fée*).
SUPERSAXO Ludwig (*Saas-Fée*).
SUPERSAXO Peter-Joseph (*Saas-Fée*).
TAUGWALDER Gabriel (*Zermatt*).
TAUGWALDER Heinrich (*Zermatt*).
TAUGWALDER Joseph (*Zermatt*).
TAUGWALDER Peter (*Zermatt*).
TAUGWALDER Rudolph (*Zermatt*).
TRUFFER Aloys (*Randa*).
TRUFFER Aloys (*Randa*).
TRUFFER Fridolin (*Randa*).
TRUFFER Johann-Jos. (*St. Nicholas*).
TRUFFER Joseph (*Randa*).
TRUFFER Jul. (*Randa*).
TRUFFER Peter-Joseph (*St. Nicholas*)
TRUFFER Samuel (*Randa*).
VENETZ P.-Joseph (*Stalden*).
WILLISCH Joseph (*St. Nicholas*).
ZEN-KLUSEN Kaspar (*Glis*).
ZUBER Franz (*Randa*).
ZUBER Peter (*Randa*).
ZUM-TAUGWALD Jul. (*Zermatt*).
ZUM-TAUGWALD Mathias (*Zermatt*).
ZUM-TAUGWALD Sebastian (*Randa*).
ZURBRIGGEN Clemens (*Saas*).
ZURBRIGGEN Clemens (*Saas*).
ZURBRIGGEN Daniel (*Saas-Fée*).
ZURBRIGGEN Franz (*Saas*).
ZURBRIGGEN Peter-Joseph (*Almagell*)

H.—Courte Note sur la Géologie du Matterhorn. Par Signor F. Giordano, Ingénieur en Chef des Mines d'Italie, etc. etc.

Le Matterhorn ou Mont Cervin est formé depuis la base jusqu'au sommet de roches stratifiées en bancs assez réguliers, qui sont tous légèrement relevés vers l'Est, savoir vers le Mont Rose. Ces roches quoiqu'evidemment d'origine sédimentaire ont une structure fortement cristalline qui doit être l'effet d'une puissante action de métamorphisme très-développée dans cette région des Alpes. Dans la série des roches constituantes du Mont Cervin l'on peut faire une distinction assez marquée, savoir celles formant la base inférieure de la montagne, et celles formant le pic proprement dit.

Les roches de la base qu'on voit dans le Val Tournanche, dans le vallon de Z'Mutt, au col de Théodule et ailleurs, sont en général des schistes talqueux, serpentineux, chloriteux, et amphiboliques, alternant fort souvent avec des schistes calcaires à noyeaux quartzeux. Ces schistes calcaires de couleur brunâtre alternent ça et là avec des dolomies, des cargueules, et des quartzites tegulaires. Cette formation calcaréo-serpentineuse est très etendue dans les environs. Le pic au contraire est tout formé d'un gneiss talqueux, souvent à gros éléments, alternant parfois à quelques bancs de schistes talqueux et quartzeux, mais sans bancs calcaires. Vers le pied ouest du pic, le gneiss est remplacé par de l'euphotide granitoïde massive, qui semble y former une grosse lentille se fondant de tous côtés dans le gneiss même. Du reste les roches du Cervin montrent partout des exemples fort instructifs de passages graduels d'une structure à l'autre, résultant du métamorphisme plus ou moins avancé.

Le pic actuel n'est que le reste d'une puissante formation géologique ancienne, triasique peut-être, dont les couches puissantes de plus de 3500 mètres enveloppaient tout autour comme un immense manteau le grand massif granitoïde et feldspathique du Mont Rose. Aussi son étude détaillée, qui par exception est rendue fort facile par la profondeur des vallons d'ou il surgit, donne la clef de la structure géologique de beaucoup d'autres montagnes des environs. On y voit partout le phénomène assez curieux d'une puissante formation talqueuse très-cristalline, presque granitoïde, régulièrement superposée à une formation schisteuse et calcarifère. Cette même constitution géologique est en partie la cause de la forme aigue et de l'isolement du pic qui en font la merveille des voyageurs. En effet, tandis que les roches feuilletées de la base étant facilement corrodées par l'action des météores et de l'eau ont été facilement creusées en vallées larges et profondes, la roche supérieure qui constitue la pyramide donne lieu par sa dureté à des fendillements formant des parois escarpées qui conservent au pic ce profil elancé et caractéristique alpin. Les glaciers qui entourent son pied de tous les côtés en emportant d'une manière continue les débris tombant de ses flancs, contribuent pour leur part à maintenir cet isolement de la merveilleuse pyramide qui sans eux serait peut-être déjà ensevelie sous ses propres ruines.

GEOLOGICAL SECTION OF THE MATTERHORN, BY SIGNOR F. GIORDANO.

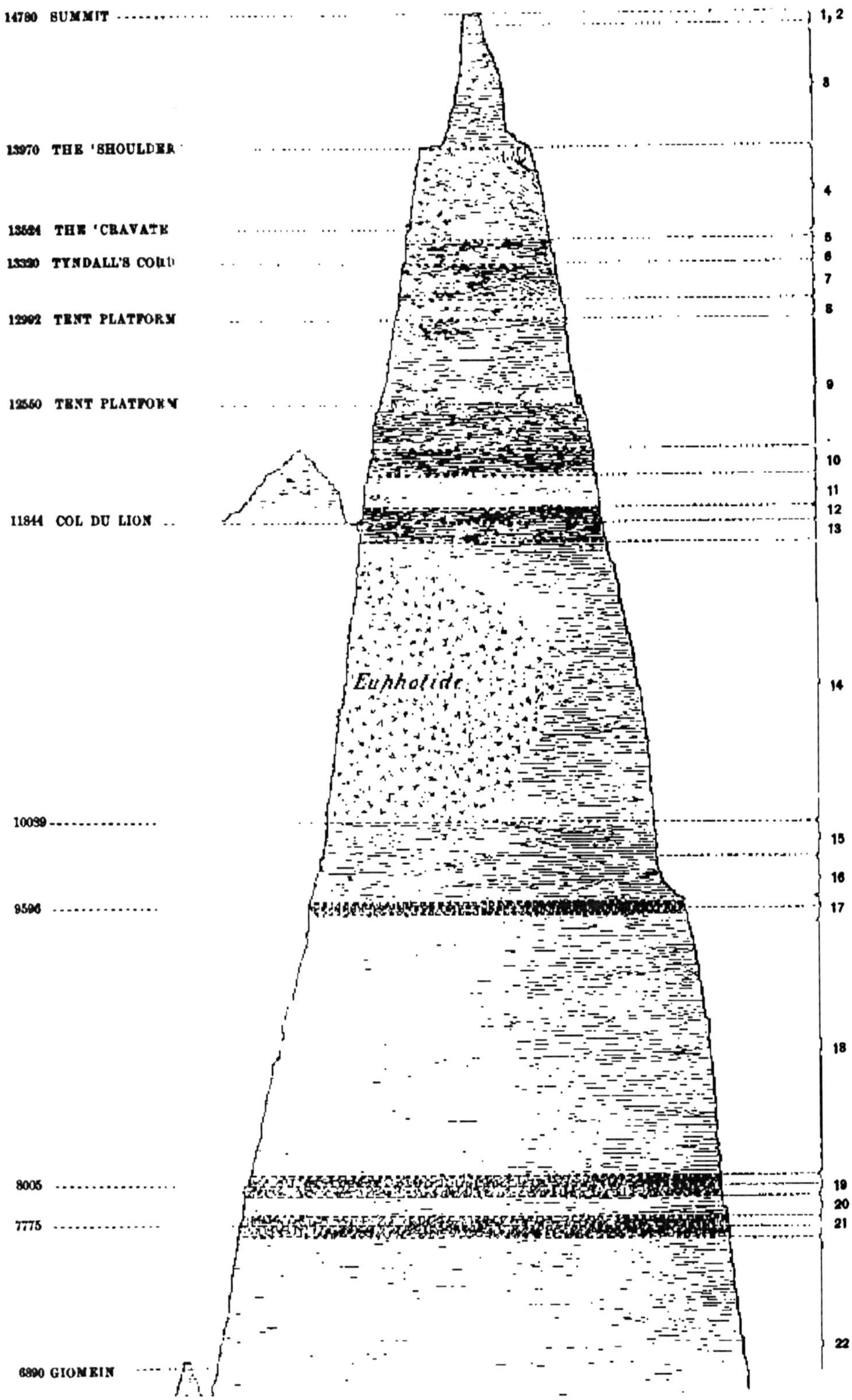

References to the Geological Section of the Matterhorn.

I. Gneiss talqueux quartzifère. Beaucoup de traces de foudres.

II. Banc de 3 à 4 mètres de schistes serpentineux et talqueux verts.

III. Gneiss talqueux à éléments plus ou moins schisteux, avec quelque lit de quartzite.

,, Gneiss et micaschistes ferrugineux à éléments très-fins, beaucoup de traces de foudre.

IV. Gnciss alternant avec des schistes talqueux et à des felsites en zones blanches et grises.

V. Petite couche de schistes serpentineux, vert sombre.

VI. Gneiss et micaschiste avec zones quartzifères rubanées.

VII. Gneiss talqueux à éléments schisteux.

VIII. *Id.* *id.* verdâtre, porphyroïde à éléments moyens.

IX. Gneiss talqueux granitoïde à gros éléments et avec des cristaux de feldspath.

X. Schistes grisâtres.

XI. Micaschistes ferrugineux.

XII. Gneiss talqueux vert sombre.

XIII. Gneiss et schistes quartzeux, couleur vert clair.

XIV. Euphotide massive (feldspath et diallage) à éléments cristallins bien développés, traversée par des veines d'eurite blanchâtre. Cette roche forme un banc ou plutôt une lentille de plus de 500 mètres de puissance intercalée au gneiss talqueux.[1]

XV. Gneiss talqueux alternant avec des schistes talqueux et micacés.

XVI. Schistes compactes couleur vert clair.

XVII. Calcaire cristallin micacé (calcschiste) avec veines et rognons de quartz. Il alterne avec des schistes verts chloriteux et serpentineux.

XVIII. Schistes verts chloriteux, serpentineux et talqueux, avec des masses stéatiteuses.

XIX. Calcschistes (comme ci-dessus) formant un banc de plus de 100 mètres.[2]

XX. Schistes verts chloriteux.

XXI. Calcschistes (comme ci-dessus).

XXII. Il suit ci dessous une série fort puissante de schistes verts serpentineux, chloriteux, talqueux et stéatiteux alternant encore avec des calcschistes. En plusieurs localités les schistes deviennent très-amphibologiques à petits cristaux noirs. Cette puissante formation calcaréo-serpentineuse repose inférieurement sur des micaschistes et des gneiss anciens.

[1] Cette roche granitoïde paraît surtout à la base ouest du pic sous le col du Lion tandis qu'elle ne paraît pas du tout sur le flanc est où elle paraît passer au gneiss talqueux.

[2] En plusieurs localités des environs, cette zone calcarifère présente des bancs et des lentilles de dolomie, dc cargueule de gypse et de quartzites.

The Death of Signor F. Giordano.

Signor Giordano, who supplied the above valuable note upon the Geology of the Matterhorn, and the accompanying section, lost his life in 1892, under very shocking circumstances. He went to Vallombrosa to pass a few days, and on the evening of the 14th of July left his hotel for a walk. As he did not return, several persons took lanterns to search the woods, and at last, attracted by moans, discovered the unfortunate engineer in a horrible state. He had tumbled over a cliff into a pool, and, having fractured his skull and a leg, was quite unable to move. Myriads of leeches from a neighbouring marsh were devouring the defenceless man alive. His hands, face, and body were covered with these bloodsuckers. He was carried back to the hotel in a dying condition, and expired in the course of the following day. Signor Giordano was very short-sighted, and this may possibly have caused the accident.

MÈTRES.	FEET.	MÈTRES.	FEET.	MÈTRES.	FEET.
1	= 3·28	50	= 164·04	100	= 328·09
2	6·56	51	167·33	200	656·18
3	9·84	52	170·61	300	984·27
4	13·12	53	173·89	400	1312·36
5	16·40	54	177·17	500	1640·45
6	19·69	55	180·45	600	1968·54
7	22·97	56	183·73	700	2296·63
8	26·25	57	187·01	800	2624·72
9	29·53	58	190·29	900	2952·81
10	32·81	59	193·57	1000	3280·90
11	36·09	60	196·85	1100	3608·99
12	39·37	61	200·13	1200	3937·08
13	42·65	62	203·42	1300	4265·17
14	45·93	63	206·70	1400	4593·26
15	49·21	64	209·98	1500	4921·35
16	52·49	65	213·26	1600	5249·44
17	55·78	66	216·54	1700	5577·53
18	59·06	67	219·82	1800	5905·62
19	62·34	68	223·10	1900	6233·71
20	65·62	69	226·38	2000	6561·80
21	68·90	70	229·66	2100	6889·89
22	72·18	71	232·94	2200	7217·98
23	75·46	72	236·22	2300	7546·07
24	78·74	73	239·51	2400	7874·16
25	82·02	74	242·79	2500	8202·25
26	85·30	75	246·07	2600	8530·34
27	88·58	76	249·35	2700	8858·43
28	91·87	77	252·63	2800	9186·52
29	95·15	78	255·91	2900	9514·61
30	98·43	79	259·19	3000	9842·70
31	101·71	80	262·47	3100	10,170·79
32	104·99	81	265·75	3200	10,498·88
33	108·27	82	269·03	3300	10,826·97
34	111·55	83	272·31	3400	11,155·06
35	114·83	84	275·60	3500	11,483·15
36	118·11	85	278·88	3600	11,811·24
37	121·39	86	282·16	3700	12,139·33
38	124·67	87	285·44	3800	12,467·42
39	127·96	88	288·72	3900	12,795·51
40	131·24	89	292·00	4000	13,123·60
41	134·52	90	295·28	4100	13,451·69
42	137·80	91	298·56	4200	13,779·78
43	141·08	92	301·84	4300	14,107·87
44	144·36	93	305·12	4400	14,435·96
45	147·64	94	308·40	4500	14,764·05
46	150·92	95	311·69	4600	15,092·14
47	154·20	96	314·97	4700	15,420·23
48	157·48	97	318·25	4800	15,748·32
49	160·76	98	321·53	4900	16,076·41
		99	324·81		

One Mètre = 3·2808992 English Feet (*Annuaire des Longitudes*, Paris).

FEET.	MÈTRES.	FEET.	MÈTRES.	FEET.	MÈTRES.
1 =	0·30	3300 =	1005·82	8300 =	2529·79
2	0·61	3400	1036·30	8400	2560·27
3	0·91	3500	1066·78	8500	2590·75
4	1·22	3600	1097·26	8600	2621·23
5	1·52	3700	1127·74	8700	2651·71
6	1·82	3800	1158·22	8800	2682·19
7	2·13	3900	1188·70	8900	2712·67
8	2·43	4000	1219·18	9000	2743·15
9	2·74	4100	1249·66	9100	2773·63
10	3·04	4200	1280·14	9200	2804·11
20	6·09	4300	1310·62	9300	2834·59
30	9·14	4400	1341·10	9400	2865·07
40	12·19	4500	1371·58	9500	2895·55
50	15·24	4600	1402·05	9600	2926·03
60	18·29	4700	1432·53	9700	2956·51
70	21·34	4800	1463·01	9800	2986·99
80	24·38	4900	1493·49	9900	3017·47
90	27·43	5000	1523·97	10,000	3047·94
100	30·48	5100	1554·45	10,100	3078·42
200	60·96	5200	1584·93	10,200	3108·90
300	91·44	5300	1615·41	10,300	3139·38
400	121·91	5400	1645·89	10,400	3169·86
500	152·40	5500	1676·37	10,500	3200·34
600	182·88	5600	1706·85	10,600	3230·82
700	213·36	5700	1737·33	10,700	3261·30
800	243·84	5800	1767·81	10,800	3291·78
900	274·31	5900	1798·29	10,900	3322·26
1000	304·79	6000	1828·77	11,000	3352·74
1100	335·27	6100	1859·25	11,100	3383·22
1200	365·76	6200	1889·73	11,200	3413·70
1300	396·23	6300	1920·21	11,300	3444·18
1400	426·71	6400	1950·68	11,400	3474·66
1500	457·19	6500	1981·16	11,500	3505·14
1600	487·67	6600	2011·64	11,600	3535·62
1700	518·15	6700	2042·12	11,700	3566·10
1800	548·63	6800	2072·60	11,800	3596·57
1900	579·11	6900	2103·08	11,900	3627·05
2000	609·59	7000	2133·56	12,000	3657·53
2100	640·07	7100	2164·04	12,100	3688·01
2200	670·55	7200	2194·52	12,200	3718·49
2300	701·03	7300	2225·00	12,300	3748·97
2400	731·51	7400	2255·48	12,400	3779·45
2500	761·99	7500	2285·96	12,500	3809·93
2600	792·47	7600	2316·44	12,600	3840·41
2700	822·94	7700	2346·92	12,700	3870·89
2800	853·42	7800	2377·40	12,800	3901·37
2900	883·90	7900	2407·88	12,900	3931·85
3000	914·38	8000	2438·36	13,000	3962·33
3100	944·86	8100	2468·84	14,000	4267·12
3200	975·34	8200	2499·31	15,000	4571·92

One English Foot = 3·0479449 décimètres (*Annuaire des Longitudes*, Paris).

GS-
668
POLLUX
13,432
SCHWARZTHOR
12,274
EASTERN END OF
THE BREITHORN
SCHWARZE GLACIER
GORNER GLACIER

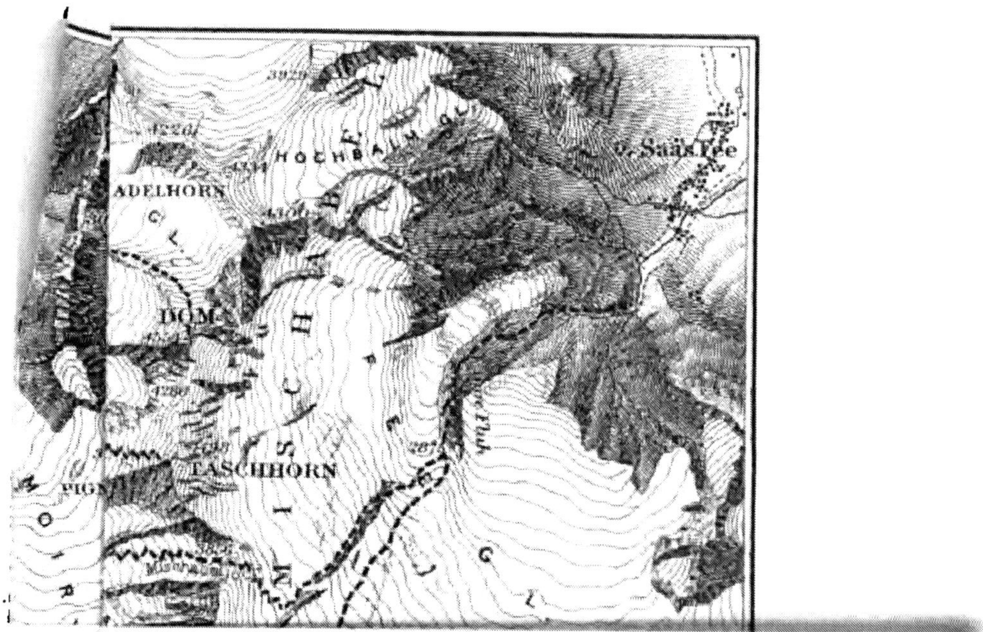
ADELHORN
DOM
TASCHHORN

LaVergne, TN USA
12 February 2010
173019LV00003B/37/P